A State of Risk

A STATE OF RISK

Will Government-Sponsored Enterprises Be the Next Financial Crisis?

Thomas H. Stanton

HarperBusiness
A Division of HarperCollins*Publishers*

Library of Congress Cataloging-in-Publication Data
Stanton, Thomas H., 1944-
    A state of risk / Thomas H. Stanton.
    p.   cm.
    Includes bibliographical references (p.) and index.
    ISBN 0-88730-419-2
    1. Government-sponsored enterprises—United States. I. Title.
    HG181.S793   1991
    353.09'2—dc20   90-24432
                                                                CIP

International Standard Book Number: 0–88730–419–2

Library of Congress Catalog Card Number: 90–24432

Printed in the United States of America

91 92 93 94 CC/HC 9 8 7 6 5 4 3 2 1

To Marty,
Benjamin, and Joshua

Contents

Preface   *xix*

CHAPTER 1
INTRODUCTION:
GOVERNMENT-SPONSORED ENTERPRISES
AND THRIFT INSTITUTIONS   *1*

What Have We Learned from the Thrift Debacle?   *1*
Large-Scale Thrift Failure: A Two-Step Process   *2*
   The First Step: Loss of Capital   *3*
   The Second Step: Gambling for Solvency   *4*
Regulatory Efforts to Reduce Gambling by Insolvent
   Thrifts Were Belated   *7*
Financial Parallels   *8*
Political Parallels   *10*
The Need for Preventive Steps   *12*

CHAPTER 2
THE HIDDEN COSTS AND PUBLIC
BENEFITS OF
GOVERNMENT-SPONSORED
ENTERPRISES   *14*

Enterprises: Government Agencies or Private Companies?   *15*
Enterprises Resemble Banks and Thrift Institutions   *17*

Enterprises Are Growing Rapidly   18
Enterprises Have a Long Tradition   19
   Farm Credit System (FCS)   20
   Federal Home Loan Bank System (FHLBS)   20
   Fannie Mae   21
   Freddie Mac   22
   Sallie Mae   23
   Farmer Mac   23
   FICO and REFCORP   24
   Other Enterprises under Consideration   25
The Development of the Federal Subsidy Implicit in
   Enterprise Lending   25
The Controversy Surrounding Government-Sponsored
   Enterprises   27
   Competitive Issues   27
The Public Benefits and Costs of Enterprise Lending   28
   The Difficulty of Protecting Taxpayers against
      Unnecessary Financial Risk   28
   Enterprises as Specialized Lenders   30
   Enterprise Lending and the Highest Public Priority
      Credit Needs   31
   The Accelerating Rate of Enterprise Growth   34

CHAPTER 3
HOW GOVERNMENT-SPONSORED
ENTERPRISES WORK

                                   39

Raising Money in the Federal Agency Credit Market   40
   The Federal Agency Credit Market   41
   The Implicit Federal Guarantee of Enterprise
      Obligations   41
Liquidity of Enterprise Obligations   44
Guaranteeing Mortgage-backed Securities (MBSs)   45
Issuing Multiclass MBSs (REMICs)   47
Farmer Mac-guaranteed MBSs   49

Enterprises as Private Lenders   50
  Making or Purchasing Loans   50
  Making Collateralized Advances to Lenders   50
  Guaranteeing MBSs: The Swap Transaction   52
How the Enterprises Make Money   54
  MBS Guarantee Fees   56
  Income from Other Services   56
  Sources of Income for Each Enterprise   57
Tension between the Private Ownership and Public
  Purpose of an Enterprise   58
  Statutory Terms and Public Purpose   58
  Incentives of Private Owners   60
  Social Responsibility and Shareholder Profit   61
Unusual Elements in Enterprise Ownership and
  Control   64
  Protection against Hostile Takeover   64
  Enterprise Directors: Appointed by the Government
    and Elected by Shareholders   65
The Quality of Enterprise Management   69
  Financial and Operational Skills   69
  Political Skills   71
  Compensation of Senior Management   72

CHAPTER 4
ENTERPRISES IN THE MARKETPLACE   75

Federal Law and Enterprise Advantages   76
  Federal Credit Support   76
  Federal, State, and Local Tax Benefits   78
  Freedom from Capital Requirements   79
  Freedom to Serve the National Market   79
Limitations Imposed on the Enterprises   81
Enterprises: Specialized Lenders Serving a Nationwide
  Market   83
  Huge Size and Rapid Growth   83

x   Contents

Longtime Dedication to a Market Segment   85
Product and Service Innovation   85
Enterprises as Competitors   86
Sallie Mae versus Commercial Banks   87
Fannie Mae and Freddie Mac versus Thrift
    Institutions   88
Fannie Mae, Freddie Mac, and the FHLBS versus
    Securities Firms   89
Turning the Competitors into Enterprise Providers   91
How the Enterprises Shape Their Markets   91
Effects of Fannie Mae and Freddie Mac on the
    Residential Mortgage Market   91
Fannie Mae's and Freddie Mac's Influence in the
    Primary Mortgage Market   92
Farmer Mac's Impact on the Agricultural Mortgage
    Market   94
The Farm Credit System and the Market for Farm
    Loans   94
Federal Advantages versus "Crowding Out"   95
How the Enterprises Improve Market Efficiency   97
Farm Credit System   97
Federal Home Loan Bank System   98
Fannie Mae   99
Sallie Mae   100
How Enterprise Contributions to Market Efficiency
Change over Time   101
Improving Market Efficiency Gains of Enterprise
    Activities   102
Delivering Federal Subsidy Benefits   103
The Economic Debate over the Effects of Enterprise
Lending   104

CHAPTER 5
THE POLITICS OF ENTERPRISE LENDING

107

Pressures to Expand Enterprise Powers · *107*
Congressional Receptivity · *108*
When Congress Declines · *111*
Political Competition between the Enterprises and Other Financial Institutions · *113*
Expanding Enterprise Powers and the Public Policy Issues · *116*
Pressures to Serve Noneconomic Segments and Reduce Profitability · *118*
The Role of Constituencies in the Creation of the Enterprises · *121*
Farm Credit System · *121*
Federal Home Loan Bank System · *121*
Fannie Mae · *122*
Freddie Mac · *122*
Sallie Mae · *123*
New Enterprises in the 1980s · *123*
The Politics of Allocating Enterprise Benefits · *125*

CHAPTER 6
ENTERPRISES AS PRIVATE FINANCIAL INSTITUTIONS

128

Fannie Mae's Financial Statements · *129*
What Fannie Mae's Balance Sheets Don't Reveal · *132*
The Financial Reports of Other Government-Sponsored Enterprises · *136*
Freddie Mac · *136*
Federal Home Loan Bank System · *140*
Farm Credit System · *141*

Sallie Mae   143
Financing Corporation (FICO)   146
Market-Value Accounting Improves the Quality of
  Enterprise Financial Disclosures   148

CHAPTER 7
THE IMPLICIT FEDERAL GUARANTEE AS A SOURCE OF RISK EXPOSURE   153

Risks of Enterprise Lending   154
  Management Risk   154
  Market Risk   155
  Other Types of Risk   155
Effects of the Implicit Federal Guarantee on Enterprise
  Risk Taking   157
  The Implicit Guarantee and Enterprise Shareholders   157
  The Implicit Guarantee and Enterprise Debt-holders   158
  Risk Taking by the FCS, Fannie Mae, and Thrift
    Institutions   159
The Extent of the Government's Risk Exposure   162
The Government's Lack of Knowledge   163
A Preliminary Assessment of the Financial Condition of
  the Enterprises   164

CHAPTER 8
SUPERVISING ENTERPRISE SAFETY AND SOUNDNESS   167

Regulation of Enterprise Safety and Soundness to
  Compensate for the Lack of Market Discipline   167
Why Capital Is Important   169
The Current State of Enterprise Regulation   171
  Safety and Soundness   171
  Capital Requirements   173

Possible Effects of Improved Financial Regulation of the
Enterprises   *174*
Enhanced Financial Disclosures   *175*
Federal Examination   *177*
Federal Authority to Enforce Safety and Soundness
and Capital Requirements   *179*
Federal Authority to Close or Reorganize a Failing
Enterprise   *183*
The Politics of Improving Federal Supervision of the
Enterprises   *185*

CHAPTER 9
ENTERPRISE ACCOUNTABILITY   *188*

Separating the Supervision of Enterprise Safety and
Soundness from Oversight of Benefits   *189*
Centralized Regulation of Safety and Soundness   *189*
The Allocation of Enterprise Benefits Raises Politically
Charged Issues   *191*
Congressional Oversight of the Allocation of Enterprise
Benefits Is Needed   *192*
Improving Congressional Oversight of Enterprise
Benefits   *193*
The Future of Government-Sponsored Enterprises   *196*

APPENDIX A
LAW, CASES, AND OTHER LEGAL
SOURCES ON
GOVERNMENT-SPONSORED
ENTERPRISES   *201*

The Laws Establishing the Enterprises   *201*
Legal Authority for Enterprise Activities   *203*

Legal Elements of the Implicit Federal Guarantee of
Enterprise Obligations   204
Government-Sponsored Enterprises as Federal
Instrumentalities   205
The Benefits of Federal Instrumentality Status   206
The Responsibilities of Enterprise Directors   207
Legal Accountability   208
Federal Regulation   209
Additional Legal Writings   210

APPENDIX B
REFERENCES   211

INDEX   219

Tables and Figures

CHAPTER 2:

Table 2–1 Government-Sponsored Enterprises:
An Overview   16

Table 2–2 Government-Sponsored Enterprises
Compared to Federally Chartered
Thrifts and National Banks   18

Table 2–3 Financial Overview, 1985–1989   19

Table 2–4 Enterprise Securities Outstanding at
the End of the Fiscal Year,
1970–1991   35

Figure 2–1 Government-Sponsored Enterprises:
Securities, Guarantees, and
Reinsurance   34

CHAPTER 3:

Table 3–1 The Financial Functions of
Government-Sponsored Enterprises   40

Table 3–2 Enterprise Returns on Average
Shareholder Equity, 1989   61

Table 3–3 Investor versus Borrower-User
Ownership and Control of the
Enterprises   65

Table 3–4 Limitations on Enterprise Ownership
by the Investing Public   66

Figure 3–1 A Typical FHLBS Debt Obligation
          Offering Notice   42
Figure 3–2 Elements of the Loan Portfolio:
          Interest Income, Term
          Intermediation, and Credit and
          Operations Risks   51
Figure 3–3 Elements of Collateralized Advances:
          Interest Income, Term
          Intermediation, Operations Risk,
          and Protection against Credit Risk   53
Figure 3–4 Elements of Guaranteed MBSs: Fee
          Income, and Credit and Operations
          Risks   54

C H A P T E R 4:

Table 4–1 Advantages Conferred on the
         Enterprises by Federal Law   77
Table 4–2 Disadvantages Conferred on the
         Enterprises by Federal Law   82
Table 4–3 Fannie and Freddie Mac: Total
         Residential Mortgage Debt and
         Total of Mortgages Held or
         Guaranteed, 1970–1989   84

C H A P T E R 6:

Table 6–1 Fannie Mae's Balance Sheets,
         1988–1989   130
Table 6–2 Fannie Mae's Financial Statements,
         1987–1989   131
Table 6–3 Fannie Mae's Income Statements,
         1987–1989   137
Table 6–4 Freddie Mac's Consolidated Balance
         Sheets, 1988–1989   139

Table 6–5 Federal Home Loan Banks: Selected
Financial Data, 1988–1989   141

Table 6–6 Farm Credit System's Combined
Statement of Condition, 1988–1989   142

Table 6–7 Sallie Mae's Consolidated Balance
Sheets, 1988–1989   144

Table 6–8 Financing Corporation's Balance
Sheets, 1987–1988   147

Table 6–9 Freddie Mac's Consolidated
Market-Value Balance Sheet, 1989   151

Figure 6–1 Fannie Mae's Asset–Liability
Duration Gap, 1985–1989   133

Figure 6–2 Selected Notes to Fannie Mae's 1989
Financial Statements   135

CHAPTER 7:

Table 7–1 Standard & Poor's Preliminary
Assessment of the Potential Risk to
the Federal Government of the
Implicit Guarantee, 31 October 1989   165

Preface

For too long, government-sponsored enterprises were shrouded in misunderstanding. They were the proverbial elephant surrounded by blind people—so vast and complex that customers, investment bankers, competitors, and federal policymakers could each feel a different part without appreciating the full dimensions of the animal. Over the 1980s, sight returned and government-sponsored enterprises came finally to be seen as the behemoths that they are. Today, everyone perched on and around the elephant can clearly see that the elephant is large and growing, and that it has strong potential for positive accomplishment, but only if we can assure that it moves in the right direction.

My introduction to the elephant came in 1982 as a senior staff member of the President's Commission on Housing. Then, from 1982 to 1985, I was assistant general counsel and then associate general counsel at Fannie Mae, the largest of the enterprises. Unexpected illness among senior management gave me the opportunity to work with the company's board of directors, policy committee, and skilled management team on a variety of exacting financial and legislative projects. This provided a firsthand view of the interplay of contending constituencies that affect the scope of an enterprise's legal authority and its activities in the marketplace. Also I learned about the difficulties that can beset financial institutions in dealing with a regulator that lacks a sophisticated understanding of the company's business.

Other federally chartered financial institutions such as banks and thrifts are free to leave many political and legislative issues to their trade associations; government-sponsored enterprises must deal with federal officials, agencies, and congressional committees and subcommittees on a continuing basis. Because of their unique charters, government-sponsored enterprises are sensitive to their congressional sponsorship and the way changes in the wording of their enabling legislation can profoundly affect their day-to-day business operations and opportunities.

In 1985, a chance meeting with an old friend convinced me that it was time to go into private practice. I left the elephant to work intensively on the 1986 Tax Reform Act. After the legislation was complete, it seemed time to return to government-sponsored enterprises.

The opportunity came in late 1986; the House of Representatives passed legislation to create a new government-sponsored enterprise, called the Corporation for Small Business Investment (COSBI), to invest in small business investment companies. Studying the legislation, I was shocked to find that the bill lacked even the most basic safety and soundness provisions familiar from the Fannie Mae charter act. I wrote up my concerns in an article for the *Legal Times*[1] and also conveyed them to the Senate Small Business Committee. A prepublication copy of my article found its way to various decision makers on Capitol Hill and in the Treasury Department. The House-Senate Conference Committee, which tentatively had approved COSBI a few days before my calls, ultimately declined to enact the legislation. This was a new view of the elephant for me—the process of creating a government-sponsored enterprise and a firsthand look at the disparity of knowledge about such enterprises between the ardent private promoters of the legislation and the congressional committees asked to conceive an enterprise.

In 1987, the Banking Research Fund of the Association of Reserve City Bankers commissioned me to write a monograph on the benefits and costs of government-sponsored enterprises as instruments of federal policy. This permitted me to become familiar with the finance and economics literature concerning financial institutions, federal guarantees, and federal regulation of safety and soundness. The Reading Committee, and its insightful

---

[1]Thomas H. Stanton, "Pending Legislation Would End Impasse over SBA Legislation: Congress May Create a New Corporation to Aid Small Business, but Has Drafted the Law in a Way That May Ultimately Expose the Government To Significant Financial Losses," *Legal Times* 6 October 1986, pp. 24–26.

adviser, Donald Jacobs, dean of the Kellogg School of Business at Northwestern University, asked hard questions whose answers improved the paper's quality; they left the policy conclusions to my independent judgment.

Members of Congress completed federal legislation to create yet another government-sponsored enterprise, Farmer Mac, in 1987. The Farm Credit Administration, regulator of the then-failed Farm Credit System, asked me to provide advice about the legislation and a possible framework for effective safety and soundness regulation of the new enterprise. With this, I had a fourth look at the elephant, this time during the birth process. From the perspective of the regulator, I could see the flip side of my previous Fannie Mae experience—the need for the regulator to obtain the most important financial information in a timely manner without becoming inundated in extensive materials that would cloud rather than enhance the quality of a regulatory approach. Here I came to appreciate the opportunities for a win-win agreement between the regulator and the regulated institution if (1) the regulatory task is expressly confined to issues relating to safety and soundness and not to larger policy questions, such as the permitted scope of enterprise powers, better left to the legislative process; and (2) both the regulator and regulated institution can establish the basis for mutual trust in an arm's-length relationship. As the earlier Farm Credit System failure had shown, there are dangers if the regulator gets too close to the elephant.

In 1987, the U.S. General Accounting Office (GAO), the congressional watchdog agency, asked me to analyze legal and competitive factors in the secondary market for guaranteed student loans and Sallie Mae. The capable and dedicated staff of the GAO deserve great respect. As an arm of Congress, they have escaped the disinvestment of people and resources that has weakened so much of the executive branch of government. My work with the GAO on this and another project concerning government-sponsored enterprises highlighted the absence of such a capable centralized federal watchdog to oversee all of the enterprises together, much as the FDIC supervises commercial banks. Just as the GAO staff learns lessons on one project that are then applied to others, so too a centralized regulator of enterprise safety and soundness could apply lessons from one enterprise to another. The GAO is an example of the benefits of designing institutions to serve the federal government over the long term.

I revisited the process of conceiving a new enterprise in 1988. The infrastructure task force of the National Association of Home Builders, a group of extremely capable individuals, asked that I design a new government-sponsored enterprise to assist in infrastructure finance. I had the task of grappling with the core question of this book: Is it possible to design a safe and sound and well-capitalized government-sponsored enterprise that can profitably and successfully provide credit support to serve a major public purpose? After interviewing experts in infrastructure finance, the infrastructure task force has indeed developed an enterprise that appears likely to meet all of these tests. The proposed National Infrastructure Bank, dubbed Infra Mae by the task force, promises to be a small but attractive creature to propose to Congress.

The savings and loan crisis caused a greater concern about government-sponsored enterprises. The year 1989 opened with the government finally acting to address the savings and loan industry debacle—a $300 billion lesson about the need for effective regulation of the safety and soundness of institutions with federal backing. The Financial Institutions Reform, Recovery and Enforcement Act of 1989 (FIRREA) restructured the thrift industry and its regulator and provided taxpayer funds for a bailout. Consumer's Union, the public interest group that publishes *Consumer Reports,* asked me to help follow FIRREA and provide advice about provisions to protect taxpayers and promote low-income housing opportunities. Working on FIRREA as it went through Congress meant taking a close look at the thrifts and at how to deal with the thrift crisis.

I also became acquainted with two outstanding members of Congress, Representatives J. J. Pickle from Texas, chairman of the Oversight Subcommittee of the House Ways and Means Committee, and Bill Gradison from Ohio, of the Ways and Means Committee. They and other members of their unusually capable committee, and their talented committee and personal staff—Charles Brain, Margaret Hostetler, Joseph Grant, Ronald Boster, and many others—added a modest but important provision to

FIRREA: the requirement that the U.S. Treasury study the financial risk posed by each of the government-sponsored enterprises and provide an annual report to Congress.

Much to everyone's surprise, Fannie Mae and Freddie Mac objected to the provision; behind the scenes, Fannie Mae fought it strenuously. As the *Wall Street Journal* observed in 1989, "Fannie Mae claims it is sound and welcomes outside scrutiny. Still, it has quietly recruited Senator Alan Cranston to kill any Treasury study of its operations."[2] Senator Cranston, from California, a senior member of the conference committee on FIRREA, was in a powerful position. He objected to an annual Treasury risk study and succeeded in limiting it to two years, 1990 and 1991.

In response, Chairman Pickle promptly convened a hearing of his Oversight Subcommittee. "If we have learned nothing else from the savings and loan experience," he said, "we surely must accept that these off-budget liabilities can have very sudden and profound on-budget consequences."[3] Pickle summoned officials from the Treasury Department, the General Accounting Office, and the chief executives from the various enterprises to answer probing questions about enterprise safety and soundness. This was the first oversight hearing on the financial condition of all of the enterprises that Congress had conducted in over thirty years.

In May 1990, the Treasury and GAO reported back to the Ways and Means Committee on the results of their studies. The two reports validate many of the contentions of this book, and especially the position that the accountability of government-sponsored enterprises must be enhanced through more effective financial supervision and increased capital standards.

The Treasury Department's *Report* provides a veritable checklist of important elements of financial risk and the extent to which each enterprise has kept the risk under control. For each government-sponsored enterprise (GSE), the Treasury provides (1) a description; (2) an overview of financial safety and soundness; (3) an assessment of business risk, credit risk, interest-rate risk, and management and operations risk; (4) an analysis of

[2]Editorial, *Wall Street Journal*, 26 July 1989, p. A-12.
[3]House Ways and Means Committee, Subcommittee on Oversight, "Government-Sponsored Enterprises," Hearing Record of 28 September 1989, p. 2.

capital adequacy; and (5) a discussion of the quality and timeliness of information provided by each GSE to the public and the federal government.[4]

The GAO *Report* similarly analyzes each GSE in terms of (1) its risks and the quality of its risk management; (2) its loss reserves and capital adequacy; and (3) the quality of current federal oversight of its risk taking and capitalization.[5] Both the Treasury and the GAO were limited in their staff resources and thus in their access to data and records; they requested information from the enterprises and did not conduct independent examinations (like those the federal government conducts for banks and thrift institutions with federally insured deposits) to validate the accuracy of the responses. Given this significant limitation, the quality of the 1990 studies is especially impressive. The 1991 studies are expected to be more thorough; the government still has much catching up to do before it is in a position to know and control the risks associated with government-sponsored enterprises.

President Andrew Jackson once observed of the Bank of the United States, the grandfather of today's elephant, that "if any private citizen or public functionary should interpose to curtail its powers or prevent a renewal of its privileges, it cannot be doubted that he would be made to feel its influence."[6] In 1990, I felt the truth of that statement myself. In February of that year, the Senate Subcommittee on Housing and Urban Affairs, led by Senators Alan Cranston and Alphonse D'Amato from New York, asked me to participate in a roundtable hearing. Both senators were well known for their political support of Fannie Mae, Freddie Mac, and their managers. In 1989, for example, Senator Cranston spearheaded the effort to weaken or eliminate the annual Treasury risk study. The invited witnesses included the chief executive officers of Fannie Mae and Freddie Mac, the undersecretary of HUD, and a virtual "who's who" of New York investment bankers whose companies do business with Fannie Mae

---

[4]Treasury Department, *Report of the Secretary of the Treasury on Government-Sponsored Enterprises* (Washington, D.C.: GPO, May 1990).
[5]General Accounting Office, *Government-Sponsored Enterprises: Government's Exposure to Risk* (Washington D.C.: GPO, August 1990).
[6]Andrew Jackson, "Bank Veto Message," 10 July, 1832. Quoted in Richard Hofstadter, *Great Issues in American History from the Revolution to the Civil War, 1765–1865* (New York: Random House, 1958), p. 293.

and Freddie Mac. Three of these New York participants were known to me as members of Fannie Mae's advisory committee. The invited witness list also included three academics, representatives of Moody's and Standard & Poor's, and me. It did not emerge until the hearing that two of the academics were not impartial witnesses; they had been hired by Freddie Mac to attest to their client's safety and soundness.

If 1989 had been a high point because of the willingness of the House Ways and Means Committee to require a risk assessment of each enterprise, the 1990 Senate Subcommittee hearing, with its carefully choreographed message of "Don't worry, be happy," was a low point. Facing the front of the elephant was at times necessary, and it did contribute to my experience in writing this book. Suddenly, I was contacted by others who had faced the tusks of the elephant. These were people afraid to make their views public because they or their firms had been silenced before, but they shared their stories. Some were people from companies that had sought to compete head-to-head with government-sponsored enterprises. While I may differ respectfully with some of their strong opinions, we have indeed shared an uncommon view of the elephant, and I am grateful for their insights.

Acknowledgments

There are many other people to thank for the knowledge that went into this book. In the early 1980s, the study of government-sponsored enterprises was an arcane legal specialty; today, the enterprises are widely understood by experts in and out of government. It is my hope that this book will help to make the general public more knowledgeable about the enterprises. In working toward this goal, I have benefited from the valuable insights, experiences, and advice from the many people who contributed to this book.

My thanks go to the friends and colleagues who explored with me and exchanged their views on the issues addressed in the book. Among them are managers and others employed by the enterprises, who took the time to engage in off-the-record discussions. My dialogue with these people reaffirmed my conviction that enterprise safety and soundness is an important goal, one that can be pursued in a win-win relationship with the responsible enterprises. Needed are mutual trust, respect, and a willingness to address problems before, rather than after, something goes wrong.

Thanks also go to Harold Seidman, the intellectual father of teachings on government-sponsored enterprises and other federal instrumentalities. (To Harold an acknowledgment: In this book, I define *government-sponsored enterprise* more narrowly than you have in your writings.) Although not an attorney, Harold Seidman has done more to improve today's knowledge of the law of public institutions than almost any lawyer I know. Many of his writings are included in the references of this book.

I also wish to thank Ronald Moe, Alan Dean, and the other members of the National Academy of Public Administration (NAPA). It is an honor to serve on the National Academy's Standing Panel on Executive Organization and Management and as a speaker at the annual NAPA seminar on government corporations. The United States is a country whose law of public institutions reached a high point in the 1930s and virtually died as a distinct academic body of law since then; we all have a great debt to NAPA and its dedication to restoring and improving this important body of knowledge.

Many people in government today have worked hard to analyze the important issues relating to the accountability of government-sponsored enterprises. Michael Basham, Deputy Assistant Secretary of the Treasury for Federal Finance, and his talented staff produced the first report on government-sponsored enterprises to examine carefully and analytically their financial strengths and shortcomings. Two leading analysts in the Congressional Budget Office, Marvin Phaup and Robin Seiler, have produced reports on federal contingent liabilities, including those of the enterprises, that have greatly enhanced the government's ability to deal with excessive risks to taxpayers. The American people are fortunate that these dedicated officials and others—in the Office of Management and Budget, the U.S. General Accounting Office, congressional offices, and the various executive departments—have remained in public service despite the great disincentives involved.

Chairman Marshall J. Breger, Executive Director William Olmstead, and the capable and dedicated staff of the Administrative Conference of the United States—notably Jeffrey Lubbers and Brian Murphy—deserve special mention in this regard. Focusing on administrative and regulatory issues of the federal government, this federal agency produces scholarly works and procedural improvements that contribute benefits far in excess of its minuscule budget. I am particularly grateful that the Administrative Conference decided in 1989 to study federal supervision of safety and soundness of government-sponsored enterprises, even before the 1990 Treasury and GAO reports confirmed the importance of this issue.

Some personal thanks are also in order. I am greatly indebted to my friend and colleague Harrison Wellford for his continuing support and enthusiasm. Thanks go also to the attorneys and staff at Olwine, Connelly, Chase, O'Donnell & Weyher, whose guidance and collegiality have been invaluable. Special thanks go to Violet R. Sewell for her good humor and amazing productivity during the preparation of the manuscript and other stages of the project.

My editor, Martha Jewett, deserves a special note of gratitude, for her strong editorial contributions to the book and her ability to deliver accurate feedback with graciousness. Thanks also to publisher Mark Greenberg, with whom I share a common background.

My greatest debt of gratitude, of course, is to my family. My wife, Martha Zaslow, and sons, Benjamin and Joshua, have borne the brunt of many long weekends and late nights spent working on the manuscript. My parents have been consistent supporters of my many ventures, including this book; I am grateful for their encouragement. My mother-in-law, Doris K. Zaslow, also deserves thanks, for her help during several weeks of especially intensive work on the book. It is a joy to be back home again, on a (more or less) regular schedule.

Washington, D.C.
November 1990

1

Introduction: Government-Sponsored Enterprises and Thrift Institutions

I am by no means an alarmist. I believe that our system, though curious and peculiar, may be worked safely; but if we wish so to work it, we must study it. We must not think we have an easy task when we have a difficult task, or that we are living in a natural state when we are really living in an artificial one. Money will not manage itself, and [they have] a great deal of money to manage.

—Walter Bagehot, *Lombard Street: A Description of the Money Market*

What Have We Learned from the Thrift Debacle?

The insolvency of hundreds of savings and loan institutions provides painful lessons about the way financial institutions can fail. It also serves as a warning of the need for serious capital requirements and more effective regulation, not only of thrifts but also of government-sponsored enterprises. While there are notable structural differences between government-sponsored enterprises and thrift institutions, enough similarities exist to per-

1

mit the lessons of thrift failures to be drawn from enterprises[1] as well.

At the root of the savings and loan debacle is that, like a government-sponsored enterprise but unlike the typical private firm, a thrift institution with federally insured deposits does not automatically go out of business when it fails. Under the law, thrifts, banks, and government-sponsored enterprises may not go bankrupt under the Bankruptcy Code; they can be closed only by their government regulators or the Congress. To the extent that the regulators fail to close insolvent institutions promptly, this can greatly compound the government's financial losses.

The thrift industry's protracted fight against financial account-ability shows how closing an insolvent financial institution is a zero-sum game. If the regulator acts, private owners lose but the public is protected; if the regulator fails to act, the owners stay in business and greatly expand the magnitude of possible public losses. It is little wonder, then, that insolvent thrifts applied con-siderable political pressure to prevent their regulator from promptly closing them when their market value net worth dropped to zero.

Large-Scale Thrift Failure: A Two-Step Process

The failure of hundreds of thrift institutions occurred in two stages. First, rising interest rates caught thrifts in a squeeze so that many lost money in their traditional mortgage portfolio lending business. Second, as many thrifts became technically insolvent, managers gambled for survival by engaging in high-risk ventures that usually compounded thrift losses and losses to the federal insurance funds.

[1]Throughout this book, the terms *enterprises* and *government-sponsored enterprises* are used interchangeably. There are eight such enterprises: Fannie Mae, Freddie Mac, Sallie Mae, the Farm Credit System (FCS), the Federal Home Loan Bank System (FHLBS), Farmer Mac, the Financing Corporation (FICO), and the Resolution Funding Corporation (REF-CORP). The term *government-sponsored enterprise* is formally defined on p. 17.

The First Step: Loss of Capital

The first stage in the large-scale thrift failure was tied to the specialized lending function of savings and loan associations. Traditionally, thrifts were confined by law to making long-term mortgage loans funded by deposits (that is, short-term money). Thrifts made money in three ways: They originated mortgages for an initial fee, serviced those mortgages out of a fee from monthly payments, and held the mortgages in portfolio, thereby benefiting from the difference in interest rates between low-yielding passbook deposits and the higher-yielding mortgages.

Until the early 1980s, passbook interest rates were kept artificially low by Regulation Q of the Federal Reserve Board. Regulation Q placed a statutory ceiling on passbook interest rates and also gave thrifts the authority to pay one-fourth of a percentage point more for their deposits than could their major competitors, the commercial banks. This comfortable state of affairs lasted for many years, leading some to describe the thrift business as a "three-six-three" business: The thrift executive paid 3 percent on passbook deposits, made mortgage loans at 6 percent, and was on the golf course everyday by three in the afternoon.

The good times ended with the drastic increase in interest rates starting in 1979. Long-term rates such as for mortgages rose significantly and short-term interest rates shot up even faster. Depositors began moving their money from thrift accounts into money-market accounts paying much higher rates of interest. Congress and the regulators quickly phased out Regulation Q, but that didn't help. Thrifts found themselves squeezed between the new high market rates of interest they paid on their deposits and the much lower rates they earned on their large portfolios of long-term home mortgages. In 1980, Congress also expanded deposit insurance coverage, from a limit of $40,000 to $100,000 per account. The federal government was taking on greater risk at just the wrong time.

By 1982, the end of the first stage in the thrift debacle, hundreds of thrift institutions had run out of capital and, according to generally accepted accounting principles (GAAP), had a negative net worth. Economist R. Dan Brumbaugh estimates that in 1982, 282 out of 3,343 insured thrifts with assets of $47 billion had a negative GAAP book value. At that point, it would have cost the government $1.2 billion to close down the insolvent thrifts or to merge them with healthy institutions.[2] Because GAAP tends to overstate actual net worth for a thrift, the situation in terms of market-value insolvencies was probably even worse than estimated by economists.

Instead of closing the failed thrifts, however, the federal government responded with solicitude. It provided so-called income capital certificates, net worth certificates, and other pieces of federally backed paper to take the place of the depleted shareholder capital. Further, "regulatory accounting" was used to puff up the book value of institutions that in fact were completely insolvent. Unlike other financial institutions, which are required to report their financial circumstances using GAAP, the Federal Home Loan Bank Board (FHLBB) permitted thrifts to overstate their net worth. This had the effect of reducing the number of insolvent thrifts that actually reported a negative net worth (from 252 to 80 in 1982, for example) to avoid being subject to closure or merger. These accounting changes and the accompanying regulatory forbearance meant that many thrifts remained in business despite their substantial negative net worth. Moreover, regulatory accounting obscured the extent of the government's losses and thereby permitted thrift industry advocates to downplay the significance of those losses.

The Second Step: Gambling for Solvency

Starting in 1982, interest rates came down. By itself, this should have brought welcome relief to many institutions. Instead, hundreds of thrifts made serious financial misjudgments that took them yet further into debt. Brumbaugh estimates that by 1986, some 468 thrifts had a GAAP negative net worth. It would have cost the government about $3.2 billion to close or merge them at this time.[3] Again, the situation in terms of market-value insolvencies was worse than reflected in the GAAP values.

In retrospect, shareholder capital is seen as a key to the thrift problem. Managers of insolvent institutions suddenly found

[2]R. Dan Brumbaugh, Jr., *Thrifts under Siege: Restoring Order to American Banking* (Cambridge, Mass.: Ballinger, 1988), 40, 53–54.
[3]Ibid.

themselves without shareholder capital. Capital is essential for a variety of reasons, especially because it can give shareholders a stake in the long-term well-being of the institution. An under-capitalized institution, and particularly one with negative net worth, is likely to take substantial risks.[4] The thrifts were no exception.

Yet no one was watching them. The people who should have been watching were the regulatory officials of the Federal Home Loan Bank Board. Even from its inception, the FHLBB was solicitous of the thrifts it was supposed to regulate.[5] Indeed, the FHLBB was in an anomalous position as a regulator, for it also was statutorily required to promote the industry it supervised.[6] Until the late 1980s, the FHLBB was unhappy at the prospect of having to close an institution in its care. Hundreds of thrifts became technically insolvent in the 1980s (that is, they had a market value less than zero), but because they reported their financial condition based on regulatory accounting their value was overstated. That fact deprived the FHLBB of the information needed promptly to close them down. The FHLBB also lacked the will and the staff to deal with the suddenly large number of failing institutions.

Starting in 1982, protected by a weak and, initially at least, friendly regulator, hundreds of failed thrifts began to try and gamble their way back to solvency. The Garn-St. Germain Act of 1982 expanded the lines of business available to thrift institutions, permitted them to make commercial and agricultural loans up to specified limits, removed loan-to-value limits on real estate loans, and even allowed thrifts to make unsecured construction loans.

State-chartered savings and loans (in Texas and California, for

---

[4]This concept is well understood by financial analysts:

> The time to really watch a bank's management is when things are going badly. At some point, management comes to the realization that they are going to lose either their jobs or, worse still, their bank unless they make a high-stake gamble and win. That stark reality—nothing to lose on a gamble and everything to win—is bound to dampen whatever natural risk aversion management may have.

Marcia L. Stigum and Rene O. Branch, Jr., *Managing Bank Assets and Liabilities* (Homewood, Ill.: Dow Jones-Irwin, 1983), 194.
[5]Marriner S. Eccles, *Beckoning Frontiers: Public and Personal Recollections* (New York: Knopf, 1951), 152–54.
[6]12 U.S.C. Section 1465 (repealed in 1989).

example), frequently had much greater latitude than federally chartered institutions. California law permitted state-chartered thrifts to invest 100 percent of their assets in service corporations authorized to engage in a broad range of higher-risk activities (for example, investing in junk bonds and a variety of commercial ventures). California- and Texas-chartered thrifts were given broad discretion, for instance, to make substantial direct equity investments in commercial real estate.

For a solvent thrift with sufficient shareholder capital at stake, the new lending powers could provide an opportunity to diversify out of the now dangerous portfolio mortgage business. For an insolvent thrift with the government's backing and no shareholder money at stake, the new activities became another way to bet the bank. Further, the government often had little ability to supervise the new activities, and FHLBB examiners did not fully understand many transactions until it was too late.

Sometimes fraud was involved, and business horror stories abounded. Yet even honest thrift managers felt the need to make high-risk bets to survive. Thrifts that did not find the new powers attractive could gamble with traditional mortgage lending instead. One institution, American Savings and Loan (ASL), operating under new management approved by the FHLBB, added $10 billion of mortgage-backed securities to its portfolio in the second and third quarters of 1986, in a bet that interest rates would fall further. ASL lost the bet and substantially increased ultimate government losses.

The thrift industry, including healthy as well as insolvent thrifts, opposed steps by the federal government to act more effectively and promptly to reduce losses.[7] The problem of regulatory delay was significantly exacerbated by the prevailing enthusiasm for wholesale deregulation. The number of FHLBB examiners dropped from 638 in 1979 to 596 in 1984, despite the substantial increase in problem institutions.[8]

Others knew better. In 1983, Federal Home Loan Bank Board Chairman Edwin Gray, a Reagan appointee, became the first

---

[7]Edwin Gray, former chairman of the FHLBB, was perhaps the most outspoken in this regard. See Michael Binstein, "They Were Calling Me the Gestapo: A Conversation with Ed Gray," *Regardie's,* Oct. 1988, p. 96.

[8]Kathleen Day, "Cutback in Oversight of Banks, S&Ls Has Proved Costly," *Washington Post,* 2 October 1988, p. H-5.

FHLBB chair actively to sound the alarm about insolvent thrift institutions. He sought more supervisory staff but was rebuffed by Director David Stockman of the Office of Management and Budget.

Capitol Hill also played a role. In 1987, when the magnitude of the impending Federal Savings and Loan Insurance Corporation (FSLIC) insolvency was increasingly apparent even to the Reagan administration, Congress passed an FSLIC recapitalization bill. Over FHLBB objections, the bill included extensive forbearance provisions permitting insolvent institutions to remain open under certain conditions despite statutory and regulatory violations.

Regulatory Efforts to Reduce Gambling by Insolvent Thrifts Were Belated

When they came, the funds were too little, too late. In 1987, the Reagan administration and Congress overcame strong industry opposition and finally legislated $10.8 billion in funds to close insolvent thrifts, but only permitted the FHLBB to spend the money over several years.

By 1987, the Federal Home Loan Bank Board also was actively trying to restore the quality of regulatory oversight lacking in the previous decades. Through delegating regulatory functions to the privately owned banks of the Federal Home Loan Bank System, the FHLBB avoided budgetary and personnel ceilings and began to hire hundreds of new examiners and other regulatory staff.

The FHLBB took other serious steps as well. The regulator imposed increasingly stringent capital requirements, limited institution growth rates, required GAAP accounting (by 1993), and imposed other safety and soundness measures. Its regulatory staff doubled from 1,093 in 1985 to approximately 2,103 several years later, and the average experience of the staff also increased notably.[9] The 1989 financial institutions legislation created the Office of Thrift Supervision (OTS) to assume the supervisory and en-

[9]M. Danny Wall, Chairman, Federal Home Loan Bank Board, testimony before the Senate Committee on Banking, Housing, and Urban Affairs, 1 March 1989, *Problems of the Federal Savings and Loan Insurance Corporation (FSLIC)*, Part II, 338.

forcement functions of the FHLBB and the FHLBS and provided
the regulator with strengthened powers and resources. Already
by 1990, though, there was serious discussion of abolishing the
OTS and giving the Comptroller of the Currency (OCC) and
Federal Deposit Insurance Corporation (FDIC) the authority to
supervise thrifts as well as commercial banks.

Financial Parallels

As institutions, enterprises share many characteristics with
thrifts. Most importantly, both thrifts and enterprises are crea-
tures of the law rather than of the marketplace. With rare exceptions, the nature of these institutions is essentially determined by
the federal credit support they receive. Thrifts receive this support from federal deposit insurance, and enterprises from an implicit federal guarantee of their obligations and mortgage-backed
securities. They also benefit from tax advantages and preferred
status under a variety of laws that restrict their competitors. The
law makes Fannie Mae and Freddie Mac, for example, into what
one analyst calls "a perfect duopoly";[10] their statutory benefits
permit them to earn handsome profits, at least in good times,
while driving competitors from large parts of the market.

The trouble comes when economic circumstances change. Like
thrifts, government-sponsored enterprises are specialized lenders. In return for their statutory benefits, they are limited by law
to serving prescribed kinds of borrowers or dealing in specified
kinds of loans. Thus, their business is much more homogeneous
than that of banks and other diversified lenders. When something
goes wrong with one part of the business of a thrift or government-sponsored enterprise, it may easily go wrong for a large part
of the business.

Because of the lack of diversity, many loans tend to respond
together to particular economic stresses. As will be discussed in
chapter 2, one systematic problem with excessive credit risk,
interest rate risk, or inadequate management and control systems

[10]Eric I. Hemel, "We Love Freddie Mac At Current Prices Which We Believe Fully
Discount Political Risks," (New York: First Boston Corporation, 21 August 1990), p. 3.

can suddenly translate into substantial financial damage. Thus, it took only two years for the thrift industry, then largely limited by law to purchasing home mortgages, to lose its entire market value net worth after interest rates rose in 1979. Fannie Mae, also limited to dealing in home mortgages, felt the impact of higher interest rates as well, and by 1981 had a market value net worth of *negative* $10.8 billion.[11]

Similarly, a downturn in the agricultural economy, compounded by the Farm Credit System's systematic mistakes in assuring high credit quality and in pricing the interest rates on its agricultural mortgage loans, brought that enterprise from high profits and an expanding market share in the late 1970s to financial failure by 1985.

So far, most enterprises seem to have been well run, despite the incentive to take risks that is created by the implicit federal guarantee. In the volatile financial markets of the 1990s, a record of past profitability is not enough. Adverse economic circumstances or management mistakes can topple a lender—and especially a specialized lender—with breathtaking speed. As we learned from federal deposit insurance, the government must carefully supervise the use of all government guarantees.

Without federal credit support, financial institutions such as thrifts and government-sponsored enterprises lose much of the market discipline—especially the signals from debtholders—that would normally help to constrain risk taking. In other companies, debtholders monitor financial leverage—the proportion of capital available to protect debtholders against losses—and risk taking. Without government backing, companies with too much leverage or too much perceived risk find that they must pay more when they raise money in the debt markets. At some point, investors simply refuse to purchase the obligations of very risky ventures.

Government guarantees undermine these market constraints because debtholders believe that they can turn to the federal government for protection against losses. Even after the Farm Credit System lost $4.6 billion in 1985 and 1986, for example, Standard & Poor's announced that FCS obligations qualified as

[11]U.S. Department of Housing and Urban Development, *1986 Report to Congress on the Federal National Mortgage Association* (Washington, D.C.: Government Printing Office, 1987), Table V-3, p. 100.

"AAA"-rated investments because of the implicit government guarantee.[12] Residual market signals meant some increase in the cost of farm credit borrowings, but these signals were too muted and came too late to protect taxpayers against losses. As was the case for thrift institutions, enhanced accountability of enterprises required effective federal oversight and increased capitalization.[13]

Political Parallels

The politics of the thrift industry's legislative efforts are also instructive. For years, the U.S. League of Savings Institutions was one of the most formidable lobbying groups dealing with Congress. From its inception, the thrift industry dominated its nominal regulator, the Federal Home Loan Bank Board. The thrift industry claimed that its public mission—to support homebuyers and the mortgage market—justified lax federal oversight and low shareholder capital. Some enterprises today foster a similar belief that somehow their public purposes justify a status quo that places taxpayers at too much risk. Today, the U.S. League is politically weakened, reflecting the collapsed state of the industry. Enterprises, by contrast, are all exceedingly influential in Congress, especially with respect to the committees and subcommittees that enact their charter legislation.

When the U.S. Treasury proposed in 1990 to impose greater financial discipline on government-sponsored enterprises, members of the House and Senate banking committees leapt to the defense of Fannie Mae and Freddie Mac.

The housing subcommittees of the House and Senate banking committees sponsored several hearings to provide a forum for the

[12]Standard & Poor's Corporation, "Farm Credit System's 'AAA' Eligibility Monitored," *Standard & Poor's Credit Week*, 20 July 1987, 13.
[13]There is a substantial body of economic literature on this point. See Mark J. Flannery, "Deposit Insurance Creates a Need for Bank Regulation," *Business Review*, January/February 1982, 17–27; Fischer Black, Merton H. Miller, and Richard A. Posner, "An Approach to the Regulation of Bank Holding Companies," *Journal of Business* 51 (March 1978): 379–412; Sherman J. Maisel, ed., *Risk and Capital Adequacy in Commercial Banks* (Chicago: University of Chicago Press, 1981), especially chapter 6. See also Kevin E. Villani, "The Federal Forecast," *Secondary Mortgage Markets* (Spring 1985): 26–33; and Edward J. Kane, "Comments," *The Federal National Mortgage Association in a Changing Economic Environment*, Symposium (Washington, D.C.: U.S. General Accounting Office, July 1985), 181–189.

enterprises and their supporters. Representatives of the housing and real estate industry, low-income housing groups, and Wall Street investment firms that sell Fannie Mae and Freddie Mac securities were invited to testify. They expressed concern about maintaining the public purpose of the two corporations and fear about the potential damage if greater financial accountability were imposed by the Treasury plan; some claimed that low-income buyers would be especially hurt by the Treasury plan.

Yet the concerns were largely misplaced. To require a high investment grade rating from Fannie Mae and Freddie Mac without regard to their federal credit support, and to provide effective financial supervision, as the Treasury proposed, was unlikely to impair the enterprises' long-term service to the housing industry. Analysts believe that Freddie Mac could achieve a high investment grade rating with fairly little effort.[14] The five-year transition period proposed by the Treasury Department would then permit Fannie Mae to reduce reliance on its burgeoning mortgage portfolio, and to adopt a Freddie Mac–type strategy of predominantly using guarantees of mortgage-backed securities to serve the housing market without incurring excessive interest-rate risk. With extra capital and less risk taking, the enterprises would be strengthened in their ability to serve borrowers in years to come.

Thus, the hearings served less to protect the interest of home buyers than to provide political cover for the Fannie Mae and Freddie Mac shareholders who would lose leverage if the companies were held to higher capital standards. Federal Reserve Board Chairman Alan Greenspan wrote to Senate Banking Committee Chairman Donald W. Riegle, Jr. that the enterprises deliver a credit subsidy whose benefits are divided between homebuyers and shareholders. He observed that as the proposals to require increased capital "have gained force, stock prices of FNMA and FHLMC have fallen, suggesting that a significant portion of the subsidy may have been going to shareholders."[15]

During the 1990 congressional budget summit negotiations,

---

[14]See, for example, U.S. Department of Housing and Urban Development, "1987 Report to Congress on the Federal National Mortgage Association," issued 27 September 1989, p. 51.

[15]Letter from Alan Greenspan, chairman, Board of Governors of the Federal Reserve System, to Donald W. Riegle, Jr., chairman, Senate Committee on Banking, Housing and Urban Affairs, 31 August 1990, p. 11.

the influence of Sallie Mae and particularly of the Farm Credit System was also felt in opposition to enactment of the Treasury proposals. As happened with congressional and regulatory approval of reduced thrift capital standards in the early 1980s, American taxpayers were the major group without adequate representation in the process.

Government-sponsored enterprises have such immense political resources at their disposal that they raise the ultimate fear of the thrift debacle: that these institutions are out of political control. Today, even while reaping generous federal benefits, enterprises exert immense political power, especially over the authorizing committees, to structure a cozy regulatory relationship—or to avoid regulation altogether, in the case of Sallie Mae—and rely on only minimal capital requirements, which may fail to protect taxpayers against financial calamity if something goes wrong.

The Need for Preventive Steps

If statesmanship is optimally the combination of sound policy and good politics, then it is time for U.S. policymakers to pay more attention to sound policies. Some longstanding principles of finance and public administration can help build institutions capable of serving the country over the long term. It is time to bring these financial and institutional principles effectively to bear, first on government-sponsored enterprises, then on federal agency credit programs, and ultimately on each government department, agency, and instrumentality.

Charles A. Bowsher, comptroller general of the United States, has spoken of the crisis that he calls the disinvestment of government, "the increasing difficulty in finding solutions to problems because of postponed decisions, neglect, or poor management."[16] As the thrift debacle has shown, the cost of such neglect is not easy to measure at any particular moment. To ignore financial soundness is to remain in a state of risk. While the probability

[16]Charles A. Bowsher, "An Emerging Crisis: The Disinvestment of Government," The James E. Webb Lecture, National Academy of Public Administration, Washington, D.C., 2 December 1988, p. 9.

of collapse of any one institution in any one year may be small, the odds mount as the years pass. We have learned from the thrift industry that taxpayers cannot afford to play the odds forever. It is time now, before another government-sponsored enterprise faces financial failure, to institute reasonable regulatory and institutional reforms that can help protect taxpayers against unnecessary losses in the future.

2

The Hidden Costs and Public Benefits of Government-Sponsored Enterprises

The most important thing to remember about our federal ties is this: the trade-off for these ties is concentration on one business and one business only—housing. We don't buy toaster loans or domed-stadium loans when rates on these loans are higher than on housing loans—as they frequently are. . . .

—David O. Maxwell, Fannie Mae
chairman and chief executive officer

Government-sponsored enterprises are among the largest financial institutions in the United States. Fannie Mae and Freddie Mac together fund one out of every four home mortgages in the country. They are each larger than Citicorp, the Bank of America, or any of America's largest bank holding companies or money center banks. Sallie Mae holds one out of every four guaranteed student loans and, directly or indirectly, funds about half of all such loans. The Farm Credit System holds one-third of the farm real estate debt in the country. The Federal Home Loan Bank System lends thrift institutions one out of every ten dollars they borrow.

Yet, despite their massive financial presence, the activities of government-sponsored enterprises remain largely misunderstood by policymakers and are virtually unknown to the public at large. Most of the enterprises are unfamiliar to the public because they provide their services to other lenders rather than to the individual borrower. Fannie Mae, Freddie Mac, Sallie Mae, and Farmer Mac are restricted by law to the secondary market; they purchase or guarantee loans that primary lenders-banks, thrifts, mortgage bankers, and others—make to the borrower. Similarly, the Federal Home Loan Banks lend money to thrift institutions rather than to the general public. Only the Farm Credit System, one of the better known enterprises at least in rural areas, has an express mandate to make loans directly to eligible individuals.

Enterprises: Government Agencies or Private Companies?

Many who know of individual enterprises still misunderstand how they work. Part of this misunderstanding occurs because the enterprises combine private and governmental characteristics in an unusual way. At first glance, they appear to be part of the government. Established by Congress, the enterprises are authorized to issue debt obligations with most of the characteristics of federal agency securities: they are governed by boards that often include governmentally and presidentially appointed directors; they usually have lines of credit to the U.S. Treasury; their obligations are implicitly guaranteed by the federal government, creating potentially open-ended claims on federal funds; and they are considered instrumentalities of the federal government with federal charters that preempt some state laws and taxes.

However, in other ways the enterprises look like private companies. They are privately owned; they sell stock to private people and institutions; their employees are exempt from federal civil service and procurement laws; they are free to make a profit; and their activities do not depend on regular federal appropriations. (Table 2–1 presents an overview of the enterprises and their functions.)

Given this confusion, it is necessary to define the term *govern-*

TABLE 2–1

Government-Sponsored Enterprises: An Overview

Enterprise	Year Established	Year of Full Private Ownership	Lending Activities	1989 Size (in $billions)	Type of Ownership
Farm Credit System (FCS)	1916 (Federal Land Banks) 1923 (Federal Intermediate Credit Banks) 1933 (Banks for Cooperatives)	1968	Makes agricultural loans (including mortgages, operating loans, loans to co-ops)	$63.6 (assets)	Cooperative borrower/ shareholders
Federal Home Loan Bank System (FHLBS)	1932	1951	Makes advances (collateralized loans) to thrifts and other lenders	$180.2 (assets)	Cooperative borrower/ member shareholders
Fannie Mae	1938	1968	Purchases home mortgages from primary lenders	$352.5 ($124.3 assets plus $228.2 mortgage-backed securities)	Investor/ shareholders
Freddie Mac	1970	1970	Purchases home mortgages from primary lenders	$308.4 ($35.5 assets plus $272.9 mortgage-backed securities)	Investor/ shareholders
Sallie Mae	1972	1972	Purchases student loans from primary lenders and makes advances (collateralized loans) to lenders	$35.5 (assets)	Investor/ shareholders
Farmer Mac	1988	1988	Guarantees pools of agricultural mortgage-backed securities	Not operating in 1989	User cooperative lender/ shareholders

TABLE 2–1 *(Continued)*

Enterprise	Year Established	Year of Full Private Ownership	Lending Activities	1989 Size (in $billions)	Type of Ownership
Financing Corporation (FICO)	1987	N.A.	Funds government closure of insolvent thrifts	$8.1 (assets)	Federal assessments/ de facto federal ownership
Resolution Funding Corporation (REFCORP)	1989	N.A.	Funds government closure of insolvent thrifts	$1.2 (assets)	Federal assessments/ de facto federal ownership

Source: Of financial information: Treasury Department, *Report of the Secretary of the Treasury on Government-Sponsored Enterprises* (Washington, D.C.: GPO, May 1990).

ment-sponsored enterprise more precisely. *A government-sponsored enterprise is a privately owned, federally chartered financial institution with nationwide scope and specialized lending powers that benefits from an implicit federal guarantee to enhance its ability to borrow money.*

Enterprises Resemble Banks and Thrift Institutions

Close analysis reveals that government-sponsored enterprises most resemble federally chartered thrift institutions and national banks. Like these thrifts and banks, the enterprises are federally chartered, privately owned instruments of federal policy. Like national banks and even more like federally chartered thrifts, the enterprises are limited in their lending to powers defined in federal law; like federal deposit insurance for thrifts and banks, implicit federal backing helps the enterprises to lower their cost of funds. Table 2–2 compares some of the important attributes of government-sponsored enterprises to those of federally chartered thrift institutions and national banks.

Just as thrifts specialize as home mortgage lenders, government-sponsored enterprises serve a variety of specialized mar-

TABLE 2–2

Government-Sponsored Enterprises Compared to Federally Chartered Thrifts and National Banks

Characteristic	Government-Sponsored Enterprise	Federally Chartered Thrift	National Bank
Private ownership	Yes	Yes	Yes
Shareholder control[a]	Yes	Yes	Yes
Federal credit support	Yes—all obligations and guaranteed securities	Yes—deposit accounts up to $100,000	Yes—deposit accounts up to $100,000
Federal charter	Yes	Yes	Yes
Lending powers defined by federal law	Yes	Yes	Yes
Specialized lender	Yes	Yes	No

[a]Some enterprises and thrifts are in mutual form, with control by shareholders who are borrowers or users as well as investors (see the last column of table 2–1).

kets. Fannie Mae and Freddie Mac purchase home mortgages in the secondary market, Sallie Mae funds student loans, the Farm Credit System (FCS) deals in agricultural loans, the Federal Home Loan Bank System (FHLBS) lends to thrift institutions and a few other housing lenders, and the Financing Corporation (FICO) and Resolution Funding Corporation (REFCORP) help provide funds for the government to close or reorganize insolvent thrift institutions. Another enterprise, Farmer Mac, is about to begin funding agricultural mortgages.

Enterprises Are Growing Rapidly

Supported by their ability to borrow virtually unlimited low-cost funds in the so-called federal agency credit market, government-sponsored enterprises can grow quite rapidly. Table 2–3 shows how the size of the major enterprises—Fannie Mae, Freddie Mac, and Sallie Mae—more than doubled in just five years. Only the Farm Credit System shrank in size, from 1985 to 1989, reflecting its collapse in 1985 and the painful process of revival since then. Omitted from table 2–3 are Farmer Mac, which is only beginning operations, and FICO and REFCORP, whose size is capped by their authorizing legislation.

TABLE 2–3

Financial Overview, 1985–1989

Enterprise	1985 Size (in $billions)[a]	1989 Size (in $billions)[a]	Growth in 1989 (%)	Five-Year Growth, 1985–1989 (%)	1989 Shareholder Equity (in $billions)	1989 Ratio of Equity to Size (%)
Farm Credit System	$ 79.8	$ 63.6	−3.2%	−20.3%	$ 3.4[b]	5.3%
Federal Home Loan Bank System	$112.1	$180.2	3.1%	60.9%	$14.2	7.9%
Fannie Mae	$154.1	$352.5	21.4%	129%	$ 3.0	0.8%
Freddie Mac	$116.8	$308	18.2%	164%	$ 1.9	0.6%
Sallie Mae	$ 14.4	$ 35.5	24.0%	146%	$ 1.0	2.9%

Sources: Calculated from information presented in the Treasury Department, *Report of the Secretary of the Treasury on Government-Sponsored Enterprises* (Washington, D.C.: GPO, May 1990).
[a]Assets plus mortgage-backed securities (MBSs).
[b]The 1990 *Report of the Secretary of the Treasury on Government-Sponsored Enterprises* expresses concern that only $2.3 billion of this amount is actually at risk; the remainder is borrower stock of a kind that was protected from loss when the government provided funds to support the system in 1987.

Another important statistic related to enterprise growth is shareholder capitalization. The Federal Home Loan Bank System is well capitalized, with shareholder equity amounting to almost 8 percent of its total size. By contrast, Fannie Mae and Freddie Mac are thinly capitalized, with shareholder equity for each amounting to less than 1 percent of total size. (Size is properly measured as an enterprise's assets plus its lending through guaranteed mortgage-backed securities, or MBSs.)

Enterprises Have a Long Tradition

Enterprises have a long tradition as instruments of federal policy. (See table 2–1 for the year each enterprise was established and the year it became fully private.) The earliest enterprises were started with capital contributions from the federal government, which were later repaid or forgiven when the government sold or gave all of its stock to private shareholders.

Farm Credit System (FCS)

The oldest enterprise, the Farm Credit System (FCS), originated in 1916, when the federal government established the Federal Land Banks and affiliated cooperative associations (later called Federal Land Bank Associations) to encourage the flow of credit for farm mortgage loans. The FCS was expanded in 1923, with the creation of the Federal Intermediate Credit Banks (FICBs) and Production Credit Associations to make farm operating loans, and again in 1933, with the Banks for Cooperatives to lend to agricultural producer cooperatives. The FCS banks, either directly or through their affiliated associations, make loans and provide a variety of other financial services to their borrowers. The associations, now called Agricultural Credit Associates, have assumed an increasing role in the FCS. From the beginning, FCS institutions—banks and associations—have been created as cooperatives owned and controlled by their borrowers.

Federal Home Loan Bank System (FHLBS)

The second oldest enterprise, the Federal Home Loan Bank System (FHLBS), was established in 1932 to provide funds to the thrift industry, which had been heavily damaged in the Great Depression. The Federal Home Loan Banks were authorized to make cash advances (that is, loans secured by collateral provided by the borrower) to thrift institutions. The FHLBS is owned and controlled by thrift institutions (and a few other specialized housing lenders) under legislation requiring all thrifts to purchase minimum amounts of stock in the FHLB serving their geographic district.

As a result of the depression, thrifts were faced with large-scale withdrawals of deposits. At the same time, deflation in real estate made it impossible to sell their portfolios of mortgages that those deposits had funded. The FHLBS cash-advance system permitted thrifts to use their mortgages as collateral and to borrow funds from the Federal Home Loan Banks.

Over time, the FHLBS advances became an inexpensive source

of funds for many thrifts. From 1966 until the mid-1980s, federal law limited the interest rates that thrifts could pay on their deposits. FHLBS advances were especially valuable as substitutes for lost deposits when market rates of interest rose above the regulatory ceiling and depositors closed their accounts to invest elsewhere, such as in higher-yielding money-market accounts. Today, FHLBS advances provide a source of funds for thrift institutions, a few commercial banks, and credit unions engaged in residential mortgage lending. Large thrifts tend to use FHLBS advances much more than smaller ones; altogether, roughly half of the institutions that are members of the FHLBS also receive advances. Since 1982, thrifts have been permitted to use market-able assets other than mortgages as collateral for FHLBS advances. Member institutions can borrow routinely from the FHLBS and advances can have maturities of up to twenty years.

Fannie Mae

In 1934, the Roosevelt administration proposed the creation of another set of enterprises, national mortgage associations, to provide a secondary market for residential mortgages. Under the original legislation, any incorporator willing to commit the necessary capital and to accept the benefits and limitations of the federal legislation was authorized to obtain a federal charter for a national mortgage association. Largely because of opposition from the thrift industry, the benefits of a national mortgage association charter were quite limited. This compounded the general economic hesitancy prevalent after 1929, and no private incorporators ever sought a charter.

Instead, in 1938, the Reconstruction Finance Corporation, an arm of the federal government, chartered the National Mortgage Association of Washington, quickly renamed the Federal National Mortgage Association (FNMA), as a mortgage-lending subsidiary. Fannie Mae was later transferred to the predecessor agency of the Department of Housing and Urban Development (HUD). Then, in 1968, it was divided into a government agency called the Government National Mortgage Association (Ginnie Mae) and a privately owned Federal National Mortgage Association (Fannie Mae). Fannie Mae has an eighteen-member board of directors; thirteen are elected by their shareholders and five are appointed by the president of the United States.

For decades Fannie Mae has served housing finance by purchasing and holding residential mortgages in portfolio. The Emergency Home Finance Act of 1970 permitted Fannie Mae to deal in conventional mortgages (that is, those with private mortgage insurance). Previously, it was restricted to mortgages insured by the Federal Housing Administration (FHA) or guaranteed by the Veterans Administration (VA). In 1981, after rising interest rates caused substantial losses from its portfolio lending business, Fannie Mae followed the examples of Ginnie Mae and Freddie Mac when it began to guarantee mortgage-backed securities as a means of funding home mortgages.

Freddie Mac

In 1970, the thrift industry persuaded Congress to create another government-sponsored enterprise to support home mortgages in the secondary market—the Federal Home Loan Mortgage Corporation, or Freddie Mac. For many years, only thrift institutions were permitted to own Freddie Mac stock. The law was revised in 1988 to permit sale of Freddie Mac stock to the general public. Another recent change concerns Freddie Mac's corporate structure. From 1970 until only recently, Freddie Mac's board of directors consisted of the same three federal officials who made up the Federal Home Loan Bank Board (FHLBB). In the 1989 legislation abolishing the FHLBB, Freddie Mac obtained a shareholder-controlled board of directors patterned on that of Fannie Mae.

From its inception, Freddie Mac chose a strategy of funding home mortgages by guaranteeing mortgage-backed securities. Today, its mortgage portfolio is only a small part of its total lending activities. Time will tell whether the changes in Freddie Mac's board of directors and corporate structure (from thrift-shareholders to general investor-shareholders) will affect its lending strategy. In contrast to its earlier years, Freddie Mac will face shareholder pressure to maximize short-term returns, and possibly to increase its risk taking and make money from increased portfolio lending. Today, Fannie Mae and Freddie Mac operate under similar charter legislation; they provide secondary market services to the same kinds of residential lenders, including thrift institutions, mortgage bankers, and commercial banks.

Sallie Mae

Congress created the Student Loan Marketing Association, or Sallie Mae, in 1972 as a means of enhancing financial support for federally guaranteed student loans. At the time, guaranteed student loans seemed small, expensive to service, and generally unattractive to commercial banks and other private lenders. Sallie Mae was authorized to purchase student loans and to make advances (that is, loans secured by student loans) to lenders. Over time, Sallie Mae expanded its activities to include the funding of student loans not federally guaranteed as well as other kinds of loans, including home-equity loans (which some home owners may use to borrow funds for their children's education).

Sallie Mae is controlled by a board of directors consisting of twenty-one members: seven elected by financial institutions, seven elected by educational institutions, and seven appointed by the president of the United States. Sallie Mae has developed economies of scale, including sophisticated loan-origination and servicing software for primary lenders. The government has expanded the kinds and amounts of student loans and has increased the subsidy paid to lenders in the guaranteed student loan program. These changes, and Sallie Mae's conspicuous success, have shown lenders that student loans can be a very profitable business, in contrast to their earlier reputation in the lending community.

Farmer Mac

The Federal Agricultural Mortgage Corporation, or Farmer Mac, was established in 1988 to provide a secondary market for agricultural loans, essentially serving much of the same market as the Farm Credit System. Farmer Mac guarantees mortgage-backed securities (MBSs) issued by private lenders, including Farm Credit Institutions, and based on pools of agricultural mortgages with characteristics specified in the law. Here Farmer Mac is solely a guarantor; it is not authorized to purchase loans or issue debt. FCS institutions, commercial banks, insurance companies, and other rural lenders originate and service the loans in the MBS pools. In addition, in late 1990, Farmer Mac obtained authority to deal in agricultural loans by the Farmer's Home Administration and to fund a portfolio of such loans by issuing debt.

Farmer Mac stock is owned by commercial rural lenders and FCS institutions. The Farmer Mac board consists of fifteen members: five elected by FCS shareholders, five elected by commercial lender-shareholders, and five appointed by the president of the United States. The absence of voting investor-shareholders means that Farmer Mac is oriented to the needs of its lender-users rather than to investors seeking to maximize Farmer Mac's profits.

FICO and REFCORP

The government established the Financing Corporation (FICO) and the Resolution Funding Corporation (REFCORP) in 1987 and 1989, respectively, as off-budget devices to help fund the federal agencies responsible for closing insolvent thrift institutions. While the other enterprises enjoy open-ended access to federal credit (which raises issues of financial risk), the dollar limits of REFCORP and FICO are capped in their enabling legislation.

Although the earlier enterprises were designed to be self-sustaining over the long term, FICO and REFCORP were created simply to defer the impact on the federal budget of paying to close thrift institutions in a more straightforward manner. At some point, U.S. taxpayers are likely to be asked to bear much of the expense in paying off FICO and REFCORP debt-holders. When pushed to this extreme, the enterprise model loses its original public purpose; it becomes simply an instrument to minimize current federal payments and thereby push today's financial burdens onto our children. More will be said about this later.

Other Enterprises under Consideration

Because of federal deficit pressures, Congress and the executive branch have considered creating new enterprises to take federal credit programs outside of the federal budget. One powerful constituent group composed of small business investment companies (SBICs) came close to enacting an enterprise that they would own and control. In 1986, the House of Representatives passed legislation to create the Corporation for Small Business Investment (COSBI) to support small business investment companies, but the bill did not win Senate approval. Leading members of the House and Senate small business committees again introduced COSBI bills, with some variations, in 1987 and 1989.

The Development of the Federal
Subsidy Implicit in Enterprise Lending

From the history and development of government-sponsored enterprises, it is interesting to trace the evolution of the federal subsidy used to lower enterprise borrowing costs. In the two decades following the creation of the Federal Land Banks in 1916, the government experimented with a variety of means to subsidize the enterprises' credit activities. The Farm Credit System and the Federal Home Loan Bank System, for example, benefited from substantial federal, state, and local tax exemptions. By contrast, the denial of comparable tax benefits made it unattractive for investors to obtain a national mortgage association charter; the national mortgage associations would have had to compete with thrift institutions, which, at the time, were completely tax exempt and had access to federal deposit insurance to lower their cost of funds.

With the widespread collapse of financial institutions during the Great Depression, the federal government increasingly used direct federal guarantees to provide credit support. The government directly guaranteed Farm Credit System and Federal Home Loan Bank System obligations and, through the Reconstruction

Finance Corporation, provided support for the newly created Fannie Mae. Direct federal guarantees and insurance were hallmarks of New Deal credit programs, in that investors were willing to buy federally backed obligations but were often unwilling to commit their money to private institutions because so many had defaulted during the depression.

The implicit federal guarantee emerged gradually as a subsidy device. The financial markets looked on the enterprises as federal agencies and inferred a moral obligation on the federal government to back them in case of default. By 1968, when the government sold all of its remaining stock in the Farm Credit System and Fannie Mae, the implicit guarantee was regarded as strong enough to reassure investors even though all of the enterprises had become completely privately owned.

The value of outstanding enterprise securities has grown in the 1970s and 1980s, and the implicit guarantee is increasingly perceived as a practical as well as a moral obligation of the federal government. There are almost a trillion dollars of enterprise securities outstanding, and the volume is accelerating. The government is unlikely to permit any one of the enterprises to default on its obligations, for fear of shaking investor confidence in all enterprise obligations and in financial institutions holding those obligations, which could cause the price of all enterprise securities to plummet.

The government faces immense pressure to stand behind a failing government-sponsored enterprise, just as it ultimately guaranteed all of the obligations of the Continental Illinois Corporation, the large and completely private holding company parent of the Continental Illinois National Bank. Only a small fraction of total Continental debt was held by depositors in the bank's federally insured accounts. The bank had about $40 billion in assets, making it a much smaller institution than are most enterprises today.

The ultimate test of the strength of the implicit guarantee came with the creation of FICO and REFCORP in the late 1980s. Unlike the other enterprises that make loans expecting to be repaid, FICO and REFCORP are mere shell corporations designed to be commercial failures. The two corporations borrow money to provide funds to the insolvent Federal Savings and Loan Insurance

Corporation (FSLIC) and its successor. Despite a variety of elaborate funding provisions, there is a strong likelihood that taxpayers ultimately will have to help pay something to satisfy holders of the thirty-year obligations of FICO and REFCORP. (Indeed, the two corporations reveal on their balance sheets a substantial negative net worth.) Nevertheless, the implicit federal guarantee—supplements in the case of REFCORP by an explicit guarantee of interest payments—is powerful enough that obligations of both enterprises are AAA-rated; investors perceive them as of such low risk that FICO and REFCORP bonds trade at spreads just above Treasury obligations.[1]

The Controversy Surrounding Government-Sponsored Enterprises

Competitive Issues

Government-sponsored enterprises have never been free from controversy. On the one hand, constituent groups such as farmers, the real estate industry, thrift institutions, and some lenders in the guaranteed student loan program have supported the enterprises because of the credit support they provide for agriculture, residential mortgages, thrift institutions, and student loans. On the other hand, many competitors have complained about the unfair advantages available under enterprise charter acts that are said to help the enterprises "crowd out" competitive firms that otherwise would serve the same market. One of these controversies concerns the extent to which the substantial advantages of Fannie Mae and Freddie Mac have helped to reduce profit margins for thrift institutions and commercial banks, such that thrifts and banks today find it difficult to compete as portfolio lenders that hold residential mortgages. Similar questions have been raised about the Farm Credit System vis-à-vis commercial rural lenders, and Sallie Mae vis-à-vis commercial banks or other hold-

---

[1]See, for example, Financing Corporation, *Information Statement Supplement: $670,000,000 8.60% Bonds Due September 26, 2019, Series D-2019* (Washington, D.C.: Financing Corporation, September 19, 1989).

ers of student loans. The evidence concerning enterprise competition and the extent to which a "level playing field" among competitors exists are explored more fully in chapter 4.

The Public Benefits and Costs of Enterprise Lending

Here, it is useful to review some of the major policy questions concerning government-sponsored enterprises from the perspectives of the government and the taxpaying public. Four issues stand out (and serve as themes through much of this book):

1. Can the government protect taxpayers against unnecessary financial risk?
2. Do we need specialized lenders?
3. Can the government direct enterprise lending to serve the highest public priority credit needs?
4. Are there limits to the enterprises' growth in their designated markets?

The Difficulty of Protecting Taxpayers against Unnecessary Financial Risk

As federally insured thrifts have taught us, the implicit federal guarantee of enterprise obligations weakens market discipline and creates an incentive to take higher risks. Economists call this the "moral hazard"; private institutions and their shareholders profit from risky ventures while taxpayers are liable to pay for most of the losses from big mistakes.

The implicit federal guarantee means that investors can look to the government rather than to an enterprise's creditworthiness for assurance that their investments will be repaid. Federal backing thereby permits enterprise management to engage in riskier activities than can comparable private firms, without fear of driving investors away or having to pay prohibitive rates of interest to attract funds. While some managers may refrain from excessive risk taking on their own, the government must protect against losses from others who may take risks and fail. Without effective oversight, the government can face substantial exposure to risky lending by some fraction of the institutions—such as thrifts, banks, and enterprises—whose activities it implicitly or explicitly guarantees.

Fortunately, the Treasury Department's 1990 review of enterprise activities indicates that none is in danger of imminent failure. Managers of most of the enterprises—especially those at the FHLBS and Sallie Mae, who have kept their capital at prudent levels—seem to be avoiding major pitfalls of moral hazard. Nevertheless, given the ability of the enterprises to increase their risk taking, and the increased incentive to take that risk during times of adversity, the government is remiss when it fails to supervise these huge institutions and their activities.

However, as the thrift debacle has shown, government regulation is not an assured solution to problems caused when the government's implicit guarantee distorts normal market incentives. Regulators are often located in the same political and psychological environment as the institutions they regulate. Congress may be sensitive to constituencies with a stake in increasing rather than reducing the federal government's risk exposure. Concern about the practical and political limits on effective federal regulation of safety and soundness has led economists and other analysts to seek new market-based solutions, such as imposing risk-related federal insurance premiums and limiting the extent of federal guarantees so that private debt-holders share in any financial losses. In its 1990 *Report on Government Sponsored Enterprises,* [2] the Treasury Department recommended a different market-based approach, in which each enterprise would be required to obtain a rating of its obligations—without regard to the government's implicit guarantee—from two nationally recognized rating agencies. Through this approach, each enterprise would be required to conduct its business with sufficient prudence and capital so as to qualify for the highest rating.

The record of federal oversight by enterprise regulators, such as the Department of Housing and Urban Development and, until

---

[2]Treasury Department, *Report of the Secretary of the Treasury on Government Sponsored Enterprises* (Washington, D.C.: GPO, May 1990), pp. 8–10.

1985, the Farm Credit Administration, is one of dominance by the regulated institutions and inability of the regulator to impose necessary safety and soundness restrictions. The question is whether the federal government can establish an effective combination of regulatory and market-based controls before another enterprise gets into trouble.

Enterprises as Specialized Lenders

Specialized lending is the essential function of a government-sponsored enterprise. The enterprises are permitted to borrow on favorable terms in the federal agency credit market. Congress has imposed limitations on the scope of enterprise lending to help assure that these benefits are directed to serving intended beneficiaries—farmers, home buyers, students, and so forth.

The problem is that specialized lenders raise special financial concerns compared to more diversified lenders such as commercial banks. Lending is a risky business. Loans involve credit risk, the chance that the borrower won't repay, as well as interest rate risk, the chance that changing interest rates will make a loan unprofitable by the time it is repaid. For example, when interest rates rise, yields on an institution's fixed-rate loans decline in value; when interest rates drop, yields on an institution's variable-rate loans can drop below the average cost of its fixed-rate debt. Thus, matching assets and liabilities can be a tricky business, especially at times of volatile interest rates.

Lending activities also involve operations risk, the chance that a failure of management information or control will lead to financial damage. Most importantly, though, a financial institution is subject to management risk, the possibility that managers, directors, and management systems will not be of sufficient quality to protect their institutions against avoidable mistakes or imprudent risk taking.

These and other kinds of risk, discussed more fully in chapter 7, affect all lenders. And for each type of loan, various kinds of risk exist in varying degrees. A prudent diversified lender is somewhat protected by its very diversity, in that a single external factor, market risk, is unlikely to affect its various kinds of loans all at once. A specialized lender does not have that protection. A problem facing a specialized lender is more likely to permeate a large proportion of its business at the same time.

For a well-managed diversified lender, the diversity in lending activities by itself helps to hedge against particular forms of risk. Each kind of loan combines different risks in different ways so that one kind of risk has less chance to plunge the institution into financial trouble. However, to the extent that they serve national markets, government-sponsored enterprises benefit from a form of diversity that is unavailable to those commercial banks or thrifts confined to serving particular states or regions.

The question regarding enterprises as specialized lenders is one of public costs and benefits. Because a government-sponsored enterprise is restricted to serving a particular market, it cannot desert that market to take advantage of more profitable opportunities elsewhere. This means that the enterprises serve their designated economic sectors in bad times as well as good ones. But this may also mean greater financial vulnerability. Can the financial risks posed by specialized lending be controlled so that they are outweighed by the benefits of enterprise support for a particular sector of the economy? That question presented itself in acute terms with the collapse of hundreds of specialized thrift institutions during the 1980s, and to varying degrees it also poses a significant issue for the enterprises today.

Enterprise Lending and the Highest Public Priority Credit Needs

The political process determines the highest priority public credit needs. It is no accident that government-sponsored enterprises serve sectors of the economy considered especially important to the public welfare: home ownership, farming, and education. The problem is that, by their very nature, the enterprises are limited in the public benefits they can provide. They are limited to providing a modest credit subsidy in the forms of slightly lower interest rates, longer-term credit than borrowers might otherwise obtain, or other benefits.

Because the enterprises do not draw on appropriated federal funds, they can only afford to fund or guarantee commercially based loans that the borrower is expected to repay. This limits the enterprises to providing their benefits largely to creditworthy borrowers who may not need the special credit support as much as borrowers who are more marginal. It is difficult, both technically and politically, to craft enabling legislation to target enterprise lending to serve the highest public priority credit needs while assuring that the enterprises remain financially viable.

Moreover, within their permitted markets, investor-owned enterprises may seek to serve the most lucrative segments. Sallie Mae, for example, tends to purchase the student loans that are least likely to involve servicing problems because of delinquencies or defaults. Ordinarily, this would be considered good business practice. The question for a government-sponsored enterprise, though, is whether service to the more profitable market segments tends to neglect borrowers whose needs may involve a higher public priority.

The cooperative structure of the Farm Credit System (FCS) overcame this problem by creating a less profit-oriented incentive structure for the enterprise. Unfortunately, the lack of profit orientation in many FCS institutions then raised the opposite kind of problem—insufficient attention to the financial strength of the institution. The Farm Credit Banks did serve less creditworthy borrowers, especially farmers who had taken on too much debt in good times, such as during the period of booming agricultural prosperity in the 1970s, and were unprepared to service that debt when the agricultural economy declined. This meant that the FCS could not sustain itself when a serious downturn occurred and large-scale borrower defaults threw the system into decline.

The tension between service to the most needy borrowers on the one hand, and the need to remain economically sound on the other, defines the limits of enterprise lending as a useful instrument of federal credit policy. If the government desires to lend to less creditworthy borrowers, it must do so with subsidies from appropriated funds to cover losses.

Another kind of tension exists between the shareholders of an enterprise, who have an incentive to keep subsidy benefits for themselves, and the nominal beneficiaries, who are supposed to be served by an enterprise (such as home buyers or students). Investor-owned enterprises may have an incentive to increase profits for shareholders, rather than passing on the benefits by lowering loan rates to the extent they otherwise could. Moreover, poorly designed federal legislation can create barriers to entry and other artificial obstacles that limit the extent to which an enterprise passes its credit advantages on to borrowers in its designated market. (Chapter 3 explores these issues in greater detail.)

Yet another problem involves the way changing markets can alter the public benefits of enterprise lending. Fannie Mae, for instance, made an important contribution to mortgage finance in its first thirty to forty years of operation, when the presence of significant market imperfections restricted the availability of mortgage money in the growing central and western states, as compared to those in the East. Today, those market imperfections have been overcome, and many competing financial institutions are available to channel mortgage money across the fifty states. This means that the potential contribution of Fannie Mae today is measurably less than it was previously. Similarly, in 1932, the Federal Home Loan Bank System (FHLBS) may have been an important means of restoring financial vitality to the thrift industry devastated by the Great Depression; today, it is not at all clear how provision of credit to profitable thrifts serves a significant public purpose. (The FHLBS does not lend to shaky thrift institutions except with very high collateral requirements or unless the federal government guarantees repayment of the loan.)

Finally, there is the problem of considerable expansion of federal credit in recent years. This includes the dramatic growth of government agency credit programs as well as enterprise lending. Over one-third of all nonfederal credit today is subsidized by the federal government, directly or indirectly. Especially with pressures to reduce budgeted federal programs, the federal government seems unable to resist the pleas of influential constituents, including the enterprises and their borrowers, to expand federally supported credit for a growing number of claimants. This tends to reduce the public benefits of the federal credit support because they are diffuse and poorly directed; at the same time, the ability of federal credit to give selected borrowers an advantage is weakened. A federal credit advantage for everyone means an advantage for no one. This raises questions about the extent to which all federal credit subsidies, including those provided by enterprise lending, are properly focused to assure that they serve high-priority credit needs and do not offset each other.

The Accelerating Rate of Enterprise Growth

Except for the financially disabled Farm Credit System, government-sponsored enterprises have grown at a phenomenal rate. Sallie Mae grew 24-fold in only ten years, between 1979 and 1988; it grew by another 24 percent in 1989 alone. Fannie Mae and Freddie Mac today are huge institutions. At year-end 1989, Fannie Mae had $124 billion in assets plus $228 billion in guaranteed mortgaged-backed securities; Freddie Mac had $35 billion in assets plus $273 billion in guaranteed securities. In 1989 alone, Fannie Mae grew by over $62 billion, and it is projected to grow even more in 1990. Figure 2–1 shows clearly how several of the enterprises—Fannie Mae, Freddie Mac, and Sallie Mae—more than doubled in size in just four years.

Table 2–4 presents a longer-term perspective of the volume of enterprise securities outstanding since 1970. The Congressional Budget Office calculates that enterprise securities have gone from $37 billion outstanding in fiscal year (FY) 1970 to $175 billion in

FIGURE 2–1

Government-Sponsored Enterprises: Securities,
Guarantees, and Reinsurance

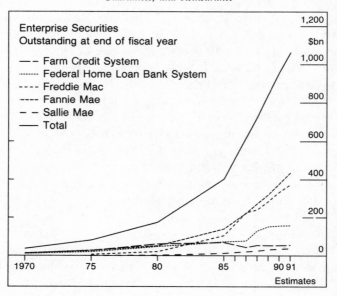

TABLE 2–4

Enterprise Securities Outstanding at the End of the Fiscal Year, 1970–1991
(in $Billions)[a]

Enterprise	1970	1975	1980	1985	1987	1988	1989	Estimated 1990	Estimated 1991
Farm Credit System (FCS)									
Banks for Cooperatives	$ 1.5	$ 3.2	$ 8.4	$ 8.1	$ 8.9	$ 11.2	$ 11.5	$ 11.8	$ 12.6
Farm Credit Banks[b]	11.3	23.7	53.6	61.8	35.3	43.4	42.1	41.2	41.2
Federal Agricultural Mortgage Corp.[d]	c	c	c	c	c	c	c	1.0	1.7
Federal Home Loan Bank System (FHLBS)									
Banks	11.2	20.6	36.6	73.6	105.1	126.7	144.3	128.4	120.7
Financing Corporation	c	c	c	c	c	3.7	8.1	8.1	8.1
Resolution Funding Corp.	c	c	c	c	c	c	c	20.4	29.8
Freddie Mac									
Debt	c	5.1	4.7	13.8	17.1	20.6	27.1	27.8	29.2
Mortgage-backed securities	c	1.2	16.8	92.0	208.9	220.7	257.9	306.0	344.3
Fannie Mae									
Debt	13.2	28.2	52.3	91.7	92.6	106.0	111.5	119.0	127.3
Mortgage-backed securities	c	c	c	48.8	130.5	167.2	208.9	258.8	308.3
Sallie Mae	c	0.2	2.3	12.7	21.3	25.0	32.0	34.8	37.8
Total	$37.2	$82.3	$174.8	$402.4	$619.7	$724.9	$843.6	$957.3	$1061.1

Source: Congressional Budget Office, *An Analysis of the Administration's Credit Budget for Fiscal Year 1991* (Washington, D.C.: GPO, April 1990), 49.
[a]This table is based on the U.S. government fiscal year: prior to 1976, the FY ends on July 31; since 1976, it ends on October 31.
[b]Before fiscal year 1987, composed of the Federal Intermediate Credit Banks and the Federal Land Banks.
[c]Not yet chartered.
[d]Guarantees.

FY 1980 and $957 billion estimated for FY 1990. That 26-fold growth over twenty years includes the creation of new enterprises, notably Freddie Mac in 1970 and Sallie Mae in 1972. By the end of FY 1989, outstanding enterprise securities amounted to an estimated $844 billion, compared to $959 billion of federally backed deposits in savings and loan institutions. Soon the trend lines will cross and the amount of outstanding enterprise securities will exceed insured thrift deposits.

Such rapid growth results from the enterprises' virtually unlimited access to low-cost federal credit as well as a variety of tax and other benefits under their charter legislation. The enterprises have access to huge amounts of money in the federal agency credit market on favorable terms compared to other financial institutions. They are exempt from state laws and taxes applicable to many competitors. As federal instrumentalities, the enterprises are not subject to burdensome requirements such as state-doing business laws and some state restrictions on the ability of creditors to foreclose on their borrowers. Further, they are free from federal securities registration requirements and, indirectly, are permitted to avoid most state securities requirements.

Moreover, the enterprises are exempted by federal law from all state and local taxes, except real property taxes. Some enterprises have additional tax benefits. The Federal Home Loan Banks, FICO and REFCORP, Farmer Mac, and the Farm Credit Banks (but not the FCS Banks for Cooperatives) are exempt from federal income taxes. Federal law exempts investors in securities of Sallie Mae, the Farm Credit System, the Federal Home Loan Banks, and FICO and REFCORP from state and local taxes on their interest income. These benefits increase the ability of government-sponsored enterprises to operate without many of the constraints and costs facing their private competitors.

Except for limitations imposed by Congress or a regulator, there seem to be few constraints to prevent the enterprises from issuing ever-increasing amounts of debt and mortgage-backed securities. On the lending side, the enterprises seem limited only by the size of their statutorily permitted markets and by competition from other institutions with governmental support. On the borrowing side, many of the enterprises face no formal limits at all. The array of enterprise advantages is also protected from competition, in that the system of specialized charters means other investors cannot enter the same line of business under a similar charter.

Largely because other competitors lack the same federal benefits, government-sponsored enterprises have grown rapidly in their designated markets. Fannie Mae and Freddie Mac are two of the largest financial institutions in the United States, and their rate of growth continues to accelerate. The Federal Home Loan Bank System is the fourth largest U.S. financial institution, and the Farm Credit System, even after its difficulties, remains larger than several money center banks and bank holding companies.

This rapid rate of enterprise growth raises two types of questions, one financial and the other political. First, what are the financial risks associated with a specialized lender like Freddie Mac or Fannie Mae that holds or guarantees over $300 billion of loans and mortgage-backed securities? At what point does such an institution represent such a concentration of political power that the federal government loses the ability to supervise such an institution or to impose the necessary safety and soundness measures? Second, at what point does Congress or the executive branch lose the political ability to direct enterprise activities to serve the highest priority public needs?

Consider first the question of safety and soundness. If an enterprise becomes powerful enough to resist measures designed to limit taxpayer risk exposure, such as the imposition of meaningful capital requirements, the potential costs of enterprise lending will increase. Some commentators believe it is already virtually impossible for the government to deal with enterprise safety and soundness. As one Wall Street analyst points out: "The probability of Fannie Mae facing higher capital requirements . . . compares with the likelihood that Congress will convert the Lincoln Memorial to a discothèque. We see no reason—based on political factors—to alter our BUY recommendations on Fannie Mae."[3]

Political power also means that an enterprise can obtain legislative changes permitting service to profitable sectors that are not

[3]Eric I. Hemel, "Flurry of Recent Articles Takes Swipes at Fannie Mae; No Reason for Investor Concern; Maintain BUY Option," in First Boston Corporation, *Equity Research Report* (New York: First Boston Corporation, 14 April 1989), 1.

high public priorities. Especially when an enterprise already provides tens of billions of dollars to fund a dominant part of its designated market, it feels intense pressure to expand its lending powers. Over time, Congress has shown a responsiveness to requests by the enterprises to expand their lending powers. Some enterprises have established political action committees, and all are supported by strong constituencies that from time to time have an interest in expanding enterprise powers.

Examples abound of enterprises entering new lines of business that involve lower priority public needs than those they were created to serve. In 1974 and 1977, for example, Fannie Mae and Freddie Mac obtained legislation greatly increasing the size of mortgage they could purchase. This permits them to serve more affluent homebuyers who generally have less need for federal credit support. In 1987, for example, Sallie Mae began to fund home-equity loans that may or may not be related to supporting a student in school. The 1989 thrift legislation gave Fannie Mae and Freddie Mac the authority to make advances to lenders using home mortgages as collateral. This represents a significant departure from the direct support of residential mortgages, since commercial banks are free to use the enterprise advances for virtually any purpose—such as foreign, industrial, or commercial loans—whether related or unrelated to residential mortgage finance.

The accelerating rate of enterprise growth and the related expansion of enterprise funding of new kinds of loans point to an important policy issue not yet well recognized by federal policymakers: With enterprise lending, as with any federal subsidy, there can be too much of a good thing.

3

How Government-Sponsored Enterprises Work

We are a private corporation and as such, with stockholders and bondholders, we have a fiduciary responsibility to those individuals. . . . We are not charged with subsidizing the guaranteed student loan program or subsidizing the students.

—Edward A. Fox, Sallie Mae
president and chief executive officer

An enterprise exhibits a confusing mix of governmental and private characteristics. It may act like a private company for some purposes and like a government agency for others. Two distinctions help to dispel much of this confusion. *First, an enterprise raises money the way the federal government does but it lends that money as a private institution.* To understand how an enterprise works, then, we need to examine the way it borrows in the federal agency credit market as well as the financial services it provides. (Table 3–1 provides an overview of the financial functions of the enterprises.) *Second, an enterprise is a privately owned and controlled institution with a public purpose.* Each enterprise charter confines the institution to serving specified borrowers or market segments. This limitation helps to give the enterprise a public purpose beyond the private interests of its shareholders. That is, the enterprises are supposed to do well by doing good.

TABLE 3–1

The Financial Functions of Government-Sponsored Enterprises

Financial Function	Fannie Mae	Freddie Mac	FHLBS	FCS	Sallie Mae	Farmer Mac
Financial Market						
Primary lender (lends to borrowers)				X		
Secondary lender (buys loans from lenders)	X	X	X		X	X
Lending Function						
Makes or purchases loans	X	X		X	X	X[a]
Guarantees MBSs	X	X				X
Advances to lenders	X	X	X		X	
Securities Issued or Guaranteed						
Issues debt obligations	X	X	X	X	X	X[a]
Issues and guarantees MBSs	X	X				X[a]
Guarantees MBSs issued by others						X

[a]Farmer's Home Administration Loans Only

To discover the financial role of a government-sponsored enterprise, we must examine the tension between its private ownership and its public purpose. An enterprise that passes on too many benefits to its designated borrowers risks financial failure; one that captures too many benefits for its shareholders loses the public policy justification for its very existence as a federally chartered corporation.

Raising Money in the Federal Agency Credit Market

Government-sponsored enterprises raise money to fund their loans in two ways: (1) they borrow money through debt obligations or (2) they guarantee mortgage-backed securities (MBSs). This distinction is important because it affects enterprise risks and profits.

Most enterprises can borrow money by issuing debt obligations—promising to repay the principal amount plus a stated rate of interest by a specified date. An example of a typical FHLBS debt-offering notice is reproduced in figure 3–1. The terms of the offering specify (1) the date of its maturity (that is, when the

FHLBS is required to repay the principal), (2) the schedule for interest payments, and (3) the minimum denominations that investors may purchase. Note that the debt is a general obligation of the FHLBS and is not secured by collateral. Further, because the debt is a consolidated obligation, all twelve Federal Home Loan Banks are jointly and severally liable to repay the debt-holders. Since large amounts of money are involved in this FHLBS debt offering, even small changes in interest rates would greatly affect returns to investors. The term sheet provides that the interest rate will be announced just before the closing date (on or about 12 June 1990).

The Federal Agency Credit Market

One striking aspect of the FHLBS offering notice is its lack of information on the creditworthiness of the Federal Home Loan Banks, which in this case are seeking to borrow over $1.3 billion. Investors are simply referred to the most recent FHLBS financial report, dated some eight months before the June closing date.

The absence of timely financial disclosure is common to most enterprise borrowings. The enterprises borrow in the so-called *federal agency credit market,* along with the Treasury and other governmental and private institutions that benefit from federal sponsorship or guarantees of their debt. The investors, in turn, purchase federal agency debt because of its perceived high-investment quality. Each obligation sold in the federal agency market is backed, not by the financial statements and perceived creditworthiness of the borrower, but by the implicit federal guarantee (or explicit guarantee, in the case of borrowing by federal government agencies). Even though the enterprises are not government agencies, their obligations are in many ways similar, such that the financial markets perceive them as federal agency debt.

The Implicit Federal Guarantee of Enterprise Obligations

Enterprise debt and government agency obligations share an array of attributes. Like U.S. Treasury obligations, enterprise

FIGURE 3–1

A Typical FHLBS Debt Obligation Offering Notice

Federal Home Loan Banks

$365,000,000 Consolidated Bonds
Non-Callable

Date of Issue June 25, 1990   **Series MM-1991**   Maturity June 25, 1991

Interest payable on December 25 and at maturity

CUSIP #313388 XK 1

$570,000,000 Consolidated Bonds
Non-Callable

Date of Issue June 25, 1990   **Series DD-1992**   Maturity June 25, 1992

Interest payable on December 25 and June 25

CUSIP #313388 XL 9

$400,000,000 Consolidated Bonds
Non-Callable

Date of Issue June 25, 1990   **Series N-1994**   Maturity June 27, 1994

Interest payable on December 27 and June 27

CUSIP #313388 XM 7

These Bonds are Joint and Several Obligations of the Federal Home Loan Banks.
Minimum amount of $10,000 with multiples of $5,000.

The Federal Home Loan Banks' most recent financial report, dated September 30, 1989, is available from any Federal Home Loan Banks' selling group member or the Office of Finance, Federal Home Loan Banks.

I. OFFERING OF CONSOLIDATED BONDS

Through the Office of Finance of the Federal Home Loan Banks, and pursuant to the authority of subsection (c) of Section 11 of the Federal Home Loan Bank Act, as amended, the Federal Housing Finance Board will offer on or about Tuesday, June 12, 1990, the above series of Bonds for subscription through the established selling groups, subject to the provisions of paragraph IV below.

The Bonds will be offered at par. The interest rate will be announced on or about Tuesday, June 12, 1990.

II. PURPOSE OF THE OFFERING

The proceeds of this offering will be used to partially refund the $1,080,000,000 of Series F-1990, the $1,270,000,000 of Series K-1990, and the $785,000,000 of Series FF-1990 Consolidated Bonds maturing June 25, 1990.

III. SUBSCRIPTIONS AND ALLOTMENTS

Subscriptions will be accepted only from members of the established selling groups at the office of the undersigned, who reserves the right to close the books as to any or all subscriptions or classes of subscriptions at any time without notice. The right is reserved to the undersigned to reject any subscription, in whole or in part, to allot less than the amount of Bonds applied for, to make allotments in full upon applications for smaller amounts, to make reduced percentage allotments upon, or to reject applications for, larger amounts, and to make different percentage allotments to members of the established selling groups, and the action of the undersigned in any or all of these respects shall be final.

Subscriptions must be entered by telephone and subsequently confirmed by letter to the office of the undersigned.

FIG. 3-1 (CON'T)

IV. CONCESSION TO DEALERS

Concessions of $1.00 per $1,000 par value of Series MM-1991, $1.50 per $1,000 par value of Series DD-1992 Bonds, and $2.00 per $1,000 par value of Series N-1994 Bonds allotted will be allowed.

V. DELIVERY AND PAYMENT

These Bonds will be delivered via book-entry directly to an individual selling group member, or to its clearing bank, either in New York City or in another Federal Reserve District, on June 25, 1990, against payment in Federal Funds at their destination. It is advisable that each non-bank selling group member check with its clearing bank to make certain that the bank has the facilities to accept the Bonds in book-entry form. There will be no definitive securities available upon issuance or for exchange.

Austin C. Dowling, Director
Jean C. Chabot, Deputy Director
Office of Finance
Federal Home Loan Banks
655 Fifteenth Street, N.W., Suite 850
June 11, 1990
Washington, D.C. 20005
Phone: 202-272-4961

obligations, with some variations, have the following characteristics:

- *Approved by the Treasury:* Enterprise obligations are issued only upon the approval of, or in consultation with, the Secretary of the Treasury, who also usually must approve the terms (such as interest rates and maturities).

- *Exempt from Securities and Exchange Commission (SEC) registration:* Obligations are exempt from regulation by the SEC except to the extent that U.S. government securities are regulated.

- *Favorable investment for banks and thrifts:* Enterprise obligations are lawful investments for federally supervised institutions, including banks, thrift institutions, and credit unions, and have favorable government-type status in the portfolios of these institutions. (For example, shorter-term enterprise obligations may be used to meet the liquidity requirements of thrift institutions, and national banks may invest and deal in enterprise obligations without limit.)

- *Lawful investment for pension and trust funds:* Obligations are lawful investments for federal fiduciary, trust, and public funds.

- *Issued and paid through the Federal Reserve System:* Enterprise obligations are issued and paid through the facilities of the Federal Reserve Banks.

- *Eligible for Federal Reserve transactions:* Enterprise obligations are eligible collateral for Federal Reserve advances and discounts and are eligible to be bought and sold in Federal Reserve open-market operations.

- *State and local tax exemption:* Most enterprises are exempt from state and local taxation.

The one important difference between enterprise securities and U.S. Treasury obligations is that the enterprises are privately owned and are not part of the federal government.

The enterprises have additional characteristics that strengthen the perception of governmental backing:

- *Federal charter:* They are federally chartered corporations.
- *Treasury line of credit:* They usually have a direct or indirect line of credit with the U.S. Treasury.
- *Publicly appointed directors:* They are controlled by boards that often include some governmentally appointed directors.

Taken together, these attributes amount to an implicit federal guarantee that the enterprises will not default on their obligations. The federal government conveys a strong message to investors by conferring on enterprise securities the same preferred investment status as U.S. Treasury obligations. The exemption from the usual SEC registration laws removes investor protections usually considered necessary for all but governmentally backed securities. Similarly, the exemption from investment restrictions on banks and thrift institutions is otherwise limited to federally backed securities. Investors perceive that the government would not permit these exemptions from basic investor protection unless enterprise securities were extremely safe. Thus, when investors look to the implicit federal backing as a guarantee of an enterprise's creditworthiness, they find it largely unnecessary to study its financial statements.

Liquidity of Enterprise Obligations

Enterprise obligations are also attractive to investors because they tend to be issued in such large quantities that there is a ready market for resale. This factor is called *liquidity.* When a large volume of a security is outstanding, buyers and sellers are readily available and brokerage fees tend to be low. Enterprise obligations have an especially broad market because of the attributes they have in common with Treasury securities. They are legal

investments for federally chartered institutions, may be purchased and held without limitation by national banks, and are
eligible collateral for Federal Reserve advances and discounts to
depository institutions. Enterprise obligations are also eligible for
purchase by pension and other trust funds. At year-end 1989, for
example, outstanding Fannie Mae obligations amounted to
$116.1 billion and FHLBS consolidated obligations to $136.1 billion.[1]

Since enterprise obligations trade in the federal agency credit
market with an implicit federal guarantee, investors consider
them almost as safe as U.S. Treasury obligations. This explains
the willingness of investors to lend money to the enterprises at
rates of interest just above Treasury rates, usually within a
quarter to a half of a percentage point above the cost of a Treasury borrowing. The difference, or "spread," above Treasuries
reflects the greater liquidity of Treasury obligations, and the
fact that Treasuries are expressly rather than implicitly backed
by the government.

Guaranteeing Mortgage-backed Securities (MBSs)

In addition to issuing debt obligations, some enterprises fund
their loans by guaranteeing mortgage-backed securities (MBSs).
An MBS issuer, such as Fannie Mae or Freddie Mac, purchases
a pool of, say, $10 million qualifying fixed-rate residential mort-
gages. These mortgages may come in a range of amounts and bear
a variety of interest rates. They may be newly originated mortgages or seasoned ones. The mortgages may come from anywhere
in the country, and may include a mix of single- and multifamily
residential mortgages. At year-end 1989, Fannie Mae had $228.2
billion and Freddie Mac $272.9 billion of MBSs outstanding.
Fannie Mae reported receiving an effective guarantee fee rate of
21 basis points; Freddie Mac reported 23 basis points. In addition,
the enterprises earn "float" income on mortgage payments received and held before being paid to MBS-holders; Freddie Mac

---

[1]Treasury Department, *Report of the Secretary of the Treasury on Government-Sponsored Enterprises*
(Washington, D.C.: GPO, May 1990).

reported its 1989 float income as an additional 11 basis points.[2]

For what is called the "plain vanilla" (ordinary) kind of MBS, the issuer takes the pool of mortgages and divides it into equal pieces, say, into denominations of $25,000 to be sold to investors. The MBS issuer then issues securities providing investors an undivided participation interest in the pool of mortgages amounting to the $25,000, or other face amount of the security. This is called *securitizing* the mortgages.

Most importantly, the enterprise guarantees the MBS and pledges to investors that it will provide timely payment of interest on the underlying mortgage loans. Fannie Mae also pledges timely repayment of principal on its MBSs; Freddie Mac pledges ultimate repayment of principal. Thus, if a home owner defaults on a mortgage, the enterprise would assume the loss and pay off investors as if the home owner had merely prepaid the mortgage, say, when selling the home. The enterprise would then attempt to reduce its loss by collecting from the mortgage insurer, by taking recourse against the company that sold it the mortgage, or by foreclosing on the home and seeking to resell it.

The mortgage-backed security offers investors a number of advantages as well as some drawbacks. Among its chief advantages is that the MBS guaranteed by a government-sponsored enterprise has the same high-quality credit of an enterprise obligation. MBSs guaranteed by Fannie Mae, Freddie Mac, and Farmer Mac are backed by the same implicit government guarantee that backs their debt obligations. Like enterprise obligations, enterprise MBSs have financial attributes (such as exemption from bank and thrift investment limits) patterned on those of Treasury obligations and other federal securities. Most notably, the MBSs issued by Ginnie Mae are expressly backed by the full faith and credit of the government.

In addition, the fixed denomination of a Fannie Mae MBS means that the real estate investor is permitted to buy as much of a mortgage pool as desired, and in denominations of the investor's choosing, rather than the entire mortgage. Moreover, the investor's mortgage-backed security represents an undivided interest in a diversified pool of mortgages. This means that the investor's fortunes are not tied to the behavior of a single mort-

[2]Ibid.

gage and home owner, thus reducing investor uncertainty about when mortgages will be paid off. Some home owners may sell their homes or refinance their mortgages after a short time; others may keep the mortgage for an entire thirty-year term. The MBS investor can analyze the characteristics of a large pool of mortgages in order to make statistical assumptions about the frequency of prepayments. Unlike purchasers of enterprise debt, MBS investors receive an offering circular and study the details of it carefully.

Further, the large volume of Fannie Mae and Freddie Mac MBSs in the market and their high-quality credit assures the MBS investor of liquidity. As with the holder of an enterprise debt obligation, this means that the MBS investor can find a ready market to sell the enterprise MBS, or to buy more, without paying substantial brokerage fees. As Fannie Mae and Freddie Mac salespeople like to say, the process of securitizing mortgages "turns frogs into princes."

The mortgage-backed security does have one major drawback compared to the debt obligation: it is a so-called *pass-through security*. When an investor buys a Fannie Mae debenture (unsecured debt obligation), the term and interest rate are fixed. For example, an investor might buy a $25,000 Fannie Mae obligation bearing an interest rate of 10 percent with a maturity of ten years. By contrast, the MBS has a flexible term and interest rate. As the underlying pool of mortgages changes composition, primarily because of mortgage prepayments, the investor's yield changes as well. If mortgage interest rates drop suddenly, many home owners would refinance their mortgages at the lower interest rates. Investors enjoying high returns on their MBSs would suddenly be faced with prepayments of their principal at a time when interest rates had dropped.

Issuing Multiclass MBSs (REMICs)

Fannie Mae, Freddie Mac, and other MBS issuers and guarantors have dealt with the pass-through security problem using a variety of ingenious structuring devices. For example, the issuer may segment an MBS into multiple classes of security, those that pay off early (since all prepayments go to the investors first) and those that pay off later. These multiclass MBSs are known as CMOs, or collateralized mortgage obligations. The 1986 Tax Reform Act gave CMOs special tax treatment and created the term REMICs, or Real Estate Mortgage Investment Conduit securities. The CMO is essentially a pass-through MBS security divided into several classes or "tranches" of varying maturities and yields. Usually, the shorter-term CMO tranches carry lower yields than the longer-term tranches. The issuer accomplishes the division of CMO classes by allocating mortgage prepayments to pay off the shorter-term security-holders, then the intermediate-term security-holders, and so forth until all tranches of the CMO are paid off and retired in order.

The point of this exercise is to obtain higher profits by paying lower overall yields to CMO investors, compared to the higher yields often required by holders of the "plain vanilla," pass-through MBS. MBS-holders may require higher yields to offset the risk caused by the uncertain cash flow and maturity from the MBS as mortgages prepay. The uncertainty is reduced for holders of CMO securities because of the better knowledge of the approximate maturity of their tranches compared to the other tranches. Sometimes CMO issuers reduce the uncertainty even more by setting express limits on the maturities of particular tranches. The issuer then makes up the temporary shortfall, or takes the temporary excess, as the case may be, if mortgage prepayments fall below or above levels promised to security-holders.

Like single-class MBSs, REMIC issuances are largely free from credit risk and sometimes from interest rate risk, depending how they are structured. Their profitability to Fannie Mae and Freddie Mac varies according to investor expectations and the slope of the yield curve. In mid-1989, for example, Fannie Mae and Freddie Mac charged up-front fees of about 20 to 25 basis points to turn single-class MBSs into REMICs, according to an estimate by the First Boston Corporation, with transaction expenses reducing net profitability by roughly 25 percent.[3] Fannie Mae issued $37.6 billion and Freddie Mac $39.8 billion of REMICs in 1989. At

[3]Eric I. Hemel, *Fannie Mae Establishes Precedent by Using Ginnie Mae Mortgage Securities for a REMIC Deal; Long Term Plus for Both Fannie Mae and Freddie Mac; Could Raise REMIC Income by 50% over Next Several Years* (New York: First Boston Corporation, 17 July 1989), p. 3.

times of an inverted yield curve, when long-term rates are below short-term rates, multiclass securities may be less attractive to investors than the "plain vanilla" MBS; it may not even be possible to sell them at all.

Freddie Mac issued the first collateralized mortgage obligation in 1983. In 1986, the Tax Reform Act assured the exemption of REMICs from income taxes at the issuer-mortgage pooler level. Taxes are paid by the security-holders. By 1989, both Fannie Mae and Freddie Mac had overcome their regulators' efforts at limiting their issuance of multiclass REMICs and had become the dominant issuers of the entire REMIC market.

In 1989, Fannie Mae went one step farther. Instead of turning only its own MBSs into REMICs, Fannie Mae issued REMICs based on Ginnie Mae MBSs. This means that Fannie Mae and Freddie Mac (if they decide this is politically acceptable) can begin collecting REMIC fees based on the huge volume of existing Ginnie Mae MBSs as well as on new Ginnie Mae MBSs. In turn, this could greatly increase the potential volume of Fannie Mae and Freddie Mac issuance of REMICs, compared to limiting their issuance to REMICs based on their own MBSs alone. In 1989, outstanding Fannie Mae and Freddie Mac MBSs amounted to $501 billion, and Ginnie Mae MBSs amounted to another $370 billion.[4]

Farmer Mac-guaranteed MBSs

Farmer Mac operates in a slightly different way than Fannie Mae and Freddie Mac. By law, Fannie Mae and Freddie Mac are required to issue the MBSs that they guarantee. Under its enabling legislation, Farmer Mac may only guarantee securities issued by others. The Farmer Mac legislation contemplates the emergence of large mortgage poolers to purchase mortgages from originators and combine them into pools backing mortgage securities to be guaranteed by Farmer Mac. Also, because Farmer Mac is just beginning operations, its guaranteed MBSs will not have liquidity; the spreads of Farmer Mac MBSs above Treasuries (the usual

[4]Treasury Department, *Report of the Secretary.*

measure of yield on an enterprise security) may remain quite high. In late 1990, Congress authorized Farmer Mac to engage in portfolio purchases and to securitize agricultural loans guaranteed by the Farmers Home Administration.

Enterprises as Private Lenders

Making or Purchasing Loans

Government-sponsored enterprises lend money in their designated sectors in a variety of ways. The Farm Credit System (FCS) is the only primary lender among the enterprises: Farm Credit Banks and associations lend money directly to farmers, ranchers, fishermen, and farm cooperative borrowers.

Unlike the FCS, the other enterprises are secondary market institutions: They provide their services to the financial institutions operating in the primary market. Fannie Mae, Freddie Mac, and Sallie Mae issue debt obligations to raise money, which they use to purchase home mortgages or student loans, as the case may be, from primary lenders like mortgage bankers, thrifts, and banks. They then hold these loans in portfolio or, in the case of Fannie Mae and Freddie Mac, they have the option of securitizing the mortgages and selling the MBSs to investors. (Figure 3–2 shows elements of Fannie Mae's 1989 loan portfolio.) Thus, enterprise growth is tied to this constant buying or guaranteeing of loans that they do not usually sell again except into MBS pools.

Making Collateralized Advances to Lenders

Another lending function, performed by the Federal Home Loan Bank System and Sallie Mae and recently extended for Fannie Mae and Freddie Mac in 1989, is the authority to make collateralized loans, or advances, to primary lenders. The Federal Home Loan Banks may make advances collateralized by any acceptable market-worthy collateral. Sallie Mae makes advances to lenders collateralized by loans that, in the opinion of Sallie Mae's board of directors, will support the credit needs of students. Fannie Mae and Freddie Mac may make advances collateralized by the same kinds of mortgages that they are eligible to purchase.

FIGURE 3–2

Elements of the Loan Portfolio: Interest Income,
Term Intermediation, and Credit, Interest, and Operations Risks

Fannie Mae (1989)

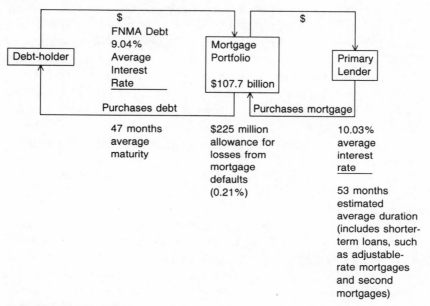

Interest-rate spread: 0.99%
Maturity gap: 6 months
Allowance for loan losses: 0.21%

Source: Calculated from Fannie Mae's 1989 *Annual Report* to shareholders.

At first glance, it seems to make little difference whether an enterprise purchases eligible loans or instead makes a loan advance based on eligible collateral provided by the primary lender. From a public policy perspective, however, the difference can be substantial. When an enterprise purchases eligible mortgages or loans, it is providing its funds directly for those loans and thereby makes those loans financially more attractive than other types of loans not eligible for funding from the federal agency credit market. By contrast, a loan advance may have a more tenuous relationship to the loan collateral. A commercial bank, for example, might provide Fannie Mae and Freddie Mac with mortgages out of its portfolio as collateral for an inexpensive loan advance. Once it receives the loan advance, the commercial bank is free to use the money for virtually any kind of permitted loan, and not merely to make new mortgages. Hence, the mortgage collateral merely serves as the basis for a commercial bank to obtain inexpensive and unrestricted enterprise credit based on the enterprise's access to the low-cost federal agency credit market.

Sallie Mae has carried this process one step further. Reasoning that a certain percentage of home-equity loans are used by parents to fund the education of their children, Sallie Mae permits commercial banks to use the loans as collateral for advances and does not require the commercial bank to certify or otherwise demonstrate a relationship between the home-equity loan and its actual use for educational needs. As with any credit advance, the bank is free to use the money for virtually any purpose. (See Figure 3–3 for the elements of collateralized advances for Sallie Mae in 1989.)

Congress has attempted to address this problem to some extent with respect to Federal Home Loan Bank advances. While thrift institutions are permitted to make a broad range of other kinds of loans, such as consumer loans, they must meet the qualified thrift lender test, which dedicates the bulk of their lending activities to residential and other specified kinds of loans. This means that thrift institutions receiving FHLBS advances, even advances collateralized by any kind of creditworthy loan, may to some extent be expected to direct the proceeds to the kind of lending activities intended by Congress. The same will be true of advances to thrifts by Fannie Mae and Freddie Mac.

Guaranteeing MBSs: The Swap Transaction

The enterprises can use mortgage-backed securities (MBSs) to fund two kinds of transactions. In the first type, discussed earlier, Fannie Mae and Freddie Mac purchase mortgages and fund them by selling MBSs to investors. They guarantee the credit quality of the mortgages, but investors still bear the risks of unfavorable interest-rate changes and prepayments. (See Figure 3–4 for elements of guaranteed MBS for Freddie Mac in 1989.)

The second kind of MBS transaction is the swap. In a swap

FIGURE 3–3

Elements of Collateralized Advances: Interest Income,
Term Intermediation, Operations Risk, and Protection against Credit Risk

Sallie Mae (1989)

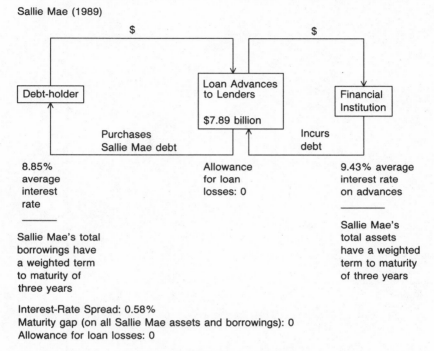

8.85%
average
interest
rate

Allowance
for loan
losses: 0

9.43% average
interest rate
on advances

Sallie Mae's total
borrowings have
a weighted term
to maturity of
three years

Sallie Mae's
total assets
have a weighted
term to maturity
of three years

Interest-Rate Spread: 0.58%
Maturity gap (on all Sallie Mae assets and borrowings): 0
Allowance for loan losses: 0

Source: Calculated from Sallie Mae's 1989 *Annual Report* to shareholders.

transaction, the seller of the pool of mortgages is the same institution that purchases the mortgage-backed securities. The most common swap transactions involve thrift institutions and commercial banks, which use swaps to convert their mortgage portfolios into MBSs. The institution continues to service its mortgages and bears the interest-rate and prepayment risks. In swapping mortgages for MBSs, it converts a portfolio of loans of passable credit quality into federally backed securities that trade in the agency credit market.

The institution obtains many advantages from the swap transactions. The MBSs count as liquid assets to meet regulatory requirements. When an institution borrows money, through short-term repurchase transactions or collateralized advances,

FIGURE 3–4

*Elements of Guaranteed MBSs: Fee Income, and
Credit and Operations Risks; No Interest Risk*

Freddie Mac (1989)

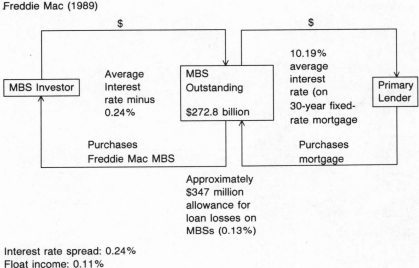

Interest rate spread: 0.24%
Float income: 0.11%
Allowance for losses: 0.13%
No maturity gap

Source: Calculated from Freddie Mac's 1989 *Annual Report* to shareholders.

MBSs provide higher-quality collateral than mortgages. Perhaps
most importantly, though, under the new risk-based capital standards, a bank or thrift may be permitted to hold less capital when
its assets consist of enterprise MBSs rather than merely mortgage
loans.

How the Enterprises Make Money

The enterprises make their money in several different ways. In
portfolio lending, an institution makes or purchases loans and
funds them by issuing debt obligations. Income from portfolio
lending comes from the interest-rate spread between the income
from the loan portfolio and the enterprise's cost of funds. To take
a hypothetical example, an enterprise might borrow two-year
money in the federal agency credit market at 7.8 percent to help

fund a portfolio of long-term mortgages with an average interest rate of 9.9 percent, for an interest-rate spread of 2.1 percent. On a $100 billion mortgage portfolio, the interest-rate spread would yield a net interest income of $2.1 billion.

Of course, portfolio lending is neither that simple nor that profitable, as many thrift institutions have found. Interest rates can be volatile. At the end of the two-year term, when the 7.8 percent obligations must be redeemed from investors, consider what would happen if short-term interest rates suddenly jumped to 10 percent. The portfolio lender, then, can be squeezed by a cost of funds higher than its portfolio income.

Two events may cause this unhappy state of affairs. First, the yield curve may become inverted. This means that, for a variety of reasons related to investors' expectations about the cost of money in the short versus the long term, short-term interest rates may suddenly jump higher than longer-term rates. Then, when the portfolio lender pays off our hypothetical two-year, 7.8 percent obligations, it might find that two-year money now costs 10 percent to borrow.

Second, lenders must be aware that the general level of interest rates may change. For instance, let us suppose that long-term mortgages are now priced at 10.9 percent in the secondary market, rather than the previous 9.9 percent. This means that the portfolio lender cannot avoid the interest-rate squeeze by selling its 9.9 percent mortgages to other investors. Any such sales would require the portfolio lender to book a loss. When mortgage rates are at 10.9 percent, investors will pay correspondingly less for a mortgage that only yields 9.9 percent. To avoid taking losses, the institution must hold on to its mortgages in the hope that interest rates soon turn around. This was the position of the thrift industry starting in 1979, when interest rates jumped and the yield curve inverted. Already by 1981, hundreds of thrift institutions had run out of capital and had an actual market value net worth that was zero or negative. They held on to their mortgages because, under applicable accounting principles, they would have had to recognize their losses on sales. By holding on to their underwater portfolios, they could maintain an accounting fiction, abetted by their regulator, that they still owned companies with positive value.

The dangers of volatile interest rates mean that portfolio lend-

ers must charge enough of a spread to protect against possible
changes. The most prudent lenders—Sallie Mae, the FHLBS, and
others—resist the temptation to play the yield curve by locking
in their spreads through a variety of hedge devices. These include
matched-duration funding (that is, funding long-term loans with
similarly long-term borrowings) and interest-rate swaps (to convert borrowings based on one interest-rate index into borrowings
based on the interest-rate index of the loans being funded).

MBS Guarantee Fees

The ultimate hedge is to push interest-rate risk off onto investors.
Fannie Mae and Freddie Mac accomplish this when they guarantee mortgage-backed securities. The investor then takes the risk
of indeterminant maturity and unanticipated prepayment of
mortgages. Fannie Mae and Freddie Mac charge management and
guarantee fees based on the outstanding principal balance of the
mortgage pools they guarantee. They also receive float income
from the mortgage payments they hold each month before passing them on to MBS investors.

It is up to the investor, when considering whether the price of
an MBS is acceptable, to determine if the spread of the MBS over
fixed-rate, fixed-term obligations (the benchmark is usually
long-term Treasury obligations) is sufficient to compensate for
the interest-rate risk. Fannie Mae and Freddie Mac MBSs may
trade at one or two percentage points above ten-year Treasury
bonds. Fannie Mae and Freddie Mac also collect management and
guarantee fees from their swap transactions with portfolio lenders, such as thrifts and commercial banks. As noted earlier, they
collect additional fees when they turn simple pass-through MBSs
into multi-class REMICs.

Income from Other Services

In addition to interest income from the loan portfolio and income
from securitizing mortgages, an enterprise with the necessary
statutory authority may earn income from fees for providing services.

The FHLBS and FCS have the express authority to provide a variety of services to their customers. Federal Home Loan Banks provide custodial facilities for the holding of securities by members and act as agents for securities transactions. Some of them also provide advisory and consulting services and furnish statistical and financial research reports to members. The 1989 financial institutions law clarifies that the Federal Home Loan Banks are authorized to engage in collection and settlement of checks, data-processing services, and correspondent banking services for their members, including servicing customer accounts and payrolls. The FHLBS also furnishes its members with letters of credit and guarantees. At year-end 1989, the Federal Home Loan Banks had approximately $4 billion in letters of credit outstanding to their member institutions. Given its authority to provide such a variety of services, there has been some conjecture that the FHLBS may seek to guarantee mortgage-backed securities in competition with Fannie Mae and Freddie Mac.

Farm Credit System institutions provide an even wider range of services to customers, including financial recordkeeping, tax planning and tax-return preparation, professional estate planning, business consulting, leasing services, credit life insurance and crop insurance, and real estate appraisals.

As with their lending activities, the enterprises are confined by law in the range of other services they may provide. Appendix A reviews some of the case law relating to litigation by competitors aggrieved about enterprise services that they believe encroach on their markets. As a practical matter today, it may be virtually impossible for most competitors successfully to challenge enterprise activities in court as exceeding statutory authority. Supervision of such matters is left largely to Congress and sometimes to a particular regulator, such as the Farm Credit Administration or the Federal Housing Financing Board.

Sources of Income for Each Enterprise

As might be expected of lending institutions, interest income provides the bulk of the revenue for the enterprises. Farmer Mac will be the one exception to this rule once it begins operations, since it is empowered only to guarantee MBSs.

Reflecting Fannie Mae's balance of portfolio lending and issuance of mortgage-backed securities, about two-thirds of its income comes from net interest on its portfolio and MBS "float" and over one-quarter from MBS fees. Interestingly, Freddie Mac earns more interest income (including "float" income on its MBSs) than it earns from guarantee and management fees on its MBS business.

The FHLBS and FCS do not have income from MBS fees, but they do earn significant fractions of their income from services to their members. However, public information is limited and the reported amounts of service income provide only general indicators of their relative importance to the enterprises.

Enterprise portfolios can contain a wide variety of investment assets besides the mortgages, student loans, advances to thrifts, and agricultural loans that are the corporations' major lines of business. Besides tax-exempt bonds, enterprise investments are reported to include airplanes, power plants, and even an oil rig. Sallie Mae's 1986 *Annual Report* referred to a sizable tax-lease portfolio at the time when such investments were profitable under the tax laws.[5] The enterprises are large financial institutions that derive their income from a variety of lending activities specified in their charter acts, but also from activities unrelated to any particular public purpose.

Tension between the Private Ownership and Public Purpose of an Enterprise

Statutory Terms and Public Purpose

A government-sponsored enterprise is established to fulfill a public purpose specified in the powers and benefits conferred by its charter. As such, it is limited to carrying out the activities expressly granted by its particular charter act, usually with limited incidental powers. (The two enterprises with exceptionally broad incidental powers are Sallie Mae and the FHLBS.)

The charter provisions are quite specific. Fannie Mae and Fred-

---

[5]Sallie Mae, *Annual Report 1986* (Washington, D.C.: Sallie Mae, 1986), p. 38.

die Mac are limited to providing a secondary market for residential mortgages of investment quality below a specified size; in 1989, the limit was $187,600 for first mortgages on single-family homes. (Although $187,600 was the legally set limit, both enterprises decided for policy reasons to limit their mortgages to $187,450 for 1989.) Similarly, Farm Credit System institutions and Farmer Mac are limited to specified kinds of agricultural lending, the Federal Home Loan Banks are limited to providing advances to thrift institutions (and, under the 1989 legislation, some commercial banks and credit unions), and Sallie Mae is largely limited to secondary market lending related to the credit needs of students.

The limited set of specified enterprise powers distinguishes the enterprises from most private companies, which, chartered under state corporation laws, may undertake virtually any activity except where prohibited by other laws. Government-sponsored enterprises are more comparable in this regard to commercial banks and thrifts, which are also considered to have a public purpose and whose enabling legislation specifies the permitted and prohibited activities for each kind of institution. As a matter of law, the public purpose of a financial institution is defined by its particular enabling law. The federal government cannot force an enterprise (or any other financial institution) to carry out additional public purposes except by amending the law under which it operates.

The issue of public purpose became especially controversial with respect to Fannie Mae in the late 1970s. Fannie Mae's nominal regulator, Department of Housing and Urban Development (HUD) Secretary Patricia R. Harris, sought to force Fannie Mae to increase its support for low-income and inner-city mortgage lending. Fannie Mae resisted, arguing that its public purpose is limited to the letter of its charter act. As Fannie Mae General Counsel (and later President) James E. Murray commented:

> The act of chartering a corporation by Congress creates no separate public purpose. . . . The Charter Act does not direct FNMA to provide subsidies to housing through below-market rate purchases.[6]

[6]James E. Murray, "FNMA: Perspectives on a Unique Institution," in *1978 General Counsel's Conference*, ed. John T. Mansfield (Washington, D.C.: Federal National Mortgage Association, 1978), pp. 3–13, at p. 11..

Faced with significant opposition from Fannie Mae and its supporters, HUD ultimately withdrew the proposal. Even without the pressure, many legal analysts doubt that HUD could have sustained its regulations as a lawful exercise of regulatory authority under the Fannie Mae charter act.[7]

The enterprise charter act defines the terms of an agreement between the private investors in stock, who own an enterprise, and the federal government, which seeks to use the institution to deliver credit support to designated borrowers and parts of the economy. Congress is free legally to amend the terms of the charter (as is discussed in Appendix A). Unless it does so, though, the government is limited to relying on the charter act as defining the terms of the agreement as well as the public purpose of the enterprise. This explains why congressional and executive branch inattention to proposed changes in charter act provisions can be so harmful; even apparently technical alterations in language can have large-scale financial consequences for the public purposes an enterprise serves.

Incentives of Private Owners

Under the terms of the enterprise charter act, private owners are legally free to make as much money as they can. (For the cooperatively structured FCS, the borrower-owners are legally free to borrow on as favorable terms as the law and their regulator permit.)

While the profit incentive of private owners is limited by political and institutional factors, it is essentially unlimited under the law. As Sallie Mae President and Chief Executive Officer Edward Fox told Congress in 1982:

> We are a private corporation, as such, with stockholders and bond holders. We have a fiduciary responsibility to those individuals. . . . We are not charged with subsidizing the guaranteed student loan program or subsidizing the students.[8]

[7]See, for example, Congressional Research Service, *Validity of Regulations Proposed by the Secretary of Housing and Urban Development Imposing the Obligation on Federal National Mortgage Association to Make Certain Percentage Loans Within Cities* (Washington, D.C.: Library of Congress, 24 March 1978).
[8]Statement of Edward A. Fox to the Senate Committee on Labor and Human Resources,

Following this philosophy, Sallie Mae has become the most profitable of the enterprises. Moreover, the company has achieved some of the highest returns on equity (ROE) of any financial institution in the United States. This can be seen in table 3–2, which gives the 1989 returns on equity of the enterprises (ROE is calculated by dividing net income by average shareholder equity).

Social Responsibility and Shareholder Profit

Most enterprises are careful to engage in some ventures that seem to embody a special attentiveness to public purposes. They have learned to avoid confrontations like Fannie Mae's feud with HUD Secretary Harris that create an image of social nonresponsiveness. Today, Fannie Mae, Freddie Mac, and a few other enterprises are exceptionally responsive socially, compared to many

TABLE 3–2

Enterprise Returns on Average Shareholder Equity, 1989[a]

Enterprise	Net Income (After Taxes)	Average Shareholder Equity (straight-line average, year-end 1989 vs. year-end 1988)	Return on Equity
Fannie Mae	$807 million	$ 2.626 billion	30.7%
Freddie Mac	$437 million	$ 1.750 billion	25.0%
FHLBS	$1.797 billion	$ 14.858 billion	12.1%
FCS	$695 million[b]	5.196 billion[c]	13.4%[b]
Sallie Mae	$258 million	$919.5 million	28.1%

Sources: Calculated from the 1989 Annual Reports to Shareholders of each enterprise and from the 1990 *Report of the Secretary of the Treasury.*
[a]The ROE figures are approximations; stock analysts are able to calculate more refined figures, such as returns on common stockholders' equity.
[b]Some FCS nominal profits arose from a $285 million reversal in a loan loss provision from the earlier years; without that accounting change, FCS net income would have been $4 million, for a return on equity of 7.9 percent.
[c]This includes "protected" borrower stock that is not at risk but that receives dividends. In 1989 $3.407 billion in FCS stock was not designated as "protected" under the law and another $1.683 billion was protected.

investor-owned competitors. Fannie Mae, for example, engages in an extensive low- and moderate-income housing program. It has purchased a considerable volume of tax-exempt housing revenue bonds, provided credit enhancement for additional housing bonds, and invested $100 million in limited partnerships and other ventures eligible for the federal low-income housing tax credit.

While the enterprises engage in some ventures that clearly serve a public purpose, they do not like to do so at the expense of profit. Fannie Mae Chairman and Chief Executive Officer David Maxwell said of his company's low-income housing initiatives, "Remember, we don't do this as a charity. We make money doing these things. I'm not hired to give away stockholders' money."[9] Nevertheless, Fannie Mae's commitment to its public purpose is strong and extends beyond a mere profit motivation. The enterprise devotes considerable staff resources to these special efforts that dollar-for-dollar might earn much more if applied elsewhere. Maxwell is personally active in advocacy on behalf of federal low- and moderate-income housing programs. From 1987 to 1988, he served as vice-chairman of the National Housing Task Force sponsored by U.S. Senators Alan Cranston and Alphonse D'Amato, the ranking members of the Senate Housing Subcommittee responsible for approving changes in Fannie Mae's charter. This relationship was good for Fannie Mae, but it also helped the cause of people who cannot afford adequate housing. In late 1990, Freddie Mac reported substantial losses in its portfolio of low-income apartment mortgages. Freddie Mac is similarly attentive to low- and moderate-income issues of special interest to the congressional housing subcommittees; by 1989, for example, it had invested $663 million in the northern Bronx area of New York City.

For one enterprise, Congress has legislated a commitment to lower-income borrowers. The 1989 thrift legislation requires the Federal Home Loan Banks to contribute $50 million or 5 percent of the prior year's income, whichever is less, to subsidizing low-income housing loans made by member institutions. After 1994,

[9]Quoted in Stephen Taub and Jackey Gold, "Twilight Zone," *Financial World,* 12 Dec. 1989, p. 46.

the legislated amounts will increase to $100 million and 10 percent, respectively. Individual Federal Home Loan Banks have objected to this assessment. The structure of the provision provides an incentive for the FHLBS to reduce reported annual income each year as a way to reduce the assessments for low-income purposes. The FHLBS is likely to reduce the pricing of its member services as one way of satisfying its members while reducing reported income and consequent assessments.

Yet the activities of Fannie Mae, Freddie Mac, and others are not just admirable examples of corporate civic leadership; they also serve practical ends. The enterprises are acutely aware that Congress can amend their charter acts if their activities seem to stray from serving a public purpose. For a $300 billion institution like Freddie Mac, a financially sound $663 million investment in low- and moderate-income housing can buy a huge amount of goodwill among the housing subcommittees of Congress that can expand or limit its charter powers.

Fannie Mae and Freddie Mac have already reaped considerable benefit from their low-income housing activities. At hearings at HUD and by the House and Senate housing subcommittees in summer 1990, a range of low-income groups testified in opposition to the Treasury Department proposal to use private ratings as a way to increase shareholder capital of the two enterprises. Allan Hunt, Director of the Vermont Housing Finance Agency, told the Senate housing subcommittee that he was "very concerned" about any tightening of regulatory requirements for Fannie Mae or Freddie Mac; Bart Harvey of the Enterprise Foundation urged that HUD be retained as the financial regulator "because we think we'd have a far better hearing there."[10] The groups were especially successful in appealing to members of the housing subcommittees who fear losing yet another source of support for low-income housing initiatives.

When used in this way, service to a high-priority public purpose can be especially profitable to shareholders by generating allies and improving the enterprise's image on Capitol Hill. Even

[10]U.S. Senate Committee on Banking, Housing, and Urban Affairs, Subcommittee on Housing and Urban Affairs, *Roundtable Hearing on HUD's Report on the Safety and Soundness of Fannie Mae and Freddie Mac* (Washington, D.C.: Typed transcript, 2 August 1990), pp. 29 and 102.

the FHLBS may discover that its low-income housing program brings significant side benefits. A good image can help soften the hard fact that, as privately owned and shareholder-controlled financial institutions, government-sponsored enterprises have an incentive to increase their returns and avoid capital requirements whether or not a public purpose is being served.

Unusual Elements in Enterprise Ownership and Control

The federal government has attempted to reduce the tension between the private ownership and the public purpose of an enterprise by imposing a variety of unusual corporate features. Each enterprise is structured so that a variety of factors may attentuate investor control over the enterprise and its profit orientation. These factors include limits on the ability of outsiders to acquire an enterprise, the presence of publicly appointed members on enterprise boards of directors, and the control of some enterprises by their customers (that is, by financial institutions or borrowers, rather than by investor-shareholders). Table 3–3 presents an overview of investor versus borrower-user ownership and control of the enterprises; table 3–4 lists the limitations of public ownership.

Protection against Hostile Takeover

To the extent that enterprise management remains in the good graces of the relevant congressional committees and subcommittees, it is free from the usual concerns about a corporate takeover that affect other corporations. Potential acquirers tend to devalue a government-sponsored enterprise because of the continuing possibility that Congress may react with legislation to confine the scope of permitted activities, or even by repealing the enterprise charter act altogether. The typical target company chartered under the general corporate laws of a state is unlikely to have such potent political protection. The continuing need for such protection provides yet another incentive for enterprise managers to curry the favor of their authorizing committees of Congress.

TABLE 3–3

Investor versus Borrower-User Ownership and Control of the Enterprises

	Fannie Mae	Freddie Mac	FHLBS	FCS	Sallie Mae	Farmer Mac
Control						
Directors elected by investor-shareholders	13 of 18	13 of 18	None	None	None	None
Directors elected by borrowers or other users of enterprise services	None	None	Majority	All	14 of 21	10 of 15
Directors appointed by the president or other federal official	5 of 18 (3 of these from user groups)	5 of 18 (3 of these from user groups)	Minority appointed by the Federal Housing Finance Board (FHFB)	None	7 of 21	5 of 15
Ownership						
% of common stock that may be held by the investing public, rather than by borrower-users	Close to 100% (a small fraction must be held by mortgage servicers)	100%	None	None	Only non-voting common stock	Only non-voting common stock

Sources: Enterprise Charter Acts.

Enterprise Directors: Appointed by the Government and Elected by Shareholders

The government-sponsored enterprise is structured to assure the presence on its board of directors of advocates on behalf of the borrowers, lenders, or others in the economic sectors to be served under the enterprise charter act. Fannie Mae and Freddie Mac each has an eighteen-member board of directors. Thirteen of these members are elected by shareholders; the remaining five are

TABLE 3–4

Limitations on Enterprise Ownership by the Investing Public

Enterprise	Limitations
Fannie Mae	A small percentage of common stock must be held by mortgage servicers doing business with Fannie Mae; otherwise, stock is publicly traded.
Freddie Mac	Voting common stock may be publicly traded except as restricted by the corporation.
FHLBS	All stock is held by member financial institutions; each institution must purchase stock equal to 1% of its mortgage portfolio or 5% of FHLBS advances it receives, and many purchase additional stock.
FCS	All stock is held by borrowers who have loans from the FCS. Stock purchases are set as a percentage (5–10%) of a borrower's FCS loans.
Sallie Mae	All voting common stock is held by two classes of user, educational institutions and education lenders. Nonvoting common stock is held by the investing public.
Farmer Mac	All voting common stock is held by two classes of user, commercial lenders and FCS institutions. Nonvoting common stock, when issued, may be held by the investing public.

Sources: Enterprise Charter Acts.

appointed by the president of the United States. The Fannie Mae and Freddie Mac charter acts prescribe that three of these appointed directors must be representatives of the groups to be served; one director is appointed from the home building industry, one from the real estate industry, and one from the mortgage lending industry.

Similarly, the boards of the Federal Home Loan Banks include a minority of public directors appointed by the federal regulator, now the Federal Housing Finance Board (FHFB). Sallie Mae's board of directors consists of twenty-one members, seven representing educational institutions, seven from educational lenders, and seven appointed by the president of the United States. The president also appoints the chair of Sallie Mae's board (though Sallie Mae is supporting legislation to remove this last requirement).

Governmentally appointed directors usually add little federal policy influence to an enterprise's board of directors. As is discussed in Appendix A, all directors owe a fiduciary responsibility to their shareholders and the corporation. There is no basis for distinguishing federally appointed directors from shareholder-elected directors in this regard. Like shareholder-elected directors, those federally appointed are accountable to shareholders and the corporation, not to a public mandate, except to the extent that these duties overlap. Only in rare circumstances, such as during Fannie Mae's controversy with HUD in the late 1970s, do shareholder-elected and governmentally appointed directors seem to differ on important issues.

Enterprises may also work to increase the identification of their appointed directors with the interests of stockholders, by offering stock-ownership plans, for example. Fannie Mae has one such plan and Freddie Mac plans to implement one for its new board of directors.

In contrast to the lack of public control through publicly appointed members of enterprise boards of directors, control by directors elected by customers or borrowers has traditionally been effective. The most extensive customer control is found in the cooperative structure of the FCS institutions, which are owned and controlled completely by their borrowers. On the one hand, this has positive consequences for FCS attentiveness to its public purposes; borrower control is an incentive for FCS institutions to provide favorable treatment to the broad range of borrowers who might otherwise be excluded from doing business with a more profit-oriented institution. On the other hand, borrower control of the FCS, combined with lax regulatory oversight, has led FCS institutions to grant overly generous loan terms that threaten its financial viability.

While a profit-oriented FCS might have been more strict in pricing its loans or shutting off credit to farm borrowers, borrower control of FCS lending policies led the system to extend loans to borrowers with unusually low creditworthiness and to price those loans below actual FCS borrowing costs. When the system took heavy losses, the FCS cooperative structure was not conducive to restoring financial soundness. Borrower-owners of FCS institutions generated intense pressure to forbear in foreclosing on defaulting loans, at a time the enterprise most desperately needed the money to stay afloat.

The newest FCS institution, Farmer Mac, has a corporate structure somewhat different from the traditional FCS cooperative approach. Unlike the FCS one-borrower, one-vote structure, the shareholder representatives on Farmer Mac's board of directors are divided into two classes, so that five directors represent commercial lenders and five directors represent the FCS institutions that will originate and pool loans and issue securities using the Farmer Mac guarantee. The remaining five directors of its fifteen-member board are appointed by the president of the United States. Farmer Mac's structure would seem to give its board of directors more of an incentive to benefit their lending institutions than in keeping the profits for Farmer Mac. Other features of the Farmer Mac charter act, such as a limitation on the guarantee fees that the enterprise may impose and the absence of authority to engage in portfolio lending, reinforce this conclusion.

The Federal Home Loan Bank System provides an example of a cooperative structure that has avoided many of the financial pitfalls affecting the FCS. In part, this is because of a healthy tension in the FHLBS structure, between the financial institutions that own FHLBS stock and seek dividend returns on their investment, and those that seek to benefit from FHLBS lending by obtaining inexpensive loan advances. All members of the FHLBS profit from dividend returns, while use of advances tends to be concentrated in a small number of larger thrifts. The views of both interests have been well represented on FHLB boards of directors. This has helped make the FHLBS a profitable institution, one that does well for its stockholders while providing loans on favorable terms to its borrowers. There is some concern that this healthy balance may shift in the 1990s, as the thrift industry declines and the relationship between the FHLBS and its member institutions changes.

Finally, Sallie Mae is perhaps the most interesting of the government-sponsored enterprises in its steadfast profit orientation, despite the absence of direct control by investor-shareholders. To some extent, Sallie Mae's peculiar corporate culture appears to reflect the strong values held by its talented top corporate management, which, until 1990, remained virtually unchanged since the enterprise was created in 1972. As is the case with some other enterprises, Sallie Mae's directors and officers do have personal incentives for the company to earn healthy profits. Sallie Mae's nonvoting common stock trades on the New York Stock Exchange, and directors and managers receive stock options whose value depends directly on the price of their Sallie Mae stock. However, it remains to be seen whether Sallie Mae's new top management will take a different approach to questions of public purpose and corporate profitability.

The Quality of Enterprise Management

Enterprise managers are necessarily different from the managers of other types of financial institutions. The more narrow lines of enterprise business mean that the enterprises can be less complicated financially to manage than banks or even some thrifts and still profitably serve their public purposes. However, the enterprises' unusual dependence on Congress and the executive branch for favorable legislation to expand their powers and increase their benefits demands enterprise managers who possess an unusual degree of political acumen.

Financial and Operational Skills

Government-sponsored enterprises are usually narrowly specialized compared to commercial banks of similar size. Banks must juggle lines of business with widely divergent marginal costs and returns, whereas enterprise assets and liabilities tend to be much more uniform. So long as enterprise managers are prudent and their markets remain healthy, the enterprises seem to be able to thrive and grow even with conservative management strategies. Yet the rapid growth of several enterprises is tied in part to state-of-the-art management-information and control systems as well as to the operational ability to handle billions or tens of billions of dollars of new business. As the 1990 *Treasury Report* indicates, Sallie Mae has an up-to-date and effective management-information system, whereas the systems of Fannie Mae and some FCS institutions need significant improvement.[11]

A number of enterprise management teams, especially those that receive competitive compensation packages, stand out in terms of ability. While their lending operations are not easily

[11]Treasury Department, *Report of the Secretary.*

evaluated by outsiders, the financial acumen of enterprise managers is widely noted by stock analysts. The enterprises are adept at using sophisticated financial techniques to bring down their funding costs as close to Treasuries as possible.

Freddie Mac issued the first collateralized mortgage obligations and Fannie Mae the first stripped mortgage-backed securities. Sallie Mae's asset-liability management practices are considered among the best of any financial institution in the country. The financial team at Sallie Mae uses interest-rate swaps and other devices to avoid basis risk, which occurs when assets and liabilities are mismatched (for example, loans pegged to the ninety-day Treasury bill rate, and liabilities that may be tied to the London Interbank Offered Rate on Eurodollar Deposits (LIBOR), a common interest rate standard. Many of the company's smaller competitors find such approaches too expensive to apply to their smaller-scale operations; just as important may be their lack of easy access to the kind of financial expertise found at Sallie Mae.

The Office of Finance of the FHLBS displays similar management skills. For example, it has achieved much lower borrowing costs for FICO bonds, which it has issued in addition to FHLBS obligations, than some specialists predicted. FICO bonds sell within one-quarter to one-half of a percentage point of Treasury obligations of comparable maturities.

Fannie Mae's finance staff is also unusually talented. In the early 1980s, Fannie Mae's chief financial officer even issued several hundred million dollars of debt at below the cost of Treasury borrowings. Enterprises use their skills to tap foreign markets. Fannie Mae, Freddie Mac, and Sallie Mae sell their obligations to foreign investors when this is advantageous, and sometimes they denominate those obligations in foreign currencies rather than in U.S. dollars.

Economies of scale help lower many enterprise costs, including personnel costs. Fannie Mae, for example, a $62 billion company in 1981, grew to a $352 billion company by 1989. In 1981, Fannie Mae had $57 million in assets and MBSs outstanding for each of its employees:[12] that amount doubled by 1988, to $114 million

[12]Roger E. Birk, "Remarks" to Fannie Mae Annual meeting of Shareholders, 18 May 1989, in Fannie Mae *Annual Report to Shareholders*.

per employee. With the exception of the FCS, the overhead expenses of government-sponsored enterprises, as a proportion of their total lending activities, tend to be much lower than those of their competitors.

Political Skills

Each enterprise was created by a committee or subcommittee of Congress with jurisdiction over the particular constituents the enterprise was expected to serve. The agricultural committees created the Farm Credit System institutions and Farmer Mac; the housing subcommittees of the congressional banking committees established Fannie Mae as a privately owned company and created Freddie Mac; the education and labor committees created Sallie Mae; and the congressional banking committees created the Federal Home Loan Bank System. The same committees and subcommittees are responsible for overseeing the activities of the particular enterprises and for proposing changes in the laws governing their operations.

Thus, the enterprises take care to remain in the good graces of their congressional authorizing committees, and enterprise managers as a result tend to be skillful at congressional relations. In 1989, the First Boston Corporation provided this analysis for investors in Fannie Mae stock:

> *Fannie Mae's leadership is extraordinarily skillful politically.* Management is intimately knowledgeable regarding the whys and wherefores of power politics. . . . We believe that political prowess is so important to the company's well-being that it is likely to be maintained regardless of future management changes.[13]

Fannie Mae's incoming chairman and CEO, James A. Johnson, continues the tradition of political strength. As chairman of the presidential campaign of former vice president Walter Mondale, Johnson has extensive political connections, especially with the Democratic leadership in Congress. Similarly, managers at Freddie Mac and Sallie Mae have won considerable respect for their political skills. The FHLBS and FCS are also ably represented in Washington, D.C. They gain strength from their decentralized

[13]Eric I. Hemel, *Flurry of Recent Articles Takes Swipes at Fannie Mae; No Reason for Investor Concern; Maintain Buy Option* (New York: First Boston Corporation, 14 Apr. 1989), p. 2.

structure and institutional presence in a large number of key congressional districts and states.

Shrewd enterprise managers tend to plan their actions with an eye to political perceptions as well as to reactions in the marketplace. One positive result of this kind of political sensitivity is the exceptional social responsiveness of some enterprises.

Compensation of Senior Management

The enterprises most geared toward profits tend to reward their executives with attractive compensation packages. Fannie Mae, for example, is a profit-oriented institution that compensates its senior executives well. According to the 1990 Fannie Mae proxy statement, Chairman and Chief Executive Officer David Maxwell received a cash compensation of $1.3 million in 1989; he also realized stock benefits that year amounting to another $3.4 million, or a total of $4.78 million. The five top officers of Fannie Mae, including Maxwell, earned $3.45 million in cash in 1989 (an average of $690,000 per officer), as well as generous performance share and stock-option benefits. Fannie Mae's top thirty-three corporate officers, including the top five, as a group, earned $8.4 million (or an average of $255,000 each) plus a variety of stock and other benefits.[14]

Sallie Mae President and Chief Executive Officer Edward Fox earned a compensation of $886,838 in 1989, as well as options on 28,500 shares of Sallie Mae stock and an incentive performance plan that, together with the stock plan, totaled $1.1 million in 1989. Sallie Mae's five top officers, including Fox, reported receiving $2.3 million (or an average of $465,000 each) in cash compensation in 1989, plus options on 57,750 shares of stock and other benefits. Sallie Mae's eleven executive officers, as a group, earned compensation totaling $3.7 million (or an average of $336,000 each) in compensation plus options on 77,250 shares of stock and other benefits.[15]

[14]Fannie Mae, *Proxy Statement: Annual Meeting of Stockholders, May 17 1990* (Washington, D.C.: Fannie Mae, 17 May 1990), p. 10; "Shaping Up Fannie Mae and Freddie Mac: Uncle Sam Sends Them Next Door," *The Economist,* 29 Mar. 1990, p. 94.
[15]Sallie Mae, *Annual Meeting of Shareholders to Be Held on May 17, 1990: Proxy Statement* (Washington D.C.: Sallie Mae, 23 Mar. 1990), p. 13.

Compensation for executives of the other enterprises is much lower. Until recently, Freddie Mac was owned by thrift institutions and controlled by a board of directors consisting of three government officials. A major complaint of Freddie Mac managers was that the arrangement kept compensation too low, especially compared to rival Fannie Mae. In 1989, for example, Leland Brendsel was Freddie Mac's president and CEO and then-chairman of Freddie Mac's new shareholder-controlled board of directors. His 1989 compensation was $367,546 in cash plus other benefits. Freddie Mac's five top officers, including Brendsel, earned $1.4 million (or an average of $278,000 each) in cash compensation plus other benefits. Now that Freddie Mac has become an investor-owned and controlled company, executive compensation is expected to increase accordingly.[16]

In 1987, the most recent year for which information was available, the Federal Home Loan Banks paid their chief executives somewhere in the range of $191,000 to $216,000. This was more than the presidents of Federal Reserve Banks earned, but below the compensation of many thrift executives.[17] It was also below the compensation of executives of centralized enterprises, even though the largest district bank—in San Francisco—by itself in 1989 was a $43 billion institution and larger than Sallie Mae.

The presidents of FCS banks traditionally tend to earn even less compensation. FCS boards of directors, usually part-time representatives of their agricultural community, compare their chief executives' compensation to that of other rural professionals and businesspeople, rather than to that of other financial services firms. The tendency to underpay was less pronounced for some of the larger FSC institutions, such as the Central Bank for Cooperatives, than for the FCS land banks. While current figures are not available, the average annual salary of an FCS CEO in 1986 was $175,000.[18] It was the system regulator, the Farm Credit Administration (FCA), that insisted on higher salaries as a way to attract more skilled professionals into the management of FCS

[16]Freddie Mac, *Proxy Statement: First Annual Meeting of Stockholders to Be Held on February 6, 1990* (Reston, Virginia: Freddie Mac, 29 Dec. 1990), p. 9.
[17]Nathaniel C. Nash, "High Salaries at Loan Banks," *New York Times*, 19 Jan. 1987, p. D2.
[18]U.S. General Accounting Office, *Farm Credit: Actions Needed on Major Management Issues* (Washington, D.C.: U.S. General Accounting Office, April 1987), pp. 38–39.

institutions. FCS boards of directors remain reluctant to provide compensation packages that may be more generous than their own farm incomes. Today, however, FCS top managers do receive stock options, which help give them a stake in the financial performance of their institutions.

Bank executives have not always done well as managers of enterprises. The job can be too constrained on the lending side and too lively on the political side. The political atmosphere of metropolitan Washington, D.C.—the headquarters of Fannie Mae, Freddie Mac, and Sallie Mae and well known to the managers of the other enterprises—is not well suited to some traditional bankers. Like their institutions, enterprise managers must develop an unusual combination of skills, public roles, and private profitability. Shareholders of the profit-oriented enterprises rightly reward successful enterprise managers with generous compensation.

4

Enterprises in the Marketplace

Legislative history suggests that the use of agency status and the special advantages that go with it should be reserved for those activities that are not, and for some reason cannot be, adequately performed by the private sector.

—Kenneth J. Thygerson, Freddie Mac president and chief executive officer, statement to the Senate Subcommittee on Housing and Urban Affairs

Government-sponsored enterprises can be formidable competitors. Limited by law to serving a defined market segment, they tend to grow to dominate that segment. The enterprises have significant competitive advantages but also some disadvantages compared to other financial institutions. These characteristics influence the commercial contest between enterprises and their major competitors; they also affect other firms and borrowers in the particular financial sectors, such as the markets for student loans, home mortgages, and agricultural loans where the competition takes place.

As government-sponsored enterprises grow, their impact on the financial markets can be substantial. Some firms are displaced by enterprise competition, while others grow by offering complementary services that the enterprises are precluded from providing directly. The behavior of enterprise customers and of the ultimate borrowers themselves is shaped by the decisions that the enterprises implement in the marketplace.

These consequences derive primarily from the federal laws that established the enterprises and define their powers and functions. Government-sponsored enterprises are not mere commercial institutions; rather, they are instruments of federal policy and their commercial impact raises questions of federal policy. To what extent does each enterprise serve valuable public purposes? To what extent does it improve market efficiency? To what extent does an enterprise effectively allocate special credit benefits that the markets or government might not otherwise be able to provide? Does today's federal legislation direct the activities of the enterprises in ways that best serve important public purposes or can this be improved? It is in terms of overall public benefits and costs that government-sponsored enterprises, as institutions of federal law, should be judged.

Federal Law and Enterprise Advantages

As corporations chartered under federal laws, enterprises gain certain benefits that contribute to their exceptional financial strength. Table 4–1 summarizes the advantages that enterprises receive under federal law. Among the most important benefits are federal credit support, tax exemptions, freedom from capital requirements, and the right to serve the national market. These and other enterprise advantages make it difficult to judge conclusively whether an enterprise is an efficient provider of financial services or if it simply displaces competitors because of the strength it gains from federal subsidies not available to other firms.

Federal Credit Support

The most important enterprise benefit is the implicit federal guarantee, which gives an enterprise a substantially lower cost of funds than most of its competitors. In 1989, for example, Fannie Mae and Freddie Mac mortgage-backed securities (MBSs) were priced at about thirty to forty basis points below AA-rated private MBSs issued by other financial institutions. Analysts esti-

TABLE 4–1

Advantages Conferred on the Enterprises by Federal Law

An implicit federal guarantee that lowers borrowing costs, provided without charge by the government

Exemption from state and local income and sales taxes, as well as from personal property taxes

For the FHLBS and some FCS banks, exemption from federal income taxes

For the FHLBS, FCS, and Sallie Mae, exemption of interest on their obligations from state and local income taxes

Favorable treatment for holdings of enterprise mortgage-backed securities when banks and thrifts calculate risk-based capital requirements

Exemption from federal SEC registration requirements and registration, as well as from most state securities requirements

Exemption from state-doing business laws and preemption of other restrictive state laws

Freedom from competition by new entrants able to obtain a similar charter

For Fannie Mae, Freddie Mac, Sallie Mae, and Farmer Mac, freedom from meaningful capital requirements

Except for the FCS (since 1985) and Farmer Mac, freedom from effective federal supervision of safety and soundness

---

mate that about half of this pricing advantage came from the government's assumption of credit risk; the remainder was related to the greater liquidity of Fannie Mae and Freddie Mac MBSs, as compared to private securities, and other factors.[1] This pricing advantage, of about a quarter to one-half of a percentage point, meant that other private firms were unable to compete against Fannie Mae and Freddie Mac in the part of the residential mortgage market—the market for "conforming" mortgages—that the two enterprises are directed to serve. Conforming mortgages are those that Fannie Mae and Freddie Mac purchase under the terms of their charter acts. For example, in 1989, conforming single-family mortgages had unpaid principal balances below $187,450, were of investment quality, and met loan-to-value requirements and other criteria established by the provisions of the charters.

The implicit federal guarantee is also an important benefit for the Farm Credit System (FCS), whose obligations would not be well rated without federal backing. In fact, it was because of the federal guarantee that FCS banks in the early 1980s were able to price their mortgage loans to farmers at rates *below* the FCS's own

---

[1]Congressional Budget Office, *An Analysis of the Administration's Credit Budget for Fiscal Year 1991* (Washington, D.C.: GPO, April 1990), 50.

borrowing costs in the federal agency credit market. Since rural banks could not match the low FCS prices, farm borrowers flocked to the FCS banks instead of to commercial lenders. Of course, the FCS's generous pricing policy was ultimately impossible to sustain. If a financial institution is losing money on every loan, it can't improve matters by increasing volume. The implicit federal guarantee permitted the FCS below-cost pricing strategy to continue long after any lender without access to such a federal credit subsidy would have failed.

The implicit guarantee provides a special benefit for the mortgage-backed securities guaranteed by Fannie Mae, Freddie Mac, and Farmer Mac. Under the risk-based capital standards now prescribed for banks and thrifts, enterprise MBSs are considered very low-risk compared to the residential or agricultural mortgages on which the MBSs are based. To reduce their risk-based capital requirements, banks and thrifts merely swap the mortgages in their portfolios for enterprise mortgage-backed securities. This expands the enterprises' MBS business and also lowers the total amount of capital that banks and thrifts must hold to back their loan portfolios. Because Fannie Mae, Freddie Mac, and Farmer Mac are free from capital requirements on the MBSs they guarantee, they are not required to increase capital to compensate for the increased risk they have taken by guaranteeing the bank and thrift mortgage portfolios. The net result is to lower the total amount of capital in the American financial system.[2]

To a lesser extent, the implicit federal guarantee benefits Sallie Mae and the FHLBS. In contrast to the other enterprises, though, these two institutions have strong balance sheets and significant capitalization. Indeed, they could probably obtain high-quality credit ratings without their federal backing; especially for Sallie Mae, the implicit guarantee is useful but not essential to its continuing financial success.

Federal, State, and Local Tax Benefits

Special tax benefits are another major advantage of government-sponsored enterprises. The FCS banks (but not the Banks for

[2]This result is discussed in Thomas H. Stanton, "Government Enterprises: Ignoring the Risk?" *Office of Thrift Supervision Journal* 20 (March 1990): 6–10.

Cooperatives), FHLBS, and Farmer Mac are exempt from federal, state, and local income taxes. Although the other enterprises must pay federal income taxes, they are exempt from state and local income taxes.

Further, interest on the obligations of the FCS, FHLBS, and Sallie Mae is exempt from state and local taxes, which is a significant benefit in improving the attractiveness of those obligations to investors. Sallie Mae benefits from a special provision that permits it to deduct interest on obligations issued to purchase tax-exempt bonds, even though the federal government does not tax the interest income from those bonds. In the 1986 Tax Reform Act, a similar interest deduction for commercial banks was restricted to a far greater extent than for Sallie Mae. Taken together, the various tax privileges give the enterprises, to varying degrees, an advantage over their competitors.

Freedom from Capital Requirements

Freedom from effective capital requirements is a special benefit for most of the enterprises, compared to other institutions that have federal backing (such as banks and thrifts). The exceptions are the Farm Credit System and Federal Home Loan Bank System, which are required to meet significant capital standards.

To the extent that the other enterprises are free from capital requirements and use that advantage to increase their own leverage, their shareholders benefit. Stockholders of institutions such as Fannie Mae, Freddie Mac, and, eventually, Farmer Mac can benefit from higher leverage than is available to shareholders of companies with significant capital requirements. (See table 2–3 in chapter 2 for the size-to-equity leverage—including MBSs as well as assets in the leverage ratio—of each enterprise.) This advantage, in turn, means that a thinly capitalized enterprise can afford to outbid its less-leveraged competitors in purchasing loans, while still providing generous returns to its shareholders.

Freedom to Serve the National Market

Government-sponsored enterprises also benefit from their ability to use federally backed funds to serve the national market. Unlike banks and thrift institutions, which, until recently, were limited by law to serving single states and now increasingly serve multistate regions, the enterprises are not subject to such branching restrictions. The centralized enterprises—Fannie Mae, Freddie Mac, Sallie Mac, Farmer Mac, and the FCS Banks for Cooperatives—are permitted to deal in loans acquired from across the country and to sell their federally backed securities to investors nationwide. Although the Federal Home Loan and Farm Credit Banks can provide their financial services only to certain restricted geographic districts, they too benefit from the freedom to sell federally backed consolidated obligations in the national market.

As federal instrumentalities, government-sponsored enterprises are exempt from state laws that would unduly burden their activities, even though those same laws are applied with strict force to private competitors. Federal law exempts Fannie Mae, Freddie Mac, and Sallie Mae from the requirement faced by nonfederally chartered companies to comply with state mandates for doing business. For example, they are exempt from licensure requirements as well as from certain state laws that subject other companies to regulatory controls, supervision, and sometimes capital standards. Again, the result is that the enterprises are permitted to serve a nationwide market largely without regard to state-by-state restrictions that may limit their competitors.

Perhaps most important, federal law protects enterprises from new entrants authorized to obtain similar charters. Sometimes an enterprise can benefit from provisions of federal law as well. The Higher Education Act, for instance, contains a provision that precludes eligible lenders in the Guaranteed Student Loan Program (now called the Stafford Loan Program) from having as their primary consumer credit function the making or holding of guaranteed student loans. The provision has a few exceptions, including one for Sallie Mae. But it may be effective in significantly restraining some competitors of Sallie Mae, in that they are thereby precluded from developing economies of scale by specializing in guaranteed student loans. In contrast, the freedom to serve the national market without such restrictions permits the enterprises to develop substantial economies of scale. On the borrowing side, the enterprises benefit from declining costs of funds as their outstanding securities amount to tens or hundreds of billions of dollars and are widely traded and held. On the lending side, the enterprises can develop impressive reductions in

the costs of dealing with each loan as they standardize and com-
puterize their loan-purchase operations. Fannie Mae has overhead expenses of roughly twenty basis points (0.2 percentage
points); to give one comparison, this amounts to only about one-
tenth of the overhead expenses of the average thrift, which
amount to about two percentage points. Unlike a thrift, Fannie
Mae does not originate mortgages or take deposits, nor does it
need expensive retail branches to support as overhead.[3]

Sallie Mae is another enterprise with impressive economies of
scale. The enterprise reports servicing costs below 70 basis points
(0.7 percentage points), compared to other lenders whose servicing costs for student loans amount to 120 to 150 basis points or
even more. Sallie Mae also has very low operating costs, reported
for 1989 at 0.22 percent of earning assets.[4] Except for the FCS, the
other enterprises also have significant economies of scale and low
overhead expenses.

Together, these benefits permit the enterprises to compete effectively against other private firms while continuing to satisfy
their shareholders. Only when federal backing abets imprudent
management decisions, or when confinement of an institution to
a risky or unprofitable economic segment stifles earnings, are
investor-shareholders of enterprises disappointed in their expectations of handsome returns.

Limitations Imposed on the Enterprises

Federal law does not just provide benefits to the enterprises; there
are restrictions, too. Table 4–2 lists some of the limitations and
disadvantages imposed on the enterprises by their charter acts.
The single major limitation on the enterprises is their confinement to a defined market segment. They may perform only the
functions specified in their charter acts, plus incidental activities.

As an enterprise develops and grows, its charter-imposed limitations can become increasingly confining. For example, an enterprise may be prevented from cross-selling products to customers
or otherwise developing economies of scope, which can occur

[3]Jonathan E. Gray and Joan M. McGettigan, *The Federal National Mortgage Association (Fannie Mae): Strategic Analysis/Financial Forecast* (New York: Sanford C. Bernstein and Co., Inc., July 1989), p. 68.
[4]Sallie Mae, *Annual Report 1989* (Washington, D.C.: Sallie Mae, 1990), pp. 2, 23.

TABLE 4–2

Disadvantages Conferred on the Enterprises by Federal Law

Limited to serving a defined market segment

Dependent on federal enabling legislation that can be amended to the disadvantage of an enterprise (for example, when the federal government assessed the FHLBS in 1987 and 1989, respectively, to provide several billion dollars for FICO and REFCORP)

Absence of a flexible corporate law to permit easy adaptation to changing circumstances

For some enterprises, oversight by a regulator that at times may be viewed as (1) incapable or (2) responsive to extraneous political concerns

---

when one institution sells a variety of products to a customer. Sallie Mae, for example, is precluded from offering credit-card services to graduating holders of its student loans; banks, by contrast, may do so. Similarly, Fannie Mae and Freddie Mac may not offer credit life insurance or other possibly attractive financial services to home owners whose mortgages they fund.

Perhaps most importantly, Fannie Mae, Freddie Mac, Sallie Mae, and Farmer Mac are limited to service in the secondary market and, as a general rule, may not become direct lenders. This prevents them from using their immense financial strength to move into the primary market by making loans directly to home buyers, students, or farmers, even if combining primary and secondary market functions would be profitable and efficient. Sallie Mae has moved closest to the primary market of any of the secondary market enterprises; it now offers computerized loan-origination services that bring the enterprise up to the point of loan origination itself.

Another enterprise difficulty caused by the federal charter relates to the temptation of congressional committees and regulators to become involved in directing enterprise activities toward socially or politically valuable purposes, to the detriment of shareholder profits. For example, Congress has taken billions of dollars from the FHLBS to fund FICO and REFCORP. As one FHLB official notes, "We would gladly substitute [Fannie Mae's or Freddie Mac's] tax liability in lieu of our congressionally mandated contributions over the years that lie ahead."[5]

The political issues of enterprise lending are the focus of chapter 5. Suffice it here to say that most enterprises have been quite

---

[5]Personal communication, June 15, 1990.

adept at holding their own in the political process. A comment in a 1989 *Business Week* article summarizes how David Maxwell, Fannie Mae's chairman and CEO, has used advocacy and support for low-income housing programs to help placate potential congressional adversaries:

> High volume, falling rates pull the money in, so he [Maxwell] stresses support for low-income housing to head off possible congressional raid on assets of federally chartered company to fund government programs.[6]

Enterprises: Specialized Lenders Serving a Nationwide Market

Unlike private companies that can grow by diversifying into a wide range of markets, government-sponsored enterprises tend to be limited to serving their designated economic segments. Federal law confines the scope of enterprise lending much more than it limits banks or even thrift institutions. However, the enterprises may also benefit from unusual combinations of powers. The Glass-Steagall Act of 1933 classifies financial institutions as those that serve banking or securities functions, usually not both. But Fannie Mae and Freddie Mac have both powers; they can buy mortgages as portfolio lenders or else securitize them and sell the MBSs, as they choose. The FHLBS has a similar set of powers, though it has chosen not to guarantee MBSs because of concerns of the thrifts that own and control the FHLBS about the way this could reduce profits from portfolio lending.

Huge Size and Rapid Growth

The concentration of enterprise lending in one economic market has several consequences. As noted earlier, it help the enterprises develop economies of scale. As a result, the enterprises tend to become huge institutions. Unlike banks and thrifts that face competition from other institutions with similar charters, enterprises

6"The Business Week Corporate Elite," *Business Week,* 20 Oct. 1989, 280.

benefit from unique charter laws and freedom from competition from new entrants, to whom the government gives similar powers and benefits.

Limited to serving their designated economic market segments but free to serve large geographic areas, government-sponsored enterprises usually direct their energies to growing within their permitted lending markets. This means that the enterprises are likely to dominate the market segments they serve. Sallie Mae, for example, directly (by purchasing loans) or indirectly (through advances to primary lenders) funds about half of the $50 billion market in guaranteed student loans. As table 4–3 shows, the market shares of Fannie Mae and Freddie Mac have grown rapidly, from about 8 percent of residential mortgage debt in 1980 to 17.6 percent in 1985. Today, Fannie Mae and Freddie Mac together fund over $650 billion of mortgages, over one-fourth of the residential mortgage debt in the United States.[7]

[7]Treasury Department, *Report of the Secretary of the Treasury on Government Sponsored Enterprises* (Washington, D.C.: GPO, May 1990), p. A–20.

TABLE 4–3

Fannie Mae and Freddie Mac: Total Residential Mortgage Debt and Total of Mortgages Held or Guaranteed, 1970–1989

| | Total Residential Mortgage Debt Outstanding | Total Residential Mortgages Held or Guaranteed | | | |
| | | Fannie Mae | | Freddie Mac | |
Year	($ Billions)	($ Billions)	(%)	($ Billions)	(%)
1970	$ 324.4	$ 16.1	5.0 %	$ 0.0	0.0 %
1975	541.0	31.9	5.9	6.6	1.2
1980	1011.6	57.3	5.7	22.0	2.2
1985	1517.4	153.2	10.1	113.9	7.5
1986	1769.1	193.4	10.9	182.8	10.3
1987	1997.5	232.5	11.6	225.6	11.3
1988	2198.8	273.2	12.4	243.8	11.1
1989	2420.7	372.2	13.5	294.7	12.2

Source: Treasury Department, *Report of the Secretary of the Treasury on Government Sponsored Enterprises* (Washington, D.C.: GPO, May 1990), p. A-20.

Longtime Dedication to a Market Segment

Government-sponsored enterprises may develop a longer time horizon for their lending activities than is possible for a competing private, shareholder-owned firm. Unlike commercial banks, which constantly evaluate marginal costs and returns for different kinds of lending, the enterprises are confined to a few lines of business. They cannot leave their designated sector when service to other borrowers suddenly seems more profitable. The long-term concentration on a single market sector means that it pays for an enterprise to make longer-term investments in product and process improvements.

Sallie Mae, for example, is dependent on high-quality management-information systems to assure effective servicing of its student loan portfolio. Sallie Mae officials told the Treasury Department that changes to the student loan program are so frequent that a servicing system has an effective life span of seven or eight years. Rather than constantly altering existing software to incorporate changes in legal requirements and technical improvements, Sallie Mae periodically develops an entirely new system. As the Treasury report concluded, this tends to maximize Sallie Mae's use of advanced systems and software improvements and to streamline its data-processing operations.[8]

Yet there are some countervailing incentives for the investor-owned enterprises to shorten their time horizons. When quarterly earnings drop, shareholders become restless. Boards of directors and enterprise managers may be directly affected by short-term changes in stock prices, in that the tendency of some enterprises to grant extensive stock options ties director and executive compensation to the stock-market value of enterprise shares on particular dates.

Product and Service Innovation

Service to a defined market segment permits the enterprises to develop new ways to serve their borrowers and to promote effi-

[8]Ibid, p. F-33.

ciencies in the lending process. After they were established in
1916, for example, the Federal Land Banks pioneered the provision of loans on an amortized basis. Until then, farmers could
only take out mortgages for a period of three to five years, at best,
with principal due at the end of that time. The Federal Land
Banks began making loans for periods of between twenty and
forty years. The new self-amortizing loans, quite common today
for a variety of loans and mortgages, provided for farm borrowers
to make annual or semiannual repayments of principal along with
the interest, to help them gradually reduce their mortgage debt.
The Farm Credit System also implemented early truth-in-lending
policies, succeeded in reducing loan fees for consumers, and pioneered variable-interest-rate loans.

Freddie Mac, following the example of the Government National Mortgage Association (Ginnie Mae), helped to develop
the mortgage-backed security as an efficient funding mechanism
that permits the lender to avoid significant interest-rate risk.
Together, Fannie Mae and Freddie Mac standardized the terms
of mortgage loan documents and helped to standardize the procedures used by mortgage sellers and servicers, thereby facilitat-
ing the emergence of a highly efficient national secondary
market for home mortgages. Sallie Mae, the largest single holder
of guaranteed student loans, pioneered computerized loan-purchase procedures. These new procedures are expected to increase the ability of originators of small numbers of student
loans to deal efficiently with Sallie Mae when they sell the enterprise their loans.

Enterprises as Competitors

The required specialization of enterprises makes them more relentless competitors in their permitted market segments than
might otherwise be the case. Unlike banks and securities firms,
government-sponsored enterprises cannot shift out of their designated markets when other lending opportunities appear more
profitable; to grow, they must expand within their permitted
market segments. They may also attempt to push back the statutory restrictions on their market segments as much as Congress

will permit, but that is a contest in the political rather than the commercial arena.

Sallie Mae versus Commercial Banks

The contest between an enterprise confined to a designated market segment and financial institutions free to leave that market segment to seek more profitable opportunities is well illustrated by the current competition between Sallie Me and commercial banks to provide a secondary market for guaranteed student loans. Such loans are small compared to a lender's cost of processing and servicing them once a student begins repayment. This makes economies of scale essential if a financial institution is to profit from purchasing and servicing student loans.

Commercial banks have some efficiencies that can make large-scale student loan activities profitable. Banks may benefit from economies of scope; they may be able to sell some other financial products to their student loan customers. They may also benefit from economies of scale; for example, in some loan processing systems and in liability management.

The major drawback for banks, however, is that student loan secondary market operations are only a fraction of their total lending activities. Commercial banks are not as committed to their student loan operations as is Sallie Mae, since Sallie Mae is restricted to this line of business. Thus, when student loans seem less profitable than other lines of business, banks sell their loan portfolios; when a bank's student loan portfolio grows to established targets, the bank will stop buying loans, or else will sell part of its portfolio to accommodate new loans.

Profitability goals based on marginal rates of return can also limit commercial banks. Successful banks are constantly assessing their lines of business against other potential lines of business. Bank profitability goals must be higher than Sallie Mae's goals because banks pay a higher marginal rate of taxes, one that includes state and local as well as federal income taxes. Banks also have higher capital requirements and higher marginal costs of funds than does Sallie Mae.

The results of this competition are not difficult to anticipate. Sallie Mae is by far the largest holder of guaranteed student loans in the United States. It buys student loans but doesn't sell them. In 1989, the company held 28 percent of the total market for guaranteed student loans.[9] The second largest holder of student loans, Citicorp, held only 4 percent of the $50 billion of guaranteed student loans outstanding.[10] There is a consensus among education lenders that Sallie Mae's share of the market is not only large but also of very high quality. Banks and state secondary market agencies often may find themselves with less profitable loan portfolios, involving smaller sizes and higher average servicing costs than the portfolios Sallie Mae can afford to buy.

Fannie Mae and Freddie Mac versus Thrift Institutions

Fannie Mae and Freddie Mac purchase home mortgages from primary lenders. They hold some mortgages in portfolio and fund most as guaranteed mortgage-backed securities. Further, although they buy mortgages, they rarely sell them to other investors, except for the mortgages they securitize.

It has been estimated that, by channeling federal agency credit into the mortgage market, Fannie Mae and Freddie Mac have helped reduce home mortgage prices by perhaps one-fourth to one-half of a percentage point.[11] Because of the dominant size of Fannie Mae and Freddie Mac in the residential mortgage market, this benefit has gone to all borrowers with conforming mortgages, not just to home owners whose mortgages Fannie Mae and Freddie Mac actually fund. One result has been a significant cost squeeze on competitors of the two enterprises, especially thrift institutions. Like Fannie Mae and Freddie Mac, thrifts were largely confined by law to residential mortgage lending, although federal law significantly loosened this restriction in 1982. Unlike Fannie Mae and Freddie Mac, many thrifts lack the low-cost structure or economies of scale to compete effectively as portfolio lenders. Even the best-run thrifts have overhead expenses, including the cost of branch offices, that are up to eight times as high as those of Fannie Mae or Freddie Mac.

9Ibid., p. F-14.
10Ibid.
11See, for example, John C. Weicher, *The Future Structure of the Housing Finance System* (Washington, D.C.: American Enterprise Institute, November 1987), p. 32.

Indeed, economist R. Dan Brumbaugh contends that the activities of Fannie Mae and Freddie Mac, and of the government MBS guarantee agency Ginnie Mae, spell the end of thrift institutions as portfolio lenders:

> A wide and growing range of non-thrift investors can buy mortgage-backed securities with the interest-risk that once had to be borne by thrifts. Opening the capital markets to mortgages means the market-driven end of thrifts as mortgage holders.[12]

Brumbaugh predicts that thrifts will ultimately function either as mortgage bankers that originate and service loans for Fannie Mae and Freddie Mac, or (if thrifts are freed of the restrictions now in federal law) as commercial banks that shift a large part of their lending activity out of the residential mortgage market entirely.

The former result may be hastened by the 1989 financial institutions legislation. That law imposes significant new capital requirements on thrift institutions and greatly increases federal deposit insurance premiums. It also increases the competitive advantage of Fannie Mae and Freddie Mac, since they have no effective capital requirements and pay no fee for federal backing that covers *all* of their liabilities (and mortgage-backed securities), not merely accounts up to $100,000. Thrifts are now selling huge volumes of their mortgages into the secondary market because they cannot support their current portfolios with the required levels of capital, nor can they afford to pay the deposit insurance premiums needed to fund them.

Fannie Mae, Freddie Mac, and the FHLBS versus Securities Firms

Fannie Mae and Freddie Mac compete even more effectively against securities firms that purchase mortgages and sell private mortgage-backed securities to investors. A recent Congressional Budget Office report notes that Fannie Mae and Freddie Mac mortgage-backed securities benefit from an edge of between 0.30 and 0.40 percentage points in yield, compared to the yield on private AA-rated mortgage pass-through securities.[13] In the

---

[12]R. Dan Brumbaugh, Jr., *Thrifts under Seige: Restoring Order to American Banking* (Cambridge, Mass.: Ballinger, 1988), p. 168.
[13]Congressional Budget Office, p. 50.

mortgage securities market, this edge is sufficient to drive out virtually all other competitors. Take the market for conventional home mortgages (that is, home mortgages that are not FHA-insured or VA-guaranteed).[14] In the late 1980s, Fannie Mae and Freddie Mac accounted for roughly nine-tenths of all mortgage-related securities, while other private securities firms accounted for less than one-tenth of that market. Indeed, the other private firms are largely absent from part of the mortgage market that Fannie Mae and Freddie Mac are limited to serving—the market for conforming mortgages. Fannie Mae and Freddie Mac together issue virtually all of the MBSs for conforming mortgages, while the private issuers are limited to securitizing so-called jumbo mortgages, with sizes above the statutory limit, and mortgages otherwise ineligible to be bought by Fannie Mae and Freddie Mac.

Sometimes private competitors can hold their own in particular market segments. Wall Street securities firms, for example, provide thrift institutions the opportunity to use their mortgage collateral for short-term borrowing through a device known as the reverse repurchase transaction. "Reverse repos" compete directly with short-term advances offered by the Federal Home Loan Bank System. Yet, despite the FHLBS's access to low-cost federal agency funds, Wall Street firms continue an active repo business with thrifts. Some analysts speculate that policy concerns have kept the FHLBS from reducing the cost of short-term advances and thereby capturing the market. In the 1980s, some FHLBs added a higher price margin to their short-term advances as a way to encourage member thrift institutions to take out longer-term advances instead, as a way of increasing the maturity match with their mortgage portfolios. It remains to be seen whether the 1989 thrift legislation and other pressures on the FHLBS to increase financial returns will change this public policy emphasis and lead the FHLBS to take a more competitive approach to pricing short-term advances.

[14]Virtually all of these FHA and VA mortgages are securitized by Ginnie Mae, an agency of the federal government whose mortgage-backed securities carry an express full-faith and federal credit guarantee. While Ginnie Mae has underpriced Fannie Mae and Freddie Mac and thereby largely driven them out of the FHA and VA markets, it has not affected their conventional mortgage activities, because by law it is not authorized to deal in such mortgages.

Turning the Competitors into Enterprise Providers

Instead of driving competitors out of the market, the enterprises sometimes turn them into providers of complementary services. Creation of a symbiotic relationship can benefit the former competitors; they pay for this with fees that must be shared with the enterprises.

The Tax Reform Act of 1986, for example, provided favorable tax treatment for a new kind of multiclass mortgage security called the Real Estate Mortgage Investment Conduit (REMIC). In 1987, Fannie Mae and Freddie Mac overcame the objections of their regulators when they began to participate heavily in the business of issuing REMICs. By 1989, 82.4 percent of all REMICs issued that year, $80.6 billion out of $97.8 billion REMICs, were issued by Fannie Mae and Freddie Mac. For the two enterprises, REMIC issuance fees provided an opportunity to earn fee income, which is free from most interest-rate and credit risks. For Wall Street securities firms, paying Fannie Mae and Freddie Mac a modest fee, largely passed forward to the mortgage sellers and back to the investors, was part of a transaction for which they continued to receive significant transaction fees.

How the Enterprises Shape Their Markets

Enterprises shape the structure of their markets, and thereby affect the functions and behavior of other firms as well as borrowers.

Effects of Fannie Mae and Freddie Mac on the Residential Mortgage Market

Certain provisions in enterprise charter legislation can benefit the companies offering ancillary services to the enterprises. For example, the Fannie Mae and Freddie Mac charter acts require that, in purchasing conventional mortgages (that is, those not guaranteed by the VA or insured by the FHA), the enterprises reduce credit risk by taking certain precautions, such as requiring mortgage insurance on mortgages with a loan-to-value ratio of 80 percent or more. The result of this provision, enacted for both enterprises in 1970, was a substantial growth in the private mortgage insurance industry during the next fifteen years or so. Private mortgage insurance for single-family homes grew from $7.3 billion in 1970 to $227 billion in 1985.[15] Even primary lenders that keep their mortgage loans in their own portfolios often seek to conform to the Fannie Mae-Freddie Mac requirements. By doing so, lenders can sell their loans in the secondary market should that become desirable.

Beginning in the mid-1980s, concern about the quality of credit in the mortgage market and the financial problems of some private mortgage insurers reduced the volume of mortgages with private mortgage insurance. Today, Fannie Mae and Freddie Mac are purchasing an increasing volume of loans that have less than an 80 percent loan-to-value ratio, thereby eliminating the need for private mortgage insurance on those loans. In 1989, only 19.1 percent of all Fannie Mae mortgages and 18.5 percent of Freddie Mac mortgages, held in portfolio or MBS pools, had private mortgage insurance.[16]

Fannie Mae's and Freddie Mac's Influence in the Primary Mortgage Market

The activities of Fannie Mae and Freddie Mac have affected the primary mortgage market in other ways as well. In 1971, the two enterprises engaged in a long collaborative process to draft standardized provisions for uniform notes and mortgage or deed of trust funds. These uniform instruments have been of value to almost all mortgage lenders in evaluating risks and in providing loan documentation on the mortgages they purchase. By 1980, about 80 percent of all conventional first mortgages were written

[15]Mortgage Insurance Companies of America, *Fact Book and Directory 1988* (Washington, D.C.: Mortgage Insurance Companies of America, 1988), p. 19; Mortgage Insurance Companies of America, *Fact Book and Directory 1976* (Washington, D.C.: Mortgage Insurance Companies of America, 1976), p. 4.
[16]Treasury Department *Report of the Secretary*, pp. A-25, B-23.

on the Fannie Mae-Freddie Mac uniform instrument forms. The prospect that loans might one day be sold into the secondary market provided an incentive for all lenders to use the forms, even when purchasing loans that at the time were larger than the Fannie Mae-Freddie Mac loan limits.

In addition, Fannie Mae and Freddie Mac have helped to promote greater uniformity in mortgage selling and servicing contracts and procedures. Although the two enterprises developed somewhat different seller-servicer guides and contracts, they have helped to standardize the terms of the relationship between primary lenders and secondary market mortgage purchasers. The increased uniformity of terms and conditions has increased the efficiency of the mortgage market and lowered transaction costs, compared to earlier days when variations among states and regions kept the mortgage market segmented into geographic regions.

To some extent, Fannie Mae and Freddie Mac have helped keep the primary market divided among a large number of relatively small originators and servicers. By providing standard servicing fees, traditionally set at a generous three-eighths of a percent of the unpaid principal balance of the mortgage, Fannie Mae and Freddie Mac have helped keep mortgage servicing profitable for smaller companies, which otherwise might have gone out of business because of their high cost structures. It is only recently, with increased economies of scale from computerized servicing systems and growing concern over the capital adequacy of mortgage originators and servicers, that large-scale servicing operations have begun to acquire a substantial market share.

Finally, along with Ginnie Mae, Fannie Mae and Freddie Mac have helped to pioneer standard terms and conditions relating to mortgage-backed securities (MBSs). MBSs benefit from liquidity (that is, the availability of a large number of similar securities such that buyers and sellers find a ready market), and their standardization has been important in producing such similar securities. Fannie Mae, Freddie Mac, and Ginnie Mae issue such huge volumes of MBSs, however, that the liquidity of the securities cannot be matched even by the large competitors. The latter, in turn, may try to issue mortgage-backed securities based on the larger-sized (so-called nonconforming) mortgages that Fannie

Mae and Freddie Mac are not eligible to purchase. These securities as well benefit from standards that Fannie Mae and Freddie Mac have set for conforming mortgages.

Farmer Mac's Impact on the Agricultural Mortgage Market

In 1988, Congress created Farmer Mac to promote a concentration, rather than a proliferation, of lenders in the agricultural mortgage market. Except for loans guaranteed by the Farmers' Home Administration, Farmer Mac is not authorized to purchase the mortgages that it helps securitize. Instead, Farmer Mac is limited to providing a guarantee for pools of agricultural mortgages assembled by mortgage marketing facilities, familiarly known as mortgage "poolers." Because mortgage-backed securities have significant funding advantages to the extent that they are issued in large standardized volumes, the poolers are expected to be large organizations. Major financial institutions, such as the Prudential and John Hancock insurance companies and Manufacturers Hanover, are likely to be among the handful of firms that will be able to compete over the long run as poolers of Farmer Mac-guaranteed securities.

The result may well be the emergence of a secondary market composed of a concentrated group of poolers with the power to dominate the originators and servicers of mortgages in the primary market. The Farmer Mac legislation, in turn, is designed to assure that Farmer Mac limits its fees for providing the guarantee and complements rather than competes with the poolers and originators. Thus, the role of this newest enterprise—to foster economic concentration in agricultural mortgage finance—is a far cry from the traditional role established for the Farm Credit System decades earlier—to move the balance of economic power forward to the borrower and away from what were considered large impersonal lending institutions.

The Farm Credit System and the Market for Farm Loans

The Farm Credit System (FCS), of course, went too far in permitting borrowers to dominate lending decisions. The generous lending practices of FCS cooperatives were noticeably influenced by FCS agricultural borrowers. In the late 1970s and early 1980s, the FCS priced its loans far below those of private competitors. By 1981, FCS mortgage loans were priced at five percentage points below those of competing rural lenders. This was a period of escalating farm incomes and land values. The low-cost FCS mortgage loans created a powerful incentive for farm borrowers to pledge their increasingly valuable land as collateral for yet greater amounts of debt. When the bubble burst, many farmers were hurt much more than they would have been if they hadn't overborrowed.

As William C. Robb, an FCS veteran from southern Illinois, warned the Farmer Mac board of directors in 1989, "Thousands of farmers in my state have failed in recent years, not as a result of their inability to produce or their operational mismanagement, but as a result of their lax discipline in the use of credit, and by standards which did not prevent excessive credit from being extended." Robb urged Farmer Mac to adopt conservative underwriting standards: "It should be made clear that the extension of credit to most farmers is not a desirable objective in, and of itself, unless someone finds virtue in farm foreclosure."[17]

As multibillion dollar financial institutions, government-sponsored enterprises can substantially affect their customers, their competitors, and their markets in positive or in negative ways. The financial advantages of the enterprises can be turned into benefits for borrowers and the marketplace or into policies that ultimately hurt rather than help the intended beneficiaries.

Federal Advantages versus "Crowding Out"

The enterprises can have profound effects on their markets because they receive federal advantages largely denied to their competitors. The government provides these advantages and thereby uses the enterprises to deliver a credit subsidy to selected borrowers and parts of the economy. The subsidy comes from the enter-

[17]William C. Robb, testimony before the Farmer Mac board of directors, 5 May 1989.

prises' access to the federal agency guarantee, which lowers their borrowing costs and provides a variety of tax and other benefits. The government does not charge the enterprises a fee for these benefits; indeed, it even exempts some of the enterprises from federal income taxes on their earnings. In some cases, the enterprises are expected to pass on a portion of their subsidy benefits to the market segments that the government is trying to help.

Given their substantial cost advantages, it is not surprising that government-sponsored enterprises can greatly alter their markets and even drive competitors out of certain lines of business. The important policy question is whether this result is appropriate and, if so, under what circumstances. That is, to what extent do the enterprises serve public purposes that other competitors would not provide adequately or at all?

To address this issue requires a focus on public costs and benefits, not on the economic fortunes of particular firms in the marketplace. Analytically, it is useful to divide the benefits of enterprise lending into two categories, efficiency gains and subsidy benefits. Efficiency gains occur when the government uses the enterprises to help overcome market imperfections and to improve the general functioning of the credit markets. Improvements in market efficiency can increase the benefits provided to some borrowers while not disadvantaging others. To economists, enterprise activity is cost-effective when it improves the allocation of resources that were previously used inefficiently. The focus of the policy issue then becomes the extent to which each enterprise is effective at overcoming market imperfections that would otherwise distort the flow of credit.

By contrast, when the government uses the enterprises to help deliver subsidy benefits to preferred borrowers and market segments, it is providing a special benefit to particular borrowers rather than improving the functioning of the credit market as a whole. Subsidy benefits mean that the government is redistributing the supply of credit by providing preferential treatment to borrowers who otherwise would have to obtain less credit or pay more for it. If loan funds are limited, the disfavored borrowers (even if they could use the money for other valued public purposes) may obtain less credit or be forced to pay more for it.

Such redistribution, in turn, causes a distortion of economic resources when it "crowds out" disfavored borrowers. Two kinds of diseconomy can occur. First, an inefficient lender may use its federal subsidy advantages to displace more efficient competitors (as the FCS Land Banks did in the 1970s). Second, the federal subsidy may cause an oversupply of credit to some borrowers (such as the farmers who took on too much debt) while constraining other borrowers who might have more productive uses for the money.

Hence, an enterprise must be assessed in terms of its value in enhancing market efficiency and in delivering subsidy benefits to meet the highest priority public purposes. For, as we have seen, the benefits of an enterprise's activities can change significantly over the years after its creation.

How the Enterprises Improve Market Efficiency

The creation of several of the enterprises—the FCS, FHLBS, Fannie Mae, and Sallie Mae—was justified on efficiency grounds. In each case, there was good reason to believe that the market by itself would not provide efficient credit support to an important group of borrowers.

Farm Credit System

Rural borrowers were long considered disadvantaged in their access to credit. In the early part of the twentieth century, rural farmers were remote from cities and banks and especially from the money center institutions of the large cities in the Northeast. The government created the Farm Credit System (FCS) institutions in three stages—in 1916, 1923, and 1933—before electricity, telephones, automobiles, and other facilities for providing financial services over long distances were widely available in rural areas. The FCS institutions were established on the premise that many creditworthy borrowers had limited access to credit and faced disadvantageous credit terms simply because of imperfections in the financial markets that impeded the flow of money to remote areas. Before rural communities were well integrated into America's financial markets, economists pointed out substantial differences in interest rates and other credit terms for rural borrowers and borrowers in urban centers.

Another market imperfection was created by bank lending limits; under federal law, banks are limited in the amount of credit (defined as a percentage of their capital base) they may extend to any single borrower. Rural banks traditionally tended to be small, and these lending limits also helped to curtail the availability of credit through the commercial banking system.

The FCS permitted farm borrowers to form cooperative financial institutions and combine their market power to tap urban investment funds. To the extent that the FCS facilitated access to credit for creditworthy borrowers and offset the market imperfections, the result was a gain in market efficiency, without significant offsetting costs. FCS activity displaced few rural lenders in the early years; in fact, rural banks often welcomed the infusion of FCS funds into the community.

Federal Home Loan Bank System

The Federal Home Loan Bank System (FHLBS) was established in 1932 during a massive market failure. Hundreds of thrifts had collapsed in the Great Depression and the rest found their mortgage portfolios greatly impaired. At the behest of the thrift industry, the Hoover administration addressed this problem by creating the FHLBS to provide advances to struggling thrifts. The Federal Home Loan Banks were supposed to provide loans for thrifts and accept the illiquid mortgages as collateral. This was intended to help thrifts stay liquid, and solvent, until the economy revived and mortgages again became a profitable asset.

The FHLBS was created before the advent of the many Roosevelt administration programs that helped pump federal credit into the housing market. At the time of its creation, the FHLBS provided a net efficiency gain, so long as the banks took care not to lose money on their advances. In contrast to the FCS, the FHLBS has taken great care in this regard and, in fact, has never lost money on an advance.

In later years, FHLBS advances also helped overcome geographical imperfections in the mortgage market. The developing communities of the Midwest, South, and West needed to fund mortgage loans, but the money was largely available in the urban areas of the Northeast. Because of legal prohibitions on thrift institutions, limiting them to providing services to one state or to a single locality, imbalances occurred between the areas possessing extra funds to deposit or invest and those areas with a need for those funds. This market imperfection was measurable; mortgage rates in large East Coast cities were noticeably lower than the rates in areas where available funds did not meet the growing demand. The FHLBS advances helped to bridge this difference by raising money from investors with extra funds and by providing advances to thrifts that needed them. Essentially, the FHLBS helped to arbitrage the mortgage interest-rate gap across the country and provided a significant net benefit without offsetting costs.

As federal regulations evolved, the FHLBS also helped to offset a different kind of market imperfection. From 1966 to the early 1980s, the government's so-called Regulation Q imposed interest-rate ceilings on thrift and bank deposit accounts. At times in the economic cycle, interest rates rose significantly above the regulated ceilings, causing substantial outflows of deposits from thrifts. At such times, the FHLBS, whose borrowings were not hampered by interest-rate ceilings, could raise money in the federal agency credit market and provide an extra volume of funds to thrifts that had lost deposits. Again, this credit flow improved market efficiency without offsetting costs, though it also helped to prop up an ultimately unsustainable system.

Fannie Mae

When Fannie Mae was created in 1938, it joined the FHLBS as an enterprise designed to help offset market imperfections and promote the free flow of funds into home mortgage lending, from cash-rich areas to developing parts of the country.

Like the FHLBS, Fannie Mae became an instrument used to offset the credit problems caused by geographic limits on banks and thrifts. By tapping the federal agency credit market, Fannie

Mae was able to borrow from investors and thereby provide mortgage money to lenders across the country. Again, to the extent that Fannie Mae did not lose money through imprudent lending, it was efficient largely without offsetting costs.

The geographic limits meant that banks and thrifts could not become efficient national providers of mortgage credit. In the developing parts of the country, bank and thrift deposits were too limited to meet market demand; Fannie Mae thus supplemented rather than displaced local lenders. Also, during the years of Regulation Q, Fannie Mae helped promote the flow of funds into mortgage lending during times of disintermediation, when banks and thrifts found themselves losing deposits. This, too, was a net efficiency gain for the credit markets.

Sallie Mae

Sallie Mae was created in 1972, seven years after the establishment of the federal guaranteed student loan program. Lenders did not consider these student loans to be a profitable line of business. The loans were small and expensive to service, and lenders did not relish trying to deal with the federal government to collect on the guarantee in case of default. Many lenders simply offered student loans as an unprofitable service to accommodate their normal customers.

The government perceived a serious need for additional federal support of the guaranteed student loan program. At the behest of the Nixon administration, Congress created Sallie Mae to purchase guaranteed student loans and provide advances to lenders. At the time Sallie Mae was established, there was no problem of displacement of other competitors; few lenders saw student loans as an attractive line of business and there was no secondary market for such loans.

Since then, however, the government has increased the amount of subsidy it provides for student loans. A 1978 change in the law removed an interest-rate cap that had periodically caused lenders to receive below-market returns on student loans. Today, the guaranteed student loan program (GSLP) provides a stated below-market rate of interest to students (currently 7 to 9 percent), reimburses lenders at a higher rate of interest (currently the

91-day T-bill rate, plus 3.25 percentage points), and makes up the difference from federal funds provided through the Department of Education. Many commercial lenders now recognize guaranteed student loans as a potentially profitable line of business.

How Enterprise Contributions to Market Efficiency Change over Time

Market imperfections are not immutable. New technologies and changing laws can erode previously insurmountable barriers to the flow of credit. As market conditions improve, then, the efficiency benefits of enterprise lending may decline.

Today, geographic restrictions on banks and thrifts have been greatly relaxed, both by changes in federal and state laws to permit multistate lending and by changes in technology that permit banks and thrifts to solicit deposits and fund loans nationwide. The three federally chartered, secondary market mortgage institutions—Ginnie Mae, Fannie Mae, and Freddie Mac—have also helped improve market efficiencies by setting the standards for mortgage instruments, transaction procedures between primary and secondary market institutions, and mortgage-backed security instruments.

These developments, and changes in the regional economies of the United States, have erased the mortgage-rate differential among parts of the country. Hence, regardless of how efficient its operations may be, the benefits that Fannie Mae can provide today are far fewer than when it first began to serve the residential mortgage market a half-century ago.

Similarly, rural areas are no longer as isolated from the national money markets. Some of the larger agricultural cooperatives served by the FCS co-op banks are among the most sophisticated corporations in America. The continuing economic concentration in American agriculture means that even farm customers for FCS mortgage loans tend to be seasoned survivors capable of managing their finances in bad times as well as good ones. Market imperfections continue to exist for many rural borrowers. However, as rural America increasingly integrates itself with the fi-

nancial markets, the net possible efficiency gains from FCS lending activities are inevitably lower than when the Federal Land
Banks first began to serve rural borrowers in 1916.

Finally, with respect to the student loan market, when Sallie
Mae was created in 1972, the original market imperfections were
based on the perception of student loans as an unprofitable line
of business. Today, because of changes in the federal program, in
the size of the student loan market, and in computerized loan
technologies, this is no longer true. The volume of student loans
and the level of federal benefits under the guaranteed student
loan program have greatly increased. As Sallie Mae has helped to
demonstrate, student loans can be a highly lucrative business for
financial institutions. An increasing number of commercial lenders argue that Sallie Mae's huge market share, fortified by restrictive provisions of the Higher Education Act, reduces their ability
to participate in the student loan business.

In contrast to the activities of Fannie Mae, Freddie Mac, and
the FCS, it is not clear whether Sallie Mae has provided significant efficiency benefits to the market. Even though the enterprise's own operations are highly efficient, the benefits go to its
shareholders. As economists Barry Bosworth, Andrew Carron,
and Elisabeth Rhyne point out, "The whole effort to develop a
secondary market has had few benefits for the government, in the
form of lower costs, or for students, through a lower loan rate."[18]

Improving Market Efficiency Gains of
Enterprise Activities

When the government establishes an enterprise to improve market efficiency, it must take steps to assure that the enterprise is
structured in such a way as to provide the consequent benefits to
the marketplace and borrowers rather than merely to shareholders. One such approach, seen during some past periods of competition between Fannie Mae and Freddie Mac, involves the
establishment of multiple enterprises to serve a single sector.
Multiple competitors can help drive down loan rates, rather than

[18]Barry P. Bosworth, Andrew S. Carron, and Elisabeth H. Rhyne, *The Economics of Federal Credit Programs* (Washington, D.C.: Brookings Institution, 1987), p. 146.

keeping prices high because of federally protected market power.

However, driving loan rates down too far in some market segments may be problematic. For example, intensified competition in the residential mortgage market could hasten the demise of many thrifts, which today rely on portfolio lending as an income-producing line of business. Striking the right balance among federal credit programs is not an easy task. The government must greatly increase its sophistication in monitoring market developments, including the implications of enterprise activities for potential competitors, to assure that the enterprises continue to provide the highest possible efficiency gains.

Kenneth Thygerson, former president of Freddie Mac, told Congress in 1983 that "the use of agency status and the special advantages that go with it should be reserved for those activities that are not, or for some reason cannot be, adequately performed by the private sector."[19] His strong statement ignores the additional value of enterprises as vehicles used to deliver a federal credit subsidy to selected borrowers. Nevertheless, Thygerson's comment serves as a warning of the need for Congress and the executive branch to be aware that other private firms may be able to provide many of the efficiency benefits now attributed to government-sponsored enterprises.

Delivering Federal Subsidy Benefits

To a significant extent, most of the enterprises are designed to deliver federal subsidy benefits, and not merely to improve market efficiency. These benefits take the forms of lower interest rates, favorable loan terms (such as longer-term loans than otherwise might be available), and increased availability of credit.

Fannie Mae and Freddie Mac are good examples of enterprises whose federal agency credit subsidy directly reduces borrowing costs for designated borrowers. Together, the two enterprises are estimated to lower home mortgage rates by about one-fourth to one-half of a percentage point for all home owners with con-

[19]Testimony in Senate Banking Committee, Subcommittee on Housing and Urban Affairs, *Secondary Mortgage Market* (Washington, D.C.: GPO, 5 May 1983), p. 121.

forming mortgages, not just for those whose mortgages are actually funded by the two institutions.[20] The impact of this benefit is made clear by comparing the interest rates on conforming mortgages with those in the nonconforming market, which includes mortgages above the $187,450 limit on mortgages purchased by the two enterprises. Even a brief inspection of the weekly real estate section of a local newspaper can help give a sense of the noticeably higher interest rates of the larger mortgages compared to conforming mortgages. Also, the larger mortgages appear to have higher origination costs.

The Farm Credit System on occasion has provided even more substantial benefits for farm borrowers. This not only displaced other rural lenders but also induced farmers to take on much higher levels of debt than they could ultimately afford to carry. The results were crippling, not only for the FCS itself but for the farm borrowers as well, who took on debt they could not afford to repay and then saw their businesses fail.

Sallie Mae stands at the other end of the spectrum: Its public purpose does not include delivering any subsidy benefits to borrowers. The guaranteed student loan program (GSLP) sets a fixed, below-market rate of interest for student borrowers. Indeed, the Higher Education Act discourages price competition in the primary market and expressly prohibits lenders from offering price incentives to attract customers. This effectively prevents Sallie Mae from using its federal agency credit to lower student interest rates below the set GSLP level. Thus, Sallie Mae's federal agency credit advantage helps subsidize the company's shareholders, but not students.

The Economic Debate over the Effects of Enterprise Lending

The extent to which the federal subsidy involved in enterprise activities distorts the nation's credit markets has not been easy to measure.[21] If the amount of credit available to U.S. borrowers

---

[20]See, for example, Weicher, *The Future Structure of the Housing Finance System*, p. 32.
[21]See, for example, William G. Gale, *Economic Effects of Federal Credit Programs*. Department of Economics Working Paper No. 483, University of California, Los Angeles, June 1988.

were strictly fixed, it would be easy to see that increased availability of loan funds to home buyers or farmers or thrift institutions would mean less availability for others. Similarly, if the markets were completely efficient, it would be easy to see that, to the extent that enterprise-supported borrowers crowded out other borrowers, the price of credit for these other borrowers would increase as they competed against one another to borrow an increasingly scarce amount of money.

While this ideal economic model is easy to understand, the extent to which it can be applied to the reality of enterprise activity is less clear. To some degree, the enterprises increase the supply of available credit to the United States as a whole. Because of the extreme creditworthiness of their obligations, the enterprises are able to market their securities to foreign investors that otherwise might not lend to the U.S. market. To the extent that this occurs, borrowers favored with enterprise loans do not displace other American borrowers or force others to pay increased interest rates. While the question of "crowding out" has drawn considerable debate, the answer awaits dispassionate economic analysis.

Moreover, even though enterprise activity involves hundreds of billions of dollars of borrowing, the economic subsidy delivered by the enterprises tends to be much less substantial than the subsidy provided by most federal government programs delivered through government agencies. This means that the potential economic distortions are likely to be less than if borrowers obtained greater subsidies. Again, economists disagree on the extent to which Fannie Mae and Freddie Mac, for example, reduce mortgage borrowing costs below efficient levels. Federal Reserve Board Chairman Alan Greenspan observes, "Although empirical studies of the credit enhancement effects vary on the amount of the impact, they generally agree that it is relatively small."[22] By contrast, the Farm Credit System clearly distorted the credit market; it provided a substantial credit subsidy that ultimately caused harm to borrowers, competitors, and the FCS alike.

Today, the collapse of hundreds of federally backed thrift in-

[22]Letter of Alan Greenspan, chairman, Board of Governors of the Federal Reserve System, to Senator Donald W. Riegle, Jr., chairman, Senate Committee on Banking, Housing, and Urban Affairs, 31 August 1990, p. 11.

stitutions warns of another kind of financial distortion, one that concerns taxpayers as well as the financial markets. As with all federally backed institutions, enterprise lending involves a huge open-ended contingent liability for federal taxpayers. If something goes wrong with an enterprise, the government faces virtually irresistible pressure to bail it out at taxpayers' expense—the subject of much of the later part of this book.

The enabling legislation for all of the enterprises could be improved, in some cases substantially, by greater attention both to enhancing the benefits of enterprise lending and to reducing the potential costs. This would help channel the relentless power of enterprise competition in directions that most benefit American borrowers and the allocation of our economic resources.

5

The Politics of Enterprise Lending

The probability of Fannie Mae facing higher capital requirements or any type of user fee compares with the likelihood that Congress will convert the Lincoln Memorial to a discothèque. . . . Fannie Mae enjoys a safe haven from regulatory interference with its operations and capital structure.

—Eric I. Hemel, First Boston Corporation

The commercial advantages that the enterprises receive from the federal government demand that they compete in the political arena to assure their financial success. A politically successful enterprise can obtain expanded authority to enter new markets and new lines of business, as well as increase the financial benefits for itself and its shareholders. Most importantly, such an enterprise can stave off unwelcome legislative or regulatory efforts that might interfere with its profits or lending activities.

Pressures to Expand Enterprise Powers

Government-sponsored enterprises feel a variety of pressures to expand their lines of business. Once an enterprise dominates much of its legally specified market segment, for instance, it may look to diversify. Sallie Mae, as it continues to increase its share of the student loan market, may face a trade-off between further expansion and a reduction in the high quality of the loans it has been able to acquire thus far. An enterprise may also feel that its dominant line of business offers attractive opportunities just beyond the reach of its legally authorized powers.

Pressures to diversify can be especially intense for the enterprise serving a stagnating or shrinking market. As the rural economy contracted after the mid-1980s, the Farm Credit System (FCS) faced a market in which many farmers were reducing rather than increasing their indebtedness. It is hard to make money in a declining market, even with access to federal agency credit. Some FCS institutions want to offer additional services to build on their large base of borrowers and thereby earn more fee income from those services.

The Federal Home Loan Banks also face uncertain market conditions, as hundreds of their potential customers disappear with the liquidation of insolvent thrift institutions. However, the increase in federal deposit insurance premiums will help the FHLBS, in that thrifts now have added incentive to rely on FHLB advances rather than on insured deposits as a source of funds. In the 1987 and 1989 legislation, the federal government assessed the FHLBS several billion dollars to help fund FICO and REF-CORP; the FHLBS now feels considerable pressure to restore earnings and is considering a wide range of options, including possibly the guaranteeing of mortgage-backed securities, as do Fannie Mae and Freddie Mac.

Congressional Receptivity

Overall, Congress has been receptive to enterprise requests to expand their authorized powers. In 1981, Congress authorized Sallie Mae "to undertake any . . . activity the Board of Directors of the Association determines to be in furtherance of the programs of insured student loans authorized under this part or will otherwise support the credit needs of students."[1] This provision gives Sallie Mae broad authority to expand its activities. In 1984, Sallie Mae used the new provision to acquire a savings and loan institution, and thereby to overcome its earlier statutory con-

[1]20 U.S.C. 1087-2(d)(1)

finement to the secondary market. The institution was the Sunbelt Savings and Loan Association of Southern Pines, North Carolina; Sallie Mae reorganized it as the First Capital Corporation.

In 1989, the Federal Home Loan Bank System obtained expanded powers. The technical language of the 1989 amendment was unobjectionable; it merely clarified that the FHLBS is authorized to conduct activities incidental to those expressly authorized by the Federal Home Loan Bank Act. However, the accompanying conference report, read by few members of Congress or their staff before it was printed, gave an extremely broad interpretation to those incidental powers. Without saying so, the conference report also overruled a major court decision, *Association of Data Processing Service Organizations, Inc. (ADAPSO) v. Federal Home Loan Bank Board* (6th cir. 1977). The court in that case held, in no uncertain terms, that the provision of data-processing services to thrift institutions is beyond the incidental powers of the FHLBS. One wonders how many participants in the 1989 legislative process, except the FHLBS itself, knew of the ADAPSO case and the consequences of the expansive conference report language.

The 1989 legislation also conferred broad new authority on Fannie Mae and Freddie Mac. It removed restrictions in Fannie Mae's charter and codified the ability of both enterprises to make advances, collateralized by home mortgages, to lenders. This new power is only loosely connected to the public purpose of providing new funds for mortgage lending. A commercial bank, for example, can use mortgages from its portfolio as collateral for Fannie Mae or Freddie Mac advances. The mortgage collateral is merely a convenient opportunity to obtain federal agency credit that can be used for a range of domestic or even foreign loans, whether or not they are related to the residential mortgage market.

In each of these cases, serious doubt exists over whether a significant number of members of Congress were properly informed about the financial and policy implications of the statutory change. The 1981 Sallie Mae charter amendment was buried in the 1981 Omnibus Budget Reconciliation Act, a massive piece of legislation amounting to almost six hundred pages of statutory text. The conference committee report alone extended over one thousand pages.

The 1989 expansion of the powers of the Federal Home Loan Banks was accomplished in conference report language that appeared only as a sweeping financial institutions bill came to a final up-or-down vote and past the point when members of Congress had the opportunity to offer amendments. The 1989 change in Fannie Mae's and Freddie Mac's powers was presented to Congress as a means for the two enterprises to provide additional funds for thrift institutions by purchasing a special kind of mortgage debt obligation, the collateralized mortgage obligation. Not spelled out, for example, was that this would place Fannie Mae and Freddie Mac in direct competition with the FHLBS.

These three examples illustrate the same lesson: Enterprises can obtain broad expansions of authority through statutory changes that few understand fully. Enterprise charter acts are highly technical and detailed pieces of legislation. The most successful efforts at expanding charter powers tend to be presented as minor technical adjustments not worthy of extended deliberation. Thus, even after a new provision is enacted, Congress may still lack accurate information about the ultimate consequences of the change.

The 1989 financial institutions legislation is replete with such provisions. In that law, Freddie Mac obtained a Fannie Mae-type charter, including a board of directors with a majority of shareholder-elected members. Although the 1989 legislation provides that HUD is to oversee Freddie Mac (as it does Fannie Mae), it was accompanied by House Banking Committee report language that largely eviscerated HUD's approval authority. In addition to the express authority to make loans on the security of mortgages, Fannie Mae and Freddie Mac obtained a large expansion of their stated statutory purposes. Until 1989, Fannie Mae's charter act provided that the corporation's purpose was to provide "supplementary assistance" to the secondary mortgage market. In 1987 and 1988, HUD had attempted to invoke this provision to limit and set conditions on Fannie Mae's authority to issue REMICs, the multiclass mortgage-backed securities. Similarly, the Federal Home Loan Bank Board, then Freddie Mac's regulator, in 1988 gave Freddie Mac only limited permission to issue REMICs.

The 1989 act changed Fannie Mae's statutory purpose. It deleted the limitation to providing supplementary assistance and stated the company's purpose as "to provide ongoing assistance" to the secondary mortgage market. In its package of 1989 statutory amendments, Freddie Mac received the same statement of purpose. The regulator has lost any legal basis for imposing limits on the extent of Fannie Mae's and Freddie Mac's authority to issue REMICs, even though they have displaced virtually all private competitors in the market for conforming mortgages.

Whether or not this is a good public policy result is an issue that was not debated in the 1989 congressional deliberations. As with Sallie Mae's expansion of powers in 1981 and the FHLBS's expansion in 1989, a major piece of legislation such as the 1989 Thrift Bailout Bill provides an opportunity for an enterprise to obtain far-reaching amendments that few comprehend fully during the process of enactment. Further, officials in the executive branch are often so busy with hundreds of other parts of a large bill that they lose the ability to focus attention on what appear to be mere technical changes advanced by the enterprises.

When Congress Declines

On some occasions, the enterprises do not succeed in obtaining the new powers they seek. This may occur with issues that become visible because of complaints from competitors in the same line of business that an enterprise seeks to enter, or from constituents who fear a loss of attention by the enterprise serving them. In such cases, Congress may deny an enterprise's request for expanded powers or even restrict existing powers believed to have been misused.

In 1982, for example, Freddie Mac proposed to expand its board of directors to include a majority of shareholder-elected directors and to permit sale of its stock to the general public. Under the proposal, Freddie Mac would have been virtually exempt from federal regulation and would have continued to be exempt from federal income taxes (as it was until a change in the tax law in 1985). Housing industry groups supported the Freddie Mac proposal, while Wall Street firms were divided. The Reagan administration and Fannie Mae strongly objected. Fannie Mae listed for Congress the competitive advantages that Freddie Mac would receive under the bill, especially the freedom from federal regulation and from federal income taxes. Unless parity existed between the two enterprises, Fannie Mae argued, Freddie Mac would benefit from unfair competition. The Freddie Mac bill died in committee after a hearing on the subject.

In 1983, it was Fannie Mae's turn to be rebuffed. Fannie Mae sought relaxation of some of its statutory restrictions, including some freedom from the dollar limits on mortgages eligible for purchase by Fannie Mae and Freddie Mac as well as from the restrictions on authority to make loans on the security of mortgages. While some housing industry groups supported the Fannie Mae proposals, others, including private issuers of mortgage-related securities and mortgage insurance companies, actively and successfully opposed the measures. Among the other opponents were the Reagan administration and—not surprising, given Fannie Mae's performance the year before—Freddie Mac. Interestingly, though the U.S. League of Savings Institutions also objected to a number of the Fannie Mae proposals, it advocated the elimination of mortgage ceilings. Unlike today, the thrift industry in 1983 did not fully perceive a financial threat from Fannie Mae and Freddie Mac. After considering various alternatives, Congress approved some modest Fannie Mae and Freddie Mac amendments, including an expansion in the size of Fannie Mae's board of directors, but not the larger benefits sought by Fannie Mae.

Sallie Mae's 1984 acquisition of the Sunbelt Savings and Loan Association met with intense opposition from financial institutions, especially those in North Carolina, where the thrift was located. The lenders sued Sallie Mae in federal district court, but lost on the ground that they had no "standing" under the structure of the Sallie Mae charter act (that is, neither competitors nor Sallie Mae stockholders had a right to bring the lawsuit). The lenders then turned to Congress. In the 1986 legislation, Congress amended the Sallie Mae charter act to prohibit the use of its expanded powers to acquire any depository institution, and also imposed other restrictions. Sallie Mae sold the thrift institution.

Political Competition between the Enterprises and Other Financial Institutions

As in the marketplace, the political relationship of government-sponsored enterprises to other financial institutions is characterized by a combination of competition and cooperation. One frequent result is to mute the voice of market participants likely to be disadvantaged by newly proposed enterprise activities.

Take again the issue of REMICs, the new mortgage securities created by the 1986 Tax Reform Act. By 1988, Fannie Mae and Freddie Mac had overcome the opposition of their regulators and began to participate heavily in the business of issuing REMICs. Some thrift institutions, particularly those originating and holding mortgages, strongly opposed the two enterprises' role as REMIC issuers. They feared that short-maturity REMICs would eventually substitute for thrift deposits and lead to an erosion of their deposit base. These thrifts also feared that REMICs would further squeeze profits from their mortgage holdings. Other thrifts, though, mainly those with operations resembling mortgage banking, favored enterprises acting as REMIC issuers. They saw REMICs as a way to improve the prices of the mortgages they sell into the secondary market.

As the General Accounting Office reported in its 1988 evaluation of the competitive effects of Fannie Mae and Freddie Mac as REMIC issuers, "the thrift industry does not speak with a unified voice on the potential impact."[2] It came as no surprise, then, that the thrift industry had little to say about the provisions of the 1989 legislation, which effectively removed all potential legal and regulatory restrictions on Fannie Mae's and Freddie Mac's activities as REMIC issuers. The thrifts were distracted by the many other parts of the bill that critically affected them, and too divided to form a strong, unified position.

The ability to complement rather than compete with the en-

---

[2]U.S. General Accounting Office, *Housing Finance: Agency Issuance of Real Estate Mortgage Investment Conduits* (Washington, D.C.: GPO, September 1988), p. 4.

terprises is a two-edged sword for competitors. On the one hand, it maximizes the competitors' ability to make money in markets that the enterprises dominate. On the other hand, it prevents the competitors from competing effectively with the enterprises in the political arena. At times, a large bank or thrift may have one department losing business to an enterprise and another department reaping the benefits of mutually favorable transactions with the same enterprise. Consider, for example, the relationship between Sallie Mae and a large commercial bank that also purchases student loans. On the one hand, the bank competes with Sallie Mae to buy the highest quality loan portfolios. The bank's student loan department may be unhappy about Sallie Mae's perceived advantages in such competition. On the other hand, the bank's liability managers may be delighted at the opportunity to borrow money at favorable rates from Sallie Mae, collateralized by home-equity or student loans. In cases like this one, few banks would risk their favorable business relationships with Sallie Mae by challenging the enterprise in the political arena.

The same is true of investment bankers. Wall Street firms may be unhappy about their inability to compete directly with Fannie Mae and Freddie Mac in issuing REMICs. At the same time, however, they actively seek business from Fannie Mae and Freddie Mac, among the selling groups that underwrite and sell enterprise securities. Thus, even though they lost the fight to limit the enterprises' role as REMIC issuers, Wall Street firms still seek to do business with Fannie Mae and Freddie Mac, dealings that involve paying the enterprises to issue REMICs for their clients.

Thrifts are in a similar position. Fannie Mae and Freddie Mac have swapped tens of billions of dollars of mortgage-backed securities (MBSs) for mortgages that thrift institutions hold in portfolio. Thrifts pay a modest MBS guarantee fee and receive in return a federally backed MBS asset that is much more liquid than the original mortgages. These transactions occurred with great frequency during the 1980s, which made it difficult for thrifts to object that Fannie Mae and Freddie Mac were applying a financial squeeze to the profitability of thrift mortgage portfolios.

For the enterprises, this state of affairs can bring a degree of satisfaction. David Maxwell, Fannie Mae's chairman and chief executive officer, told the *Institutional Investor* in 1988 that it was the large California-based thrift institutions that had most often complained about Fannie Mae's competition with their portfolio business; but "now [that] we've been doing a lot of [swap] business with big thrifts, they've been a lot quieter."[3]

Enterprises have considerable economic power, which also serves to reinforce their political strength. During the 1987 controversy over REMICs, for instance, Salomon Brothers, Inc. contended that, "in retaliation, it and its clients have been cut off from most of its Fannie Mae business."[4] Fannie Mae's chief financial officer said Salomon Brothers had been dropped "because of our perception that they value our business very highly."[5] Once the controversy ended, though, the two firms resumed an amicable business relationship.

Similarly, in June 1990, Fannie Mae withdrew its advertising account from *The Economist* of London, an apparent response to news stories and a cartoon[6] on the 1990 Treasury *Report on Government Sponsored Enterprises.* (The cartoon is reprinted on the next page.) Fortunately, though, most of the enterprises may realize the negative implications of applying economic pressures; they know that their financial strength alone gives them a sufficient advantage in the political arena.

Interdependence, and the well-founded belief that acrimony is bad business, together mean that discord between the enterprises and their competitors tends to be muted, with increased tension arising if political or marketplace changes create new friction. Most of the time, though, it is easier for competitors to get along and conduct profitable business with the enterprises rather than to engage in political confrontation. While this may be restful for the Congress, it contributes to the federal government's lack of important information about the value of enterprise activities in serving public purposes.

[3]Fran Hawthorne, "Fannie Mae Flexes Its Muscles," *Institutional Investor,* Nov. 1988, 85.
[4]"Debate on New U.S.-Backed Mortgage Security Stirs Charges of Greed, Government Domination," *Wall Street Journal,* 20 Apr. 1987, p. 48.
[5]Ibid.
[6]"Shaping Up Fannie Mae and Freddie Mac: Uncle Sam Sends Them Next Door," *The Economist,* 19 May 1990, p. 92; Carol Matlack, "Getting Their Way," *National Journal,* 27 October 1990, pp. 2584–2588.

"Uncle Sam Sends Them Next Door"

Source: Reprinted by permission from *The Economist,* 19 May 1990, p. 94.

Expanding Enterprise Powers and the Public Policy Issues

The debate over expanding enterprise powers often centers on issues of efficiency and subsidy. Without the assistance of extensive economic analysis, Congress does not always seek to distinguish the efficiency gains from the subsidy benefits of enterprise activities. However, recognizing that enterprise financing provides a significant benefit for constituents, Congress sometimes looks to target these benefits to serve higher-priority credit and constituent needs. Thus, Fannie Mae and Freddie Mac are limited to funding mortgages below a given amount ($187,450 in 1990) because, Congress reasons, home owners who can afford higher-priced homes do not need the benefits provided by these two enterprises. The Housing Subcommittee of the House of Representatives, in particular, has repeatedly sought to direct Fannie Mae and Freddie Mac toward serving low- and moderate-income home buyers rather than funding all residential mortgages.

Many of the limits on enterprise authority represent compromises or subjective judgments. Thus, the 1990 single-family mortgage limit of $187,450 applies to mortgages on homes valued at a maximum of $234,000. (This assumes that the mortgage is worth up to 80 percent of the total value of the home.) That figure is well above the mid-1990 median price of an existing home of $97,500 and of a newly constructed home of about $129,000.[7] The mortgage limit is a compromise between housing and lending institutions that may seek a complete removal of the Fannie Mae and Freddie Mac mortgage limits, and lenders and constituents that may want to direct Fannie Mae and Freddie Mac to focus exclusively on low- and moderate-income housing. The thrift industry is again split, with the institutions favoring higher loan limits (so Fannie Mae and Freddie Mac can purchase or securitize more mortgages than they originate or hold in portfolio) on one side, and the institutions favoring lower loan limits (so the enterprises do not depress their profits from holding mortgages in portfolio) on the other side.

Sometimes there is open discussion of the advantages and disadvantages of expanding enterprise powers. One example is the ongoing debate over the extent of permitted Farm Credit System activities, which continues to intensify as FCS institutions seek new ways to return to financial health. Some FCS institutions are contemplating additional services, such as assisting in the sales of money-market mutual funds, cash-management accounts, and credit cards; establishing a credit union to offer checking services, savings accounts, IRAs, and other products; and possibly even expanding into farm realty brokerage services. FCS institutions argue that these new services are a logical extension of their existing lending activities. They point to the expansion of commercial banks into an even more extensive range of services. From the FCS perspective, many of the proposed services would assist borrowers and the FCS alike by increasing the quality of borrowers' financial management. From the perspective of the commercial bank, however, the proposed expanded activities of the FCS would be a federally subsidized intrusion into areas already well served by the private sector. Indeed, the authority to offer an array of financial services is

---

[7]National Association of Realtors, *Home Sales* (Washington, D.C.: National Association of Realtors, August 1990), pp. 10, 19.

important to commercial banks. It helps them offset the financial advantage of the government-sponsored enterprise backed by relatively inexpensive federal credit. Moreover, bankers argue that FCS safety and soundness would decline because of the enterprise's lack of experience in the proposed new lines of business. Farm Credit institutions counterargue that they would be better able to satisfy that need to increase safety and soundness if they were permitted to expand their narrow range of services, diversify their sources of income, and strengthen their relationship with borrowers. So far, however, FCS institutions have not gained the new powers they seek.

Similar policy issues arise, though sometimes not publicly, when other government-sponsored enterprises seek to provide new services that complement their existing lending functions. From the enterprise perspective, such expansion would bring increased service and reduced cost to the borrower. From the competitor's view, it would be merely an extension of an already generous, open-ended federal subsidy used to support services less important than those originally contemplated by Congress. Since economic analysis is only rarely available, these disagreements are more often settled on the basis of political strength than through a systematic process of assessing the benefits and costs of opening particular activities to participation by government-sponsored enterprises.

Pressures to Serve Noneconomic Segments and Reduce Profitability

The enterprises need political strength not only to seek expanded statutory authority but also to resist the efforts of those who look to restrict their powers. In 1977, for example, when Fannie Mae was actively resisting the efforts of the Carter administration to force the corporation to fund additional low-income and center-city mortgage loans, Fannie Mae managed to block legislation introduced by Wisconsin Senator William Proxmire, chairman of the Senate Banking Committee. Proxmire's bill would have expanded Fannie Mae's board of directors by adding a majority of governmentally appointed members, who would have helped direct the corporation toward greater support for low- and moderate-income mortgages. Fannie Mae and its allies objected strongly, and the bill never emerged from the Banking Committee.

In 1978, the secretary of Housing and Urban Development (HUD) proposed regulations to increase the proportion of Fannie Mae's activities directed to low-income and center-city mortgages. As former HUD attorney Irwin Margulies recalls, "The regulations were an absolute failure."[8] The issue never reached the stage of legal analysis; instead, Fannie Mae marshaled intense political support. HUD received 1,233 comments on the proposed regulations and all but 16 were negative. The opponents of the regulation included more than a dozen national industry trade associations, many individual members of Congress, the congressional rural caucus (140 members), and many local and regional trade associations. As the regulator noted:

> With the help of numerous supporters, FNMA thwarted HUD's efforts to channel the corporation's activities towards greater support for low- and moderate-income housing and housing in older urban areas.[9]

The FHLBS has also been successful at resisting pressures to make noneconomic loans. In early 1989, the Bush administration sought to use the FHLBS to provide advances to help prop up faltering thrift institutions. The most powerful FHLB, the Federal Home Loan Bank of San Francisco, agreed to provide emergency funding to thrifts, but only if the advances were secured by sufficient collateral. According to the *Washington Post,* an unnamed administration official charged that "the directors of the bank are acting as if the private sector interests supersede the public interest duties the banks were created to fulfill." The directors of the San Francisco FHLB agreed to support the lending plan, but only "while fulfilling their fiduciary duties to the

---

[8]U.S. General Accounting Office, *Symposium: The Federal National Mortgage Association in a Changing Economic Environment* (Washington, D.C.: GPO, July 1985), pp. 233–234.
[9]Department of Housing and Urban Development, "Analysis of the Development of the Regulations Governing the Operations of the Federal National Mortgage Association," in *1986 Report to Congress on the Federal National Mortgage Association* (Washington, D.C.: Department of Housing and Urban Development, 1987), p. 166.

bank and its shareholders."[10] As with Fannie Mae's objections to serving lower-income home buyers with noneconomic loans, the FHLB prevailed. The Bush administration agreed that it would not require the FHLB to make loans against collateral that the FHLB considered inadequate; in return, the FHLB helped the government save face by agreeing to participate in the administration's emergency plan.[11]

The enterprises have also been successful at defeating other disadvantageous proposals. Fannie Mae, Freddie Mac, and other enterprises consistently thwarted the Reagan administration's attempts to impose "user fees" on the enterprises to help offset the advantage of federal agency credit. The enterprises blocked other Reagan administration proposals to reduce their access to the federal agency credit market. Although the Bush administration advocates user fees, the enterprises and their authorizing committees again are likely to resist successfully.

Despite their overall legislative success in 1989, the enterprises did suffer one major political setback. Led by Oversight Subcommittee Chairman J. J. Pickle from Texas and Representative Bill Gradison from Ohio, the House Ways and Means Committee reported an amendment that requires the Treasury Department to conduct an annual study of financial risk of each enterprise. Fannie Mae and Freddie Mac strongly objected. Fannie Mae obtained the services of a senior Senate conferee, the chairman of its authorizing subcommittee, Alan Cranston from California, to try to kill the measure, but failed. Senator Cranston did succeed in limiting the study to two years, 1990 and 1991, with the possibility that subsequent legislation may extend the Treasury studies into annual reports on enterprise safety and soundness. As Pickle later recounted, "I can say without hesitation that this was the most hard fought study requirements I had seen in my twenty-five years in the Congress."[12]

Enterprise hostility toward an annual study of an issue of legit-

[10]Kathleen Day, "S.F. Home Loan Bank Refuses S&L Plan Role; Federal Officials Call Decision 'Outrageous' and 'Irresponsible,' " *Washington Post,* 25 Feb. 1989, p. D-10.
[11]G. Christian Hill, "Home Loan Bank Agrees to Be Part of Lending Plan," *Wall Street Journal,* 9 Mar. 1989.
[12]Representative J.J. Pickle, "Remarks Before the Institute of Strategy Development Conference on Government-Sponsored Enterprises," 19 June 1990, p. 2.

imate importance to taxpayers was surprising. Some of the enterprises may have opposed the studies because of concern that they could lead to effective financial oversight. Fannie Mae and Freddie Mac show a strong preference for oversight by a department they can control, such as HUD. The enterprises also find their authorizing subcommittees to be more favorably disposed on regulatory matters than might be the case with a committee such as Ways and Means, which tends to focus on taxpayers and to insist on safety and soundness and effective oversight.

The Role of Constituencies in the Creation of the Enterprises

The interplay of markets and politics is perhaps most clear when the government decides to establish a new enterprise. Some enterprises were created at the behest of the president of the United States, as a part of a comprehensive set of legislative proposals. Most enterprises were created by constituencies that pointed to similar federally backed financial institutions providing benefits to other borrowers or lenders. The history and development of each enterprise is useful in identifying the constituencies and congressional committees with a political stake in the enterprise.

Farm Credit System

The oldest enterprise, the Farm Credit System (FCS), was created to provide credit to rural borrowers. Advocates pointed to the national bank system's tendency to serve urban areas and commercial borrowers. They requested the creation of the FCS as a second national bank system to serve rural areas and agricultural borrowers. The FCS legislation is a product of the congressional agricultural committees, consisting of representatives and senators responsive to rural areas and interests.

Federal Home Loan Bank System

In 1932, the thrift industry pointed to the Federal Reserve System and the Farm Credit System as institutions supporting commer-

cial bankers and rural areas, respectively. Thrift industry advocates argued that a Federal Home Loan Bank System (FHLBS)
was needed to provide Federal Reserve-type support to thrift
institutions and FCS-type support to urban borrowers, home
buyers in particular. As enacted, the FHLBS legislation provides
more substantial benefits to thrifts in the form of advances than
are available to commercial banks when they borrow from the
Federal Reserve Banks. The Federal Home Loan Bank Act is a
product of the congressional banking committees that traditionally include representatives and senators responsive to the interests of the thrift industry.

Fannie Mae

In 1938, the Roosevelt administration created the Federal National Mortgage Association as a subsidiary of the Reconstruction
Finance Corporation. Fannie Mae was one part of the panoply of
new institutions, including the Federal Housing Administration
and the Home Owners' Loan Corporation, designed to deal with
the impact of the Great Depression on housing. For many years,
Fannie Mae largely served mortgage bankers that originated and
serviced the FHA and VA loans it purchased. Because mortgage
bankers lacked the capital needed to hold mortgages, they had to
sell them to Fannie Mae and other institutions. Under the law,
mortgage bankers were required to purchase stock in Fannie Mae;
when the institution became privately owned in 1968, mortgage
bankers were major shareholders. Fannie Mae is overseen by the
housing subcommittees of the House and Senate banking committees, which traditionally support housing, real estate, and residential lender interests with special attention to low- and
moderate-income housing needs.

Freddie Mac

In 1970, the thrift industry repeated its feat of 1932. Pointing to
Fannie Mae and its close association with mortgage bankers,
thrifts persuaded Congress to create Freddie Mac as an enterprise
that they could own and deal with. Through their control of the
Federal Home Loan Bank Board, designated as Freddie Mac's

board of directors, thrifts could also control Freddie Mac. While Fannie Mae adopted a strategy of funding mortgages through a large portfolio, Freddie Mac chose to fund mortgages by issuing guaranteed mortgage-backed securities. This strategy permitted Freddie Mac to provide a substantial service for thrift institutions, by securitizing thrift portfolios of mortgages in swap transactions. Today, Fannie Mae and Freddie Mac serve the broad range of primary mortgage lenders, including mortgage bankers, thrifts, and commercial banks, virtually without distinction.

Sallie Mae

In 1972, the Nixon administration persuaded Congress to create Sallie Mae as a part of its package of revisions to the federal student loan assistance program. Sallie Mae was designed to purchase student loans from a broad range of lenders. The administration pointed to Fannie Mae as a model for the proposed new institution. Sallie Mae is overseen by the Education Subcommittee of the Senate Labor and Human Resources Committee and the Postsecondary Education Subcommittee of the House Education and Labor Committee. These subcommittees have not created a regulator for Sallie Mae; by law, the Treasury and the Department of Education are expressly precluded from controlling Sallie Mae or its activities.[13]

New Enterprises in the 1980s

For many years, Congress refrained from creating new enterprises. In 1986, as federal budget pressures intensified, two new enterprises were proposed. The House Small Business Committee submitted legislation to create a new enterprise to fund small business investment companies. The committee pointed to the success of the enterprises serving "food, shelter, and education" and other high-priority sectors of the economy.[14] That bill passed the full House of Representatives, but failed in the House-Senate Conference Committee.

[13]Higher Education Act, 20 U.S.C. 1087-2(h)(2).
[14]House of Representatives, Small Business Committee, *Report: Omnibus Budget Reconciliation Act of 1986* (Washington, D.C.: GPO, 1986), p. 381.

Also in 1986, the Reagan administration, despite its general opposition to government-sponsored enterprises, supported the creation of a new enterprise, called the Financing Corporation (FICO), to provide funds for the failing Federal Savings and Loans Insurance Corporation (FSLIC). In modified form, the congressional banking committees passed that legislation in 1987; FICO is helping to provide up to $10.8 billion of funds to pay for closing insolvent thrift institutions.

Congress created a new enterprise affiliate in 1986, the College Construction Loan Insurance Association, or Connie Lee. A jointly owned venture between the government and Sallie Mae, Connie Lee is authorized to guarantee, provide letters of credit, or otherwise enhance the credit rating of bonds or obligations used to fund educational facilities (such as universities and teaching hospitals). The private financial guarantee industry objected on the grounds that Connie Lee would encroach on their traditional lines of business (for example, bond insurance). In response, Congress greatly limited Connie Lee's powers, which has hampered the association's efforts to achieve market share. Although Connie Lee is a corporate affiliate of Sallie Mae, it is not by itself a government-sponsored enterprise. Connie Lee's obligations are rated according to its own balance sheets and without an implicit federal guarantee. Moreover, because it is partly government owned, it should be (but is not now) included in the federal budget.

In 1987, Congress passed legislation to bail out the failed Farm Credit System. The congressional agricultural committees created a financing corporation, called the FCS Financial Assistance Corporation, to issue fully government-guaranteed debt to raise money to close or reorganize failed FCS institutions. Rural commercial lenders strongly objected during the legislative process. They pointed to the below-cost pricing strategies adopted by the FCS and the adverse consequences for competing commercial financial institutions. They sought to obtain for themselves federal agency credit advantages similar to those of the FCS. Commercial banks and insurance companies requested that Congress create Farmer Mac as a secondary market institution to serve them as well as the FCS. The FCS bailout bill, which includes provisions to create Farmer Mac, became law in early 1988. It appears that the major benefit of the new enterprise will be for rural lenders—banks, insurance companies, and FCS institutions—to securitize their existing loan portfolios and thereby gain a variety of advantages, including possibly reduced federal risk-based capital requirements for banks.

Finally, in 1989, the Bush administration successfully supported the creation of the Resolution Funding Corporation (REFCORP) to provide an additional $30 billion to help fund the closure of insolvent thrift institutions. The creation of off-budget financing corporations, including FICO, REFCORP, and the Farm Credit System Financial Assistance Corporation, is unnecessarily costly to the government. It remains to be seen whether Congress will permit the executive branch to adopt such a haphazard approach each time the federal government needs funds, or whether the government will finally decide to consolidate the various funding devices into a single large-scale financial assistance agency or enterprise.

Competitively, off-budget financing enterprises like FICO and REFCORP have no commercial purpose. They are shell corporations and involved in none of the competitive issues raised by the other enterprises. The financing corporations serve carefully defined governmental purposes, but they are inefficient and unnecessarily expensive as a source of funds for the government. Indeed, it would cost less to borrow directly through the Treasury Department.

The Politics of Allocating Enterprise Benefits

Depending on its particular structure, an enterprise can use its borrowing advantages to reduce borrowing costs and to improve loan terms for home buyers, farmers, thrift institutions, and other borrowers in its designated market. Most of the enterprises were established to serve carefully targeted purposes. Over time, however, changes in the marketplace can reduce the value of these original enterprise services. Also, as enterprises seek and often obtain statutory changes that permit them to serve a broader market, their activities seem less closely connected to the initial priority credit needs.

Not all claimants for inexpensive federally supported credit can be accommodated. Indeed, much of the value of federally supported credit is in the edge it provides borrowers over others (especially competitors) lacking access to such credit. The history of enterprise legislation reveals how several enterprises were created by politically powerful constituencies seeking access to favorable credit. These constituencies maintain a continuing stake in the distribution of the benefits of enterprise operations. This means that congressional changes in the scope of enterprise activities (that is, allocating benefits) can involve a high degree of political activity among the contending interests, at least to the extent that the legislative proposals are understood by the interested groups. Sometimes the political action plays out entirely behind the scenes; other times it erupts into open controversy. Because of the many business relations that exist among the political interests, they have an incentive to resolve their differences as quickly as possible. Rarely is the executive branch a significant factor in this regard.

The public is in many ways poorly served when the federal government fails to oversee the allocation of enterprise benefits. First, as too many FCS borrowers have painfully learned, not all extensions of federal credit are helpful, and some are more helpful than others. For example, Fannie Mae and Freddie Mac offer lower home mortgage interest rates, but Sallie Mae does not lower borrowing costs for students and the FHLBS, which draws on huge volumes of federal agency credit, lends only to profitable thrift institutions. There is serious doubt about the degree to which such lending practices serve high-priority public purposes.

Further, markets change over time so that enterprises no longer serve their original functions. In part, the effective actions of the enterprises themselves—such as of Fannie Mae and Freddie Mac in helping to standardize the relationship of primary lenders to the secondary market, or of Sallie Mae in demonstrating the profitability of a large-scale student loan business—can facilitate the emergence of new firms able to perform similar functions. Unfortunately, however, the federal government has not monitored such developments to redirect the scope of permitted enterprise activities so that they continue to serve high-priority public purposes. The government's inattention to the diffusion of enterprise lending benefits, together with the haphazard legislative expansion of enterprise lending authority, has meant that the institutions increasingly distribute their benefits to borrowers and market segments that instead may be well served by private lenders without access to federal agency credit. Too often, the proliferation of loans backed by federal agency credit may push potentially capable private institutions to the margins of market segments or else limit them to serving enterprise borrowers with complementary services.

The allocation of enterprise benefits, to paraphrase author William Greider, is too important to be left to the enterprises by themselves.[15] It is time for the public and its designated officials to become more actively involved.

[15]William Greider, *The Trouble with Money: A Prescription for America's Fever* (Knoxville: Whittle Direct Books, 1989), p. 94.

6

Enterprises as Private Financial Institutions

No bank or thrift can hope to compete with Fannie Mae. Its agency status allows it to raise enormous sums in the credit markets (it is the second largest borrower after the U.S. Treasury) at a cost just 30–40 basis points above the Treasury itself, and without the need to incur substantial G&A [General and Administrative] expense in the operation of retail branches. It also pays no insurance premiums.

—Sanford C. Bernstein & Company, Inc., *The Federal National Mortgage Association (Fannie Mae): Strategic Analysis/Financial Forecast*

That the enterprises are more like private firms than government agencies is revealed perhaps most clearly by their financial statements. Although the enterprises are generally exempt from the registration requirements of the Securities and Exchange Commission (SEC), they are required to provide investors with financial statements and other disclosures. These statements and disclosures provide important clues about how the enterprises operate.

Freddie Mac, one of the more financially sophisticated enterprises, provides the most detailed and informative financial disclosures. Unlike the other enterprises, which use only traditional cost-accounting methods, Freddie Mac discloses its financial well-being on a market-value basis as well. To understand why this is important, we need first to examine the traditional financial statements of the largest (Fannie Mae) through the smallest

128

(Sallie Mae) enterprises, and then to compare these against Freddie Mac's market-value-based disclosures.

Fannie Mae's Financial Statements

Fannie Mae, the nation's first government-sponsored enterprise with shareholders and publicly traded stock, provides a good example of the traditional cost-accounting-based financial disclosure. An examination of Fannie Mae's 1989 balance sheets, shown in table 6–1, reveals several important facts about the enterprise.

Fannie Mae is a specialized lender with a highly concentrated portfolio of assets. Of Fannie Mae's total assets of $124.3 billion (see section a in table 6–1), $107.8 billion were home mortgages (see section b) in 1989. When something happens to the residential mortgage market, whether positive or negative, Fannie Mae is likely to feel the impact across virtually its entire lending portfolio. Unlike a commercial bank with a diversified portfolio of loans (commercial, agricultural, foreign, and consumer loans, for example), Fannie Mae's fortunes rise and fall with those of the residential mortgage market. That the enterprise's balance sheet includes a category of assets for "acquired property and foreclosure claims" underscores this fact. Fannie Mae reported $448 million of such assets (see section c) on hand at year-end 1989, amounting to about 0.4 percent of the company's total assets. Analysts study changes in this number (and other indicators of losses from foreclosures) each year, to determine the credit quality of the company's loans. Fannie Mae's full financial statement (not shown in table 6–1) indicates that in 1989 it received another $519 million in proceeds from the disposition of foreclosed properties.

Fannie Mae's balance sheets reveal another important fact. Even though detailed numbers are not presented, it appears that Fannie Mae funded its portfolio of longer-term mortgages with somewhat shorter-term borrowings in 1989. As indicated in the top half of table 6–2, Fannie Mae's borrowings in 1989 averaged 28 months' maturity (see section a in the table). This implies some interest-rate risk; that is, if the yield curve was to change, causing shorter-term interest rates to jump suddenly compared to Fannie

TABLE 6–1

Fannie Mae's Balance Sheets, 1988–1989 (in $ millions)

		December 31	
		1989	1988
Assets			
Mortgage portfolio, net	ⓑ	$107,756	$ 99,867
Investments		6,656	5,289
Cash and cash equivalents		5,214	2,859
Accrued interest receivable		1,064	939
Receivable from currency swaps		1,796	1,717
Acquired property and foreclosure claims, net	ⓒ	448	418
Other assets		1,381	1,169
Total assets	ⓐ	$124,315	$112,258
Liabilities and Stockholders' Equity			
Liabilities			
Debentures, notes, and bonds, net:			
Due within one year		$ 36,346	$ 36,599
Due after one year		79,718	68,860
		116,064	105,459
Accrued interest payable		2,424	2,173
Payable from currency swaps		1,355	1,150
Mortgagors' escrow deposits		346	353
Deferred federal income taxes		153	157
Other liabilities		982	706
Total liabilities		$121,324	$109,998
Stockholders' Equity [1]			
Common stock, $2.10 stated value, no maximum authorization, issued—247,646,455 shares (1989) and 246,155,232 shares (1988)		520	517
Additional paid-in capital		787	777
Retained earnings		1,771	1,067
		3,078	2,361
Less treasury stock, at cost, 8,756,473 shares (1989) and 10,168,733 shares (1988)		87	101
Total stockholders' equity	ⓓ	2,991	2,260
Total liabilities and stockholders' equity		$124,315	$112,258

Source: Fannie Mae, *1989 Annual Report* (Washington, D.C.: Fannie Mae, 1989), 22.
[1]Amounts and number of shares reflect a three-for-one stock split effective in October 1989. See notes to financial statements in figure 6–2.

Mae's portfolio of longer-term mortgages, then how well has the company protected itself against financial loss? The average maturity of Fannie Mae's borrowings hovers around four years, amounting to 48 months at year-end 1987 and 47 months at year-end 1989 (see section b in table 6–2).

TABLE 6–2

Fannie Mae's Financial Statements, 1987–1989 (in $ millions): Selected Disclosures

Debt Issued and Outstanding		1989	1988	1987	% Change 1989 Over 1988	% Change 1988 Over 1987
Debt issued during year						
Amount		$ 78,568	$ 64,260	$45,726	22%	41%
Average cost[1]		8.60%	7.84%	7.49%	10	5
Average maturity (months)	(a)	28	20	36	40	(44)
Debt redeemed during year						
Amount		$ 68,043	$ 55,766	$42,519	22	31
Average cost[1]		8.77%	8.18%	8.42%	7	(3)
Debt outstanding at year-end						
Amount, net		$116,064	$105,459	$97,057	10	9
Average cost[1]		9.04%	9.20%	9.46%	(2)	(3)
Average maturity (months)	(b)	47	43	48	9	(10)

Mortgage Portfolio, Net (at December 31)		1989	1988
Single-family mortgages			
First mortgages			
Government insured or guaranteed	(d)	$ 11,857	$ 12,235
Conventional fixed-rate	(f)	66,804	60,997
Conventional adjustable-rate	(g)	22,020	21,040
Second mortgages		1,614	1,561
		$102,295	$ 95,833
Multifamily mortgages			
Government insured		4,361	4,397
Conventional		4,065	2,783
	(e)	8,426	7,180
Total unpaid principal balance[2]	(c)	$110,721	$103,013
Less:			
Unamortized discount and loan fees		2,740	2,914
Allowance for losses		225	232
Total mortgage portfolio		$107,756	$ 99,867

Source: Fannie Mae, *1989 Annual Report* (Washington, D.C.: Fannie Mae, 1989), pp. 19, 25.
[1]Includes commissions, hedging costs, and the effect of currency and interest-rate swaps.
[2]Includes $11.7 billion and $8.1 billion of Fannie Mae MBSs held in portfolio at December 31, 1989 and December 31, 1988, respectively.

The bottom half of table 6–2 gives some indication of the maturity of Fannie Mae's mortgage portfolio. The total unpaid principal balance of its portfolio loans was $110.7 billion in 1989 (see section c). Of this, $11.9 billion of government-insured or guaranteed first mortgages (see section d in the table) and $8.4 billion of multifamily mortgages (see section e) are likely to be of fairly long maturities, averaging, say, ten years or more (the actual maturities are not disclosed in the financial statements). The $66.8 billion of conventional fixed-rate mortgages (see section f) may have an average life somewhat under ten years; and the $22 billion of adjustable-rate mortgages (see section g) are considered short-maturity assets, with annual interest-rate adjustments. The small holdings of second mortgages are also helpful in reducing the average term of Fannie Mae's assets.

The important issue here is whether Fannie Mae is increasing or decreasing the mismatched maturities of its assets and liabilities and thereby its interest-rate exposure. This cannot be calculated from the company's financial statements. However, a graph in the *1989 Annual Report* (see figure 6–1) indicates that Fannie Mae's assets–liabilities duration gap (a measure of interest-rate exposure) shortened during 1989, from ten months' to about six months' maturity. Further, the 1989 duration gap was an improvement over the wide gaps in 1986 to 1988.

Another important issue is shareholder equity (see table 6–1). Shareholder equity is defined as the difference between a company's total assets ($124.3 billion for Fannie Mae in 1989) and its total liabilities ($121.3 billion). Fannie Mae reported shareholder equity of about $3 billion in 1989 (see section d), which amounts to 2.4 percent of its total assets on a book-value basis.

What Fannie Mae's Balance Sheets Don't Reveal

Perhaps most important is what Fannie Mae's balance sheets fail to reveal. The volume of Fannie Mae's major line of business, for example, is absent from the balance sheets (see table 6–1). To understand the nature of a company, it is necessary to read the notes that accompany such a disclosure. Figure 6–2 re-

FIGURE 6–1

Fannie Mae's Asset–Liability Duration Gap, 1985–1989

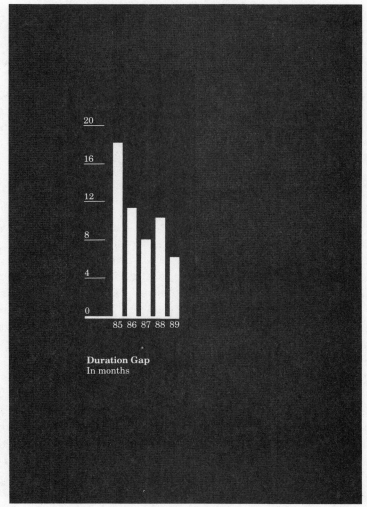

Source: Fannie Mae, *1989 Annual Report,* p. 18.

produces two notes of special importance from Fannie Mae's 1989 financial disclosure.

The first note explains why Fannie Mae does not reveal its $228.2 billion of outstanding mortgage-backed securities (MBSs) on its balance sheets: MBSs are neither assets nor liabilities, but contingent liabilities that, under generally accepted accounting principles (GAAP), need not be included on the balance sheet. Yet Fannie Mae's substantial volume of mortgage-backed securities, funding almost twice the volume of mortgages held in its portfolio, provides important insight into several issues. One is that MBSs are a useful way for an institution like Fannie Mae to earn mortgage-related income from guarantee fees without taking on extra interest-rate risk. However, MBSs also represent a substantial contingent liability for Fannie Mae, because of the credit, business, and operations risks they involve. As the company points out in the second note, Fannie Mae assumes the ultimate risk of loss on all MBSs it issues and guarantees.

Another issue highlighted by the addition of MBSs to the financial picture of Fannie Mae's operations is the corporation's significant rate of growth. In 1988, Fannie Mae had a portfolio of $99.9 billion in mortgages and outstanding MBSs of $178.3 billion, for a combined mortgage lending of $278.2 billion. By 1989, that total increased to $336 billion, including $107.8 billion in Fannie Mae's mortgage portfolio and $228.2 billion in MBSs. The corporation expanded its net mortgage lending by $57.8 billion in one year alone. Given that the amount of net new residential mortgage lending—including single- and multifamily, a FHA, VA, and conventional mortgages—amounted to only $222 billion in 1989, Fannie Market has a significant share of the market.

Further, Fannie Mae's high volume of MBSs is important in terms of shareholder capital. Fannie Mae shareholders have contributed $3 billion of capital supporting a total lending (all assets plus all MBSs) of $352.5 billion. In other words, Fannie Mae's capital ratio is only 0.85 percent when MBSs are included—a relatively small amount compared to the risk-based capital requirements now being phased in for commercial banks. Under a multinational agreement known as the Basle Accords, financial institution regulators from eleven countries (including the United States) have agreed to apply capital requirements on the basis of

FIGURE 6–2

Selected Notes to Fannie Mae's 1989 Financial Statements

Guaranteed Mortgage-Backed Securities
The corporation guarantees the timely payment of principal and interest on MBS. These securities represent beneficial interests in pools of mortgages or other MBS held in trust by the corporation. The pools of mortgages or MBS are not assets of the corporation, except when acquired for investment purposes, nor are the related outstanding securities liabilities of the corporation; accordingly, neither is reflected in the accompanying balance sheets. The corporation receives monthly guaranty fees for each MBS pool based on a percentage of the pool's outstanding balance.

Mortgage-Backed Securities
As issuer and guarantor of MBS, the corporation is obligated to disburse scheduled monthly installments of principal and interest (at the certificate rate) and the full principal balance of any foreclosed mortgage to MBS investors, whether or not any such amounts have been received. The corporation also is obligated to disburse unscheduled principal payments. Either the corporation or the participating lender from whom the mortgages were acquired can assume the primary foreclosure loss risk on the mortgages in a pool. The corporation, however, assumes the ultimate risk of loss on all MBS.

The total outstanding principal balance of MBS guaranteed by the corporation was $228.2 billion at December 31, 1989, compared with $178.3 billion at December 31, 1988. These amounts include $133.9 billion at December 31, 1989 and $94.1 billion at December 31, 1988 of securities (of which $11.1 billion and $11.2 billion, respectively, are backed by government insured or guaranteed mortgages) for which the corporation has assumed the primary foreclosure loss risk.

At December 31, 1989, the corporation had outstanding $8.4 billion of mandatory delivery commitments to issue and guarantee MBS, compared with $7.2 billion at December 31, 1988. At December 31, 1989, the corporation also had commitments outstanding to issue and guarantee $34.2 billion of MBS, upon delivery of the related mortgages by participating lenders at their option, compared with $14.5 billion at December 31, 1988.

Source: Fannie Mae, *1989 Annual Report* (Washington, D.C.: Fannie Mae, 1989), pp. 24, 26.

financial risk, and to include off-balance sheet contingent liabilities in computing those capital levels. For a commercial bank holding high-quality residential mortgages, for example, the risk-based capital requirements are 4 percent of the combined amount of mortgage portfolio assets and MBSs. If Fannie Mae had to meet the same requirements applied to banks, it would have to raise about $8.4 billion of additional capital by 1992. To meet the requirements of thrifts, Fannie Mae would still need to raise a substantial amount of capital. According to Treasury Department estimates, if Fannie Mae were a thrift, it would be required to raise about $6.2 billion of capital by 1992.[1]

Fannie Mae's low capitalization raises questions about its financial leverage. Fannie Mae is a $352 billion financial institution. It reported a net income of $807 million for 1989 (see section a of table 6–3), which represented 27 percent of its 1989 year-end shareholder equity of $3 billion. Now, if Fannie Mae had been better capitalized, that $807 million of income would have been spread over a much larger capital base and amounted to a much lower return on equity. Fannie Mae's $3.10 reported 1989 earnings per share would have dropped to perhaps one-third of that amount. It is not surprising, then, at Fannie Mae's high leverage, that investment bankers rated the company's stock enthusiastically in 1989, nor that numerous investment bankers have turned up at congressional oversight hearings to argue against imposing capital requirements on Fannie Mae.

The Financial Reports of Other Government-Sponsored Enterprises

Fannie Mae's financial statements shed light on those of the other enterprises.

Freddie Mac

Freddie Mac's balance sheet, shown in table 6–4, reports assets of $35.5 billion for 1989 (see section a), of which $21.8 billion was

---

[1]Treasury Department, *1990 Report of the Secretary of the Treasury on Government Sponsored Enterprises* (Washington, D.C.: GPO, May 1990), pp. A-86, A-87.

TABLE 6–3

Fannie Mae's Income Statements, 1987–1989 (In $ millions, except per-share amounts)

Types of Income	December 31		
	1989	1988	1987
Interest income			
Mortgage portfolio, net of servicing fees	$10,103	$ 9,629	$9,586
Investments and cash equivalents	977	597	257
Total interest income	11,080	10,226	9,843
Interest expense	9,889	9,389	8,953
Net interest income	1,191	837	890
Other income			
Guaranty fees	408	328	263
Gain (loss) on sales of mortgages	9	12	(81)
Miscellaneous, net	60	69	53
Total other income	477	409	235
Other expenses			
Provision for losses	310	365	360
Administrative	254	218	197
Total other expenses	564	583	557
Income before federal income taxes	1,104	663	568
Provision for federal income taxes			
Current	358	285	203
Deferred	(61)	(129)	(11)
Total provision for federal income taxes	297	156	192
Net income (a)	$ 807	$ 507	$ 376
Per share[1]			
Earnings			
Primary	$ 3.14	$ 2.14	$ 1.55
Fully diluted	3.10	2.11	1.54
Cash dividends	.43	.24	.12

Source: Fannie Mae, *1989 Annual Report* (Washington, D.C.: Fannie Mae, 1989), p. 21.
[1]Per-share amounts reflect a three-for-one stock split effective in October 1989.

Freddie Mac's mortgage portfolio (see section b). According to its reported asset size, Freddie Mac seems to be a much smaller institution than Fannie Mae. But what about mortgage-backed securities?

Unlike Fannie Mac, Freddie Mac includes MBSs on its balance sheet. In 1989, Freddie Mac MBSs (referred to as "mortgage participation certificates" and "guaranteed mortgage certificates") amounted to $272.9 billion of securities outstanding (see section c). Including assets and MBSs, Freddie Mac that year was a $308 billion financial institution, close to the size of Fannie Mae. By contrast, the nation's largest bank, Citibank, had assets of $162 billion and its parent Citicorp had assets of $231 billion in 1989. Citicorp also had roughly $100 billion of letters of credit plus other contingent liabilities in that year.[2] Fannie Mae, Freddie Mac, and the other enterprises are large financial institutions, larger than most of the nation's major commercial banks and other lenders.

Like Fannie Mae, Freddie Mac specializes heavily in residential mortgages. Its assets included $271 million of real estate owned in 1989 (see section d of table 6–4). In the notes to its financial statements, Freddie Mac reveals that in 1989 it disposed of another $419 million of real estate that it owned. The company acquires such real estate when home owners default on their mortgages and lose their homes in foreclosure. Freddie Mac's delinquency and foreclosure rates were consistently lower than those of Fannie Mae during the years 1983 to 1989.[3]

Freddie Mac has shareholder equity of $1.92 billion (see section e of the table), or 0.62 percent of its assets and MBSs. Like Fannie Mae, Freddie Mac is significantly undercapitalized compared to the risk-based capital requirements of commercial banks. Freddie Mac's emphasis on guaranteeing MBSs, rather than on holding a significant mortgage portfolio, permits the corporation to avoid significant interest-rate risk; nevertheless, its MBS business involves substantial credit, management, and operations risks.

Freddie Mac is growing rapidly, though not as fast as Fannie Mae. Its mortgage-backed securities grew by $46.5 billion and its mortgage portfolio by $4.4 billion, a total growth of $50.9 billion in mortgage lending in 1989. Together, mortgage lending by Fannie Mae and Freddie Mac grew by $108.7 billion in that year, compared to $222 billion of new net mortgage originations. The two companies scooped up about half of all net new mortgage lending in 1989.

Like Fannie Mae, Freddie Mac is quite profitable. Its net income of $437 million in 1989 represented a return on year-end equity of 22.8 percent. Stock analysts like Freddie Mac's earnings, especially at such significant leverage.

[2]This is an estimate. Personal communication by an official of the Standard & Poor's Corporation, June 1990.
[3]See, for example, Treasury Department, *1990 Report of the Secretary of the Treasury on Government Sponsored Enterprises*, pp. B-28, B-29.

TABLE 6–4

Freddie Mac's Consolidated Balance Sheets, 1988–1989 (in $ millions)

		December 31	
		1989	1988

Assets

Mortgages, at unpaid principal balances (including approximately $3.0 billion and $0.6 billion held for sale, respectively):				
Single-family fixed-rate		$	12,318	$ 9,218
Single-family adjustable-rate			868	1,033
Multifamily			3,034	1,878
Mortgages financed by multiclass debt securities			5,632	5,296
	(b)		21,852	17,425
Less—Unamortized mortgage purchase discount, fees and other related items			(404)	(507)
—Reserve for losses on retained mortgages			(119)	(103)
Total mortgages, net			21,329	16,815
Cash and investments			5,397	5,525
Mortgage securities purchased under agreements to resell (market value of $5.8 billion and $9.1 billion, respectively)			5,765	9,107
Unamortized mortgage sales discount, fees and other related items			928	1,172
Accounts receivable and other assets	(d)		1,547	1,321
Real estate owned, net			271	224
Accrued interest receivable			225	188
Total assets	(a)	$	35,462	$ 34,352

Liabilities and Stockholders' Equity

Debt securities, net				
Notes and bonds payable				
Due within one year		$	16,384	$ 18,482
Due after one year			2,426	1,620
Total notes and bonds payable			18,810	20,102
Multiclass debt securities				
Due within one year			289	265
Due after one year			5,003	4,479
Total multiclass debt securities			5,292	4,744
Total debt securities, net			24,102	24,846
Accrued interest and other accrued expenses			259	370
Income taxes payable			123	216
Principal and interest due to Mortgage Participation Certificate investors			6,670	5,011
			31,154	30,443
Reserve for losses on sold mortgages			347	289
Contingencies				
Guarantees				
Single-class Mortgage Participation Certificates			225,297	215,529
Multiclass Mortgage Participation Certificates			47,573	10,877
Less—Underlying mortgages sold	(c)		(272,870)	(226,406)
			—	—
Subordinated borrowings			2,045	2,036

TABLE 6–4 *(Continued)*

		December 31	
		1989	1988
Stockholders' equity:			
Capital stock:			
Voting common stock, $2.50 par value, up to 60,500,000 and 60,000,000 shares authorized, 59,993,360 and 59,917,376 shares issued, 59,986,200 and 59,910,216 shares outstanding, respectively		150	150
Nonvoting common stock, $1,000 par value, 100,000 shares issued and outstanding		100	100
Additional paid-in capital		105	104
Retained earnings		1,561	1,230
Total stockholders' equity	(e)	1,916	1,584
Total liabilities and stockholders' equity		$ 35,462	$ 34,352

Source: Freddie Mac, *Freddie Mac 1989 Annual Report* (Reston, VA: Freddie Mac, 1990), 41.

Federal Home Loan Bank System

The Federal Home Loan Bank System (FHLBS) is also a specialized lender. The Federal Home Loan Banks (FHLBs) lend to thrift institutions. As table 6-5 indicates, in 1989 the FHLBS grew only slightly, from $74.81 billion to $180.2 billion in assets (see section a). Contingent liabilities (such as the estimated $4 billion in outstanding FHLBS letters of credit) are not required in financial disclosures, so the FHLBS does not report them.[4] (The new rules of the Financial Accounting Standards Board [FASB], an independent accounting standards-setting institution, may make disclosure of contingent liabilities mandatory.)

Traditionally, the FHLBS has been financially conservative. The system carefully hedges its interest-rate risk and also takes great care with credit risk. The FHLBS deals only with credit-worthy thrifts, or requires government guarantees (for example, FSLIC or Resolution Trust Corporation) before it lends to less-sound institutions. The FHLBS also requires significant overcollateralization to secure its loan advances. Indeed, the system has thus far avoided any losses on its advances. In contrast to the

[4]Ibid., p. C-7.

TABLE 6–5

Federal Home Loan Banks: Selected Financial Data, 1988–1989 (in $ millions)

	December 31	
	1989	*1988*
Assets		
Cash and investments	$ 35,195	$ 18,530
Advances	141,797	152,781
Other assets	3,258	3,533
Total assets (a)	$180,250	$174,844
Liabilities		
Deposits	$ 25,897	$ 19,031
Consolidated debt[1]	136,086	136,513
Other liabilities	4,070	3,780
Total liabilities	$166,053	$159,324
Capital		
Stock	$ 13,385	$ 13,177
Retained earnings[2]	811	2,342
Total capital (b)	$ 4,196	$ 15,519

Source: Treasury Department, *1990 Report of the Secretary of the Treasury on Government-Sponsored Enterprise,* (Washington, D.C.: GPO, May 1990), p. C-7.
[1]Less pass-throughs to Freddie Mac.
[2]Less contributions to FICO and REFCORP.

other enterprises, the FHLBS is well capitalized. Its 1989 capital of $14.2 billion (see section b of table 6–5) amounted to 7.9 percent of its total assets.

The most important issue facing the FHLBS today is the impact that the continuing decline of the thrift industry—its customer base—will have on its balance sheets.

Farm Credit System

The financial statements of the Farm Credit System (FCS) tell a different story (see table 6–6). In 1989, the FCS reported assets of $64 billion, compared to $61.6 billion the year before (see section a of the table). However, loans (less allowance for loan losses) actually declined in volume, from $49.6 billion to $49.1 billion (see section b). The FCS did report a positive income of $695 million in 1989, but $285 million of this resulted from an

TABLE 6–6

Farm Credit System's Combined Statement of Condition, 1988–1989 (in $ thousands)

	December 31	
	1989	1988
Assets		
Loans, less allowance for loan losses of $1,577,827 and 1,857,545 in 1989 and 1988, respectively ⓑ	$ 49,128,758	$ 49,570,468
Cash	273,427	237,615
Investments	11,235,745	8,703,208
	60,637,930	58,511,291
Accrued interest receivable on loans	1,658,192	1,693,938
Other property owned	468,350	662,521
Premises and equipment, less accumulated depreciation	388,786	414,287
Other assets and deferred charges	450,764	334,124
Restricted assets—Farm Credit Insurance Fund under the control of the Farm Credit System Insurance Corporation	349,875	
Total assets ⓐ	$ 63,953,897	$ 61,616,161
Liabilities and Capital		
Consolidated systemwide bonds and medium-term notes	$ 37,535,500	$ 37,519,010
Consolidated bank and other bonds	2,049,535	1,983,101
Consolidated systemwide discount notes	16,310,423	14,430,707
Financial Assistance Corporation bonds ⓓ	843,235	687,816
Notes payable and other interest-bearing liabilities	92,683	110,591
Accrued interest payable	1,141,193	1,122,446
Other liabilities	540,827	461,837
Total liabilities	58,513,396	56,315,508
Contingent liabilities		
Protected borrower capital ⓒ	1,683,272	3,288,528
Capital stock and surplus		
Capital stock and participation certificates	1,116,654	227,185
Restricted capital—Farm Credit Insurance Fund under the control of the Farm Credit System Insurance Corporation	349,875	
Surplus	2,290,700	1,784,940
	3,757,229	2,012,125
Total liabilities and capital	$ 63,953,897	$ 61,616,161

Source: Federal Farm Credit Banks Funding Corporation, *Farm Credit System Annual Information Statement 1989* (New York: Federal Farm Credit Banks Funding Corporation, 2 March 1990), F-3.

accounting change, reducing an earlier provision for loan losses.
Like the FHLBS, the FCS is structured on a cooperative basis, without publicly traded stock. The curious entry for "protected borrower capital" (see section c of table 6–6) gives one sign of the difference between an FCS cooperative and an investor-owned institution. FCS shareholders are also borrowers from the system;

that is, they contribute so-called capital when taking out a loan. This contribution is essentially an offsetting balance, which traditionally was repaid when the loan was paid off. Congress enacted a special provision in the Agricultural Credit Act of 1987 that protects FCS shareholder-borrowers from loss of their "capital," even though the FCS by then needed federal funds to pay for its losses. Unlike normal contributors of equity capital, FCS borrowers are thus protected from losing their equity stake, even though the financial institution they own has experienced a significant negative net worth. Since 1987, the FCS has begun to turn its borrower capital into something closer to an actual equity stake in each FCS institution. However, the Treasury Department's 1990 *Report on Government Sponsored Enterprises* expresses concern that borrower capital may again be protected from loss if the FCS begins to falter.[5]

The government responded to the FCS failure with a taxpayer bailout similar to that proposed for the savings and loan bailout. This is seen in the FCS balance sheet entry "Financial Assistance Corporation bonds," amounting to a liability of $843 million (see section d of table 6–6). A note to the financial statements indicates that the FCS Financial Assistance Corporation (FAC) has the authority to issue up to $4 billion of federally guaranteed debt to provide funds for closing or merging or otherwise dealing with insolvent FCS institutions. The 1989 balance sheets of the FCS show a troubled institution that the government is trying to restore.

Sallie Mae

Sallie Mae is a relatively well-capitalized institution with conservative financial practices. It is also a fast-growing enterprise. As table 6–7 indicates, Sallie Mae grew by over 24 percent in 1989, from $28.6 billion to $35.5 billion in assets (see section a of the table).

Sallie Mae is a specialized lender in student loans, with a portfolio of some $16 billion of insured or guaranteed student loans in 1989 (see section b). In addition, the enterprise made $8.6 billion of warehousing advances (that is, secured loans to lenders)

[5]Treasury Department, *Report of the Secretary*, pp. D-53, D-54.

TABLE 6–7

Sallie Mae's Consolidated Balance Sheets, 1988–1989 (in $ thousands, except per-share amounts)

		December 31	
		1989	**1988**
Assets			
Loans			
Insured student loans purchased, unpaid principal		$16,164,716	$13,320,647
Deferred income		(135,766)	(118,992)
Insured student loans purchased, net	ⓑ	16,028,950	13,201,655
Warehousing advances	ⓒ	8,600,998	7,989,489
Total loans		24,629,948	21,191,144
Cash and investments		9,839,675	6,567,475
Other assets, principally accrued interest receivable		1,018,782	869,143
Total assets	ⓐ	$35,488,405	$28,627,762
Liabilities			
Short-term borrowings		$14,965,348	$ 9,819,717
Long-term notes		18,622,968	16,963,663
Other liabilities, principally accrued interest payable		862,546	844,019
Convertible subordinated debentures		—	199,742
Total liabilities		$34,450,862	$27,827,141
Stockholders' Equity			
Preferred stock, par value $50.00 per share, 5,000,000 shares authorized and issued, 4,290,150 and 4,389,650 shares, respectively, outstanding		214,507	219,483
Voting common stock, par value $.20 per share, 125,000,000 shares authorized, 21,749,888 and 29,000,000 shares, respectively, issued		4,350	5,800
Nonvoting common stock, par value $.20 per share, 125,000,000 shares authorized, 96,752,752 and 75,957,828 shares, respectively, issued		19,351	15,192
Additional paid-in capital		360,109	142,580
Retained earnings		976,352	767,128
Stockholders' equity before treasury stock		1,574,669	1,150,183
Common stock held in treasury at cost, 19,934,420 and 14,889,940 shares, respectively		537,126	349,562
Total stockholders' equity	ⓓ	1,037,543	800,621
Total liabilities and stockholders' equity		$35,488,405	$28,627,762

Source: Sallie Mae, *Annual Report 1989* (Washington, D.C., Sallie Mae: 1990), p. 25.

collateralized by student loans in that year (see section c). These advances are secured, so Sallie Mae has recourse to the lenders to whom it loans the money. In 1990 it was revealed that Sallie Mae had lent about $800 million in collateralized advances to the Higher Education Assistance Foundation, a student loan guarantee agency that failed thereafter. Sallie Mae makes advances to creditworthy commercial banks and other financial institutions, not to the students directly.

In contrast to other enterprises, Sallie Mae hedges its interest-rate risk so that the weighted average maturity for its loan assets matches that of its borrowings at year-end. Credit risk is also low for Sallie Mae because its portfolio consists primarily of student loans guaranteed by the federal government. However, there is some operations risk in Sallie Mae's activities: The government will not pay off on defaults of guaranteed student loans that it believes Sallie Mae has not serviced properly. This risk is within Sallie Mae's control, so long as the corporation exercises diligence in servicing its loan portfolio. On loans collateralizing Sallie Mae's warehousing advances, though, the borrowing lender, not Sallie Mae, primarily bears the servicing risk.

Sallie Mae has more capital than Fannie Mae or Freddie Mac but less than the FHLBS. Sallie Mae's 1989 shareholder equity of $1 billion (see section d of table 6–7) amounts to 2.9 percent of its total assets, or slightly less than the capital-to-asset ratio required of well-managed commercial banks. Because so many of Sallie Mae's assets consist of guaranteed student loans with high-quality credit, the enterprise could probably meet the risk-based capital requirements (but not the required minimum capital ratio) for banks. The Treasury Department concluded in its 1990 *Report* that Sallie Mae is well capitalized; the enterprise could receive the top "AAA" rating for its obligations even without the government's implicit guarantee.[6]

Sallie Mae's financial statements reveal another distinctive characteristic of the enterprise. In 1989, the company earned a net income of $257.6 million on average stockholder equity of $919.1 million (that is, the average of reported equity at 1989 and 1988 year-end), or 28 percent. That calculation, derived from table 6–7

[6]Ibid.

and other Sallie Mae 1989 income statements, is only an approximation. Stock analysts are able to calculate a more accurate figure by obtaining from the company other important information, such as the weighted average annual amount of equity.

Financing Corporation (FICO)

The Financing Corporation (FICO) is an especially interesting institution because, unlike the other enterprises, it is not designed to be a commercial success. FICO is a financing mechanism similar in concept to the FCS Financial Assistance Corporation: It borrows money to finance the closing of insolvent thrift institutions with federally insured deposits.

FICO's balance sheets for year-end 1988 are shown in table 6–8. (The enterprise does not update its balance sheets on a timely basis—a striking sign of investor indifference.) Note the difference between the assets and liabilities of the enterprise: Assets are reported at $663 million (see section a) and liabilities at $5.99 billion (see section b), leaving a capital *deficit* of $5.3 billion (see section c) in 1988.

FICO raises money in the agency credit market and then spends that money to purchase FSLIC securities that are unlikely to be repaid. In a note to the 1988 financial statements, FICO reports that the FSLIC securities are only "contingently recoverable" (in other words, there is a significant chance they will not be repaid). FICO's accountants require FICO to record these FSLIC securities as a direct charge to the institution's capital deficit.

Another note to FICO's 1988 financial statements reveals the immense financial power of the federal implicit guarantee of enterprise obligations. Despite its substantial negative net worth, clearly disclosed to investors, FICO issued seven series of thirty-year obligations at interest rates between 9.4 and 10.35 percent in 1988, amounting to about half a percentage point above the rate of Treasury borrowings. Investors in this FICO debt looked largely to the implicit guarantee for confidence in the security of their investment, rather than to FICO's balance sheets. FICO is structured so that it has assets in the form of a thirty-year zero-coupon government bond, which it holds to pay for the principal

TABLE 6–8

Financing Corporation's Balance Sheets, 1987–1988

		December 31		
		1988		**1987**
Assets				
Cash and short-term investments				
General operating account		$ 147,247,438	$	26,959,947
Issuance and custodial account		75,803		77,255
General administrative account		21,755		48,198
Total cash and short-term investments		147,344,996		27,085,400
Accounts receivable—administrative costs				5,988
Segregated account investments, net		499,070,519		154,424,120
Concession fees paid on obligations		16,681,200		7,461,223
Total assets	(a)	$ 663,096,715	$	188,976,731
Liabilities and Capital (Deficit)				
Liabilities				
Obligations, net		$ 5,820,387,234		$ 1,198,759,597
Accrued interest payable on obligations		107,470,556		19,156,944
Accounts payable				
Bond issuance costs		37,900		24,389
General administrative costs		2,014		
Deferred assessments collected from FSLIC-insured institutions		60,526,463		13,167,864
Deferred assessments collected from FHL Banks for general administrative costs		19,740		54,187
Total liabilities	(b)	$ 5,988,443,907		$ 1,231,162,981
Capital (deficit)				
Nonvoting FICO capital stock issued to FHL Banks		497,000,000		155,500,000
Accumulated excess of assessments and investment income over costs		27,652,808		2,313,750
FSLIC redeemable nonvoting capital stock		(497,000,000)		(129,500,000)
FSLIC nonredeemable capital certificates		(5,353,000,000)		(1,070,500,000)
Total capital (deficit)	(c)	(5,325,347,192)		(1,042,186,250)
Total liabilities and capital (deficit)		$ 663,096,715	$	188,976,731

Source: Financing Corporation, *Information Statement Supplement, $530,000,000 Financing Corporation 9.70% Bonds Due, April 5, 2019, Series B-2019* (Washington, D.C.: Financing Corporation, 29 March 1989), A-3.

amount of its obligations, as well as some income from assessments on solvent thrifts to pay interest. However, the government's implicit guarantee is essential to FICO investors, who would otherwise have to worry about the extent of the shortfall in thirty years.

When pushed to the extreme of FICO, the enterprise model

loses all semblance of its original public purpose. FICO cannot make a profit on its FSLIC contributions; it is merely a device to spread over thirty years the cost of paying off today's obligations. When REFCORP soon begins to report its financial statements, it will look much the same as FICO.

Market-Value Accounting Improves the Quality of Enterprise Financial Disclosures

In late 1989, Freddie Mac became the first major financial institution to publish a market-value-based balance sheet. That balance sheet restates the cost-accounting figures for year-end 1989. Freddie Mac now publishes this information in its annual and quarterly reports.

To understand the importance of market-value disclosures, one needs to know the limitations of cost accounting. Under principles of cost accounting, a company records its assets at the cost of purchase and its liabilities at the value at time of issuance. Balance sheets thus become a summary of past transactions rather than a statement of outstanding assets and liabilities valued according to current market prices. Over time, changes in market circumstances (such as in interest rates) can cause a discrepancy between an institution's actual net worth (on a current market-value basis) and its net worth as reported in cost-accounting-based financial statements. Institutions holding long-term assets like fixed-rate mortgages may experience substantial discrepancies as interest rates change. When interest rates rise, a portfolio of long-term mortgages loses value because it yields less than current mortgages with the same face amount. When interest rates drop, the portfolio gains in value because it yields more than current mortgages. Under the principles of cost accounting, such external changes remain hidden until an institution actually sells an asset or repurchases a liability, or otherwise engages in a transaction that must be "recognized" in the financial statements.

In the 1980s, the distortions created by cost accounting became a serious problem for thrift institutions. Thrift balance sheets failed to reflect the significant loss in net worth caused by a major jump in interest rates; moreover, thrifts failed to sell mortgages to minimize these losses because they would have been required to recognize the losses in their financial statements. And, as soon as a thrift recognized its loss, its reported low net worth would likely attract unwelcome regulatory intervention, and uninsured depositors (with accounts above the federal insurance limit of $100,000) would rush to remove their money. Also, while losses were hidden on the balance sheets, thrifts could continue to pay handsome dividends to shareholders and generous salaries to managers. As long as the accountants and regulator acquiesced, no one wanted to stop the current payouts by recognizing a loss. Financial managers had considerable incentive to manage the institution so as to maximize accounting benefits, even if this impaired the institution's actual market position.

Market-value accounting is thus increasingly recognized as a major improvement over cost-accounting methods. It permits— indeed, requires—managers to make decisions according to current market conditions. Under market-value accounting, assets and liabilities are reported on a current-value rather than a historical basis.

Market-value accounting is important to the government as well as to private investors. Market-value net worth is a measure of the government's financial risk from its backing of bank and thrift deposits, enterprise obligations, and MBSs. As market-value net worth increases, the government's risk exposure declines because more shareholder equity is available to absorb unforeseen losses; as an institution's market-value net worth declines, the government stands to bear a higher proportion of any losses.

In 1989, the House Ways and Means Committee required the Treasury Department to assess the financial status of government-sponsored enterprises on a market-value basis. Although the concept had been widely discussed in academic circles for many years, this was the first time Congress actually sought to implement market-value accounting requirements.

Freddie Mac took the concept one step further. Besides complying with the Treasury study, Freddie Mac published its own market-value balance sheet for the use of investors and analysts. Several important conclusions emerge from that balance sheet, shown in table 6–9. First, note that at current interest rates, the market-value net worth of Freddie Mac is close to its book value (section a). We cannot know with certainty from a single report whether this is a coincidence or the result of Freddie Mac's management of assets and liabilities—this remains to be seen in future Freddie Mac reports, when interest rates may change.

Second, note that market-value accounting also has its shortcomings. For example, Freddie Mac's $272.9 billion in guaranteed MBSs (see section b) remains an off-balance sheet item. The outstanding MBS guarantee fees do appear as a new item called "servicing on pass-through financed mortgages" (see section c), with a positive net worth, calculated by taking the present value of expected future earnings. Moreover, market-value accounting does not necessarily accelerate the recognition of credit risk. Thus, Freddie Mac's 1989 financial statements, based on both cost accounting and market-value accounting, did not reveal the significant losses on multifamily mortgages that the company announced in the third quarter of 1990.

Third, note the advantages and disadvantages of market-value accounting. The big advantage is that gains and losses from interest-rate changes show up more promptly than on the cost-accounting balance sheet. The big disadvantage is the amount of judgment the institution must use in calculating market values. For example, what is the correct discount rate to use when computing the present value of future MBS servicing income? Also note how changes in the market can substantially change market-value accounts between reporting periods.

Despite its shortcomings, though, market-value accounting is a major step forward in providing a more accurate assessment of the financial state of an institution. Such disclosures are certainly a valuable complement to the other required financial statements. Freddie Mac Chairman and CEO Leland Brendsel deserves recognition for his leadership in adopting this important management and accounting policy.

TABLE 6–9

Freddie Mac's Consolidated Market-Value Balance Sheet, 1989 (in $ millions)

	December 31	
	GAAP Value[1]	Market Value[1]
Assets		
Mortgages		
Mortgages with matching prepayable financing		
Mortgages financed by multiclass debt securities		
CMO/MCF mortgages	$2,900	$2,900
Mortgages financed by multiclass PCs with MPOs	2,700	2,700[2]
Multifamily mortgages with prepayment lockouts	2,000	2,100
ARMs without interest-rate caps	500	500
Mortgages without prepayable financing	13,700	13,900
Less—Unamortized mortgage purchase discount, fees, and other related items	(400)	n/a
—Reserve for losses on retained mortgages	(100)	(100)
Total mortgages, net	$21,300	$22,000
Cash and investments	5,400	5,400
Mortgage securities purchased under agreements to resell	5,800	5,800
Unamortized mortgage sales discount, fees, and other related items	900	n/a
Accounts receivable, accrued interest receivable, and other assets	1,800	1,800
Real estate owned, net	300	300
Off-balance sheet items		
Contingencies		
Mortgage Participation Certificates	272,900	n/a
Less—Underlying mortgages sold	(272,900)	n/a ⓑ
Servicing on pass-through financed mortgages	—	3,500 ⓒ
Outstanding commitments to purchase mortgages	n/a	100
Total assets	$35,500	$38,900

Liabilities, Net Market Value, and Stockholders' Equity

Debt securities, net		
Prepayable financing matching mortgages •		
Multiclass debt securities		
CMO/MCF debt securities	$2,600	$2,400
Multiclass PCs with MPOs	2,700	2,700[2]
Callable debt funding multifamily mortgages with prepayment lockouts	1,200	1,200
Notes funding ARMs without interest-rate caps	500	500
Other notes and bonds	17,100	17,100
Total debt securities, net	$24,100	$23,900
Principal and interest due to mortgage participation certificate investors	6,700	6,700
Income taxes payable, accrued interest, and other accrued expenses	400	400
Reserve for losses on sold mortgages	300	300

TABLE 6–9 *(Continued)*

| | December 31 | |
	GAAP Value[1]	Market Value[1]
Subordinated borrowings		
Callable debt funding multifamily mortgages with prepayment lockouts	800	800
Other subordinated borrowings	1,300	1,700
	33,600	33,800
Net market value—before tax	n/a	5,100
Estimated income taxes on difference between market values and GAAP values	n/a	1,100
Net market value—after tax	n/a	4,000 (a)
Stockholders' equity	1,900	n/a
Total liabilities, net market value, and stockholders' equity	$35,500	$38,900[3]

Source: Freddie Mac, *Freddie Mac 1989 Annual Report* (Reston, Va.: Freddie Mac, 1990), 38.
[1]GAAP values represent amounts derived from the consolidated financial statements prepared in accordance with generally accepted accounting principles. Market values have been estimated, and GAAP values rounded, to the nearest $100 million.
[2]The market value of servicing on these PCs is included in "Servicing on pass-through financed mortgages." GAAP value has been included as market value for these assets and liabilities.
[3]Amount includes total liabilities, estimated income taxes, and "net market value—after tax."
n/a: not applicable.

7

The Implicit Federal Guarantee as a Source of Risk Exposure

A feature of the [Agricultural Credit Act of 1987] illustrates so vividly a philosophy of government that is current just now. The feature is the public guarantee of privately floated financial obligations. The philosophy is privatization of profit and socialization of risk.

—Professor Harold F. Breimyer

Federal credit programs have their costs as well as their benefits. The programs are similar to federal deposit insurance in that taxpayers may be called on to make good on the implicit government guarantee of enterprise obligations. Indeed, this event happened in the mid-1980s with the failure of the Farm Credit System, and it almost happened in the early 1980s with Fannie Mae. However, there is one important difference between federal deposit insurance and federal credit support of the enterprises in terms of taxpayer risk. The government charges thrifts and banks a fee for deposit insurance; the deposit insurance funds thereby accumulate to at least a few billion dollars, providing a cushion before bank or thrift losses require taxpayer assistance. In contrast, the government does not charge the enterprises for its implicit guarantee of their obligations, nor does it set aside an insurance fund to pay for possible losses. Hence, enterprise losses put taxpayer money immediately at stake. The only exception is the Farm Credit System, which under provisions of the 1987 act has begun to set aside insurance premiums to fund a new FCS Insurance Corporation.

To some extent, the risk of taxpayer losses can be reduced if the enterprises are well managed and prudent in their decisions. However, lending is inherently a risky business. The government's implicit guarantee compounds that problem by providing an incentive for enterprise managers to take far greater risks than they would if only shareholders' money was at stake.

Risks of Enterprise Lending

Financial institutions are subject to various types of risks associated with their lending activities generally or with specialized kinds of lending activity. New forms of risk emerge as markets change. Of the various risks involved in enterprise lending, two are especially important: the risks associated with an institution's management and its market.

Management Risk

Management risk involves the possibility that some enterprise managers may not be of the highest quality. Although most enterprise managers today appear to be of high quality, increasing financial pressures, changes in control, or other problems can change this state of affairs. Especially if unforeseen problems threaten to cause significant losses, ordinarily cautious managers may be tempted to make a financial gamble to cover themselves.

Management risk may be the single most important factor in the performance of a financial institution. Managing an enterprise is not an easy task; new systems and controls must be adopted to cope with high rates of enterprise growth as well as with changing external factors, such as the volatile interest rates and problems with credit quality of the 1980s. As an enterprise grows in size, its management risk becomes increasingly concentrated. The decisions of a handful of managers can affect the financial future of institutions with hundreds of billions of dollars of loans and guaranteed securities.

Market Risk

As specialized lenders, government-sponsored enterprises are vulnerable to economic changes in the markets they serve. The Farm Credit System, for example, was harmed by the decline in U.S. agriculture in the early 1980s. Similarly, Fannie Mae and Freddie Mac are vulnerable to the possibility of a decline in the housing market, which could affect the credit quality of some of their mortgage holdings.

Economists Guttentag and Herring of the Wharton School of Finance have written extensively about the need to protect against the risks associated with market changes. These risks have potentially damaging consequences for financial institutions, taxpayers, and the entire financial system in general.[1]

Other Types of Risk

Financial institutions are also susceptible to other types of risk exposure, including credit, interest-rate, and operations risk.

Credit Risk

Credit risk exists in the possibility that a borrower may fail to make timely payments of principal and interest on a loan held or guaranteed by a government-sponsored enterprise or other lender. For the enterprises, credit risk applies both to loans held in portfolios and to those in pools of guaranteed mortgage-backed securities (MBSs). Because an enterprise guarantees the payment of principal and interest on its obligations and MBSs to investors, it is responsible for continuing those payments if a borrower defaults. In this case, the enterprise must seek recourse from the borrower, servicer, originator, or insurer of the delinquent loan. It must also supervise the process of foreclosing on

[1]See, for example, Jack M. Guttentag and Richard J. Herring, "Disaster Myopia in International Banking," *Essays in International Finance* 164 (September 1986).

collateral or otherwise reducing its losses from a defaulted loan. Secondary market lenders also risk primary lenders' selling them a large number of bad loans.

Interest-Rate Risk

Interest-rate risk exists in the possibility of losses from rate changes. One kind of interest-rate risk affects an enterprise's portfolio lending and assets, such as mortgages and derivative securities that it may own, but not its guaranteed mortgage-backed securities owned by other investors. For example, an institution that funds a portfolio of long-term loans with short-term borrowings (or vice versa) can either profit or lose according to changes in the yield curve (that is, the relationship between long- and short-term interest rates). Some kinds of derivative mortgage-backed securities have much higher interest-rate volatility than ordinary MBSs, while other derivative securities may have less interest-rate risk.

Other interest-rate risk can arise when interest rates rise or decline significantly. For mortgage lenders, this includes prepayment risk when interest rates drop, inducing borrowers to refinance their mortgage loans and thereby reducing the yield on lenders' mortgage portfolios. Conversely, a significant increase in interest rates may discourage borrowers from taking out new loans and thereby reduce the volume of lenders' new business. The uncertainty of mortgage prepayment rates can also create risk for issuers of special kinds of MBSs, such as the multiclass collateralized mortgage obligations that guarantee investors a maximum or minimum term for their security.

Operations Risk

Operations risk involves the possibility that an enterprise may not manage its business effectively. Government-sponsored enterprises are multibillion-dollar institutions that can grow by tens of billions of dollars in net new business each year. Sophisticated computer operations are required to assure that the enterprises manage the literally millions of transactions that may occur each month, including the processing of loan payments and distributions to holders of guaranteed MBSs and enterprise obligations. In one of its most striking findings, the Treasury Department reported in 1990 that Fannie Mae lacked the ability to query its integrated reporting and accounting system, called LASER, "for data in an accurate, consistent, or timely manner."[2]

For Sallie Mae and other guaranteed student loan lenders, servicing risk is important. As a result of increased defaults on guaranteed student loans, the Department of Education now withdraws its guarantee when it finds that the student loan holder failed to exercise due diligence in dealing with delinquent loans and in attempting to prevent defaults. This means that student loan holders must assure that the servicing of their portfolios conforms to the regulatory requirements of the Department of Education.

Effects of the Implicit Federal Guarantee on Enterprise Risk Taking

The temptation to take excessive risk is inherent in the implicit government backing that permits the enterprises to issue and guarantee billions of dollars of securities. Because the government guarantee makes much of the usual market discipline unnecessary, effective government regulation of enterprise safety and soundness is essential to limiting an enterprise's risk taking and assuring its long-term viability. Investors in enterprise debt obligations and MBSs rely far less on the creditworthiness of an enterprise or the quality of loans it makes than on the implicit government backing for assurance that their investments are secure.

The Implicit Guarantee and Enterprise Shareholders

For the ordinary corporation without federal backing, investor concern about creditworthiness provides an important constraint

[2]Treasury Department, *Report of the Secretary of the Treasury on Government Sponsored Enterprises* (Washington, D.C.: GPO, May 1990), p. A-65.

on risk taking. To the extent that shareholders are aware of material changes in a company's circumstances, they have a long-term interest in protecting and enhancing their capital investment in the company. For a government-sponsored enterprise, however, the financial stake of equity investors is usually low compared to the volume of enterprise activities. An extreme example of this is Freddie Mac's shareholder capital in 1989, amounting to 0.6 percent of the corporation's assets and outstanding mortgage-backed securities. Freddie Mac's shareholders thus benefited from a leverage of 161 to 1.[3] Further, evidence from the banking literature suggests that outside shareholders and stock analysts may not be able to detect the true extent of an institution's financial difficulties until after serious damage has occurred.[4]

Although enterprise management may develop prudent business policies, there is still the fundamental problem known to economists as the "moral hazard." The implicit federal guarantee provides considerable incentive to seek extra returns by taking excessive risks. Shareholders of a government-sponsored enterprise can increase their returns by increasing risks and then leverage the benefits by greatly increasing the ratio of outstanding debt to shareholder equity. The federal government receives no compensation for bearing the increased risks of these activities, but it assumes potentially unlimited liability for them should an enterprise fail.

The Implicit Guarantee and Enterprise Debt-holders

Market discipline is enforced by debt-holders as well as by shareholders. A corporation without federal backing is subject to financial restraint when it issues debt obligations or guarantees securities. Debt-holders and purchasers of these guaranteed securities limit the degree of risk by demanding increasing returns for themselves to the extent that shareholders make their investment more risky, for example by increasing the debt-to-equity leverage of the company. Before investors rely on a corporation's ob-

[3]Freddie Mac, *Freddie Mac 1989 Annual Report* (Reston, VA: Freddie Mac, 1990), p. 41.
[4]Richard E. Randall, "Can the Market Evaluate Asset Quality Exposure in Banks?" *New England Economic Review* (July/Aug. 1989), 11.

ligation or guarantee, they require assurances about the company's financial backing. They look not only to the balance sheets of the corporation for such assurances but also to the credit quality of the assets standing behind the obligation or guarantee. Before purchasing the unsecured debt obligations of a private corporation, investors carefully assess the corporation's balance sheet, the credit quality of assets it holds, its debt-to-equity ratio, and its general creditworthiness. Similarly, before purchasing mortgage-backed securities issued or guaranteed by a private corporation, investors require assurances about the credit quality of the underlying loans and loan pools, as well as the safeguards imposed to assure that investors will have sole recourse to mortgage assets in case of default.

Investors in enterprise obligations and MBSs, however, do not impose such market discipline. They are spared the need to examine as carefully the creditworthiness of the enterprise, its assets or asset pools, and the quality of its management. Although enterprise investors investigate factors relating to yield (such as the composition of MBS pools), they rely largely on the implicit federal backing for assurance of the credit quality of enterprise obligations and guarantees. Thus, the major credit-rating services such as Standard & Poor's Corporation give all of the enterprises—even FICO and the FCS—the top "AAA" credit rating, regardless of their independent financial strength.

The overwhelming reliance on the government's implicit guarantee, rather than on an enterprise's creditworthiness and financial condition, means that an enterprise can largely disregard the usual debt-holder concerns and engage in risk-taking ventures that a private company would not even consider. Thus, the federally backed enterprise has an extensive market for its debt obligations and guarantees, even if it is undercapitalized or does not adequately police the credit quality of the assets it buys or the securities it guarantees.

Risk Taking by the FCS, Fannie Mae, and Thrift Institutions

The concerns about enterprise risk taking are not merely hypothetical. The banks of the Farm Credit System adopted an aver-

age-cost pricing policy for mortgage loans, which permitted
FCS institutions to use long-term debt to fund variable-rate
loans on the basis of FCS average debt funding costs. As interest rates rose during the 1970s, new debt tended to be priced
somewhat higher than the average price of outstanding debt.
Through the pricing of loans according to the average cost of
outstanding debt rather than the cost of new debt, FCS institutions could offer borrowers lower-priced loans than those available from competing lenders. By 1981, FCS banks were pricing
their real estate loans almost five percentage points below the
rates of their commercial competitors.

The FCS policy provided immediate rewards to managers and
borrower-shareholders. FCS managers, rewarded by an increasing market share, constructed lavish new office buildings, hired
staff, and generally expanded the organization. Unlike shareholders in corporate institutions, who receive stock dividends, FCS
shareholders received their benefits largely in the form of lower
loan rates. This, in turn, encouraged shareholders to take out a
greater than optimal volume of loans from FCS banks.

As the agricultural economy declined, the number of FCS loan
delinquencies and defaults rose significantly. Then, as interest
rates dropped, the FCS's average-cost pricing strategy became
impossible to sustain. The high volume of outstanding long-term
debt issued by the FCS at times of high interest rates now meant
higher rates for borrowers. As a result, creditworthy FCS borrowers refinanced their loans with competing lenders at the lower
interest rates.

Starting in 1985, the FCS began reporting huge annual losses.
The governor of the Farm Credit Administration announced that
the Farm Credit System would require a massive infusion of
federal funds within two years to remain in business. Even after
this announcement, the implicit federal guarantee was perceived
as strong enough to allow the FCS to continue selling its debt less
expensively than most private corporations. There was some residual market pressure, and the spreads of FCS obligations over
Treasury obligations widened noticeably; however, FCS borrowing costs remained below the borrowing costs of "A"-rated private corporations even after its disclosure of billions of dollars of
losses. The federal government has now taken steps to pay for

FCS losses resulting directly from excessive FCS risk taking, which, initially at least, provided substantial benefits to FCS managers and shareholders.

Fannie Mae underwent a similar experience, but managed to emerge from it more successfully than the FCS. During the 1970s, when short-term interest rates were less expensive than long-term rates, Fannie Mae was able to purchase billions of dollars of long-term mortgages and fund them with short-term debt. Because short-term debt was at that time less expensive than long-term debt, shareholders received immediate returns, above the normal returns expected from funding done on a more matched-maturity basis. Fannie Mae's funding system was made possible by the implicit government guarantee, which allayed the concerns of its debt-holders about the added risk involved. Without the implicit guarantee, the debt-holders would have become increasingly unwilling to lend money inexpensively to Fannie Mae because of the growing interest-rate risk in its operations.

Starting in 1979, short-term borrowing costs rose dramatically relative to long-term rates. Fannie Mae's debt costs soon exceeded returns on its portfolio of long-term mortgages bearing relatively low interest rates. By 1981, Fannie Mae had a market-value negative net worth of $10.8 billion. Fortunately, with energetic new management strategies, a charter that permitted Fannie Mae to develop a strong MBS business earning fee income largely insensitive to interest rates, and, after 1982, declining interest rates that reduced the company's exposure, Fannie Mae avoided the fate of the Farm Credit System. Again, while the federal government reaped few of the benefits from Fannie Mae's risky funding strategy, it stood to lose if the ultimate result was failure.

It is easy enough for an ordinary company to fail in the marketplace. Government-sponsored enterprises are at even greater risk of failure, without marketplace discipline fully imposed through higher costs and an ultimate limit on the ability to sell debt obligations and other securities. The implicit guarantee dampens these market signals and permits even enterprises with poor balance sheets to continue selling obligations and guarantees at favorable interest rates. Indeed, the Farm Credit System and Fannie Mae consistently recorded substantial profits in the years before the potential risk exposure turned into actual corporate losses.

When a high-risk enterprise strategy is successful, the benefits go primarily to the shareholders; when the strategy fails, the federal government is under virtually irresistible pressure to make good on its guarantee. The failure of hundreds of thrifts with federally insured deposits is perhaps the most striking example of how federal backing undermines the usual market discipline that helps to limit the losses of a faltering or failed institution. The thrift debacle also shows how, as capitalization drops to low levels, managers face pressure to take high-risk gambles that, if they fail, only compound the losses substantially. The process of the thrift institution collapse provides an expensive lesson, revealing the interplay of market and management risk, capital inadequacy, and regulatory failure.

The Extent of the Government's Risk Exposure

Because enterprises are privately owned institutions that have access to virtually open-ended amounts of federally backed credit, the amount of enterprise obligations and mortgage-backed securities outstanding has grown dramatically over the past twenty years. However, as with its inability to monitor enterprise benefits, the federal government lacks information about the contingent liability represented by these outstanding hundreds of billions of dollars of securities. This is in distinct contrast to a private lender or guarantor, which polices the risks taken by its borrowers to keep contingent liabilities within reasonable bounds.

The Congressional Budget Office and the Department of Housing and Urban Development (HUD) have published studies with risk-related information about Sallie Mae and Fannie Mae, respectively. For most of the enterprises, though, the actual amount of the government's financial exposure remains a matter of conjecture. When the federal government allocated up to $4 billion to bail out the insolvent Farm Credit System in 1987, Congress was uncertain about whether this was the appropriate amount. The Farm Credit Administration estimated the necessary federal funds at a much higher level. At Senate hearings in early 1990, HUD announced that it would rely on data furnished by the enterprises themselves. It turned out that the agricultural economy improved and the needed funds were much less.[5]

The Government's Lack of Knowledge

There is no single source of information within the federal government about government-sponsored enterprises. This is unfortunate, because the enterprises are involved in issues of law, economics, and finance that come together in unusual ways. Statistics are often unavailable except from the enterprises themselves.

Information about particular enterprises is collected by a variety of federal agencies and organizations. HUD collects information from Fannie Mae and Freddie Mac; the Farm Credit Administration receives reports of condition from Farm Credit institutions; and the new Federal Housing Finance Board is responsible for gathering information from the Federal Home Loan Banks.

The Office of Management and Budget (OMB) provides a central source of expertise on a variety of federal programs but does not dedicate the same resources to government-sponsored enterprises. As privately owned, off-budget entities, the enterprises are beyond the scope of direct OMB authority. When the OMB publishes an annual report on enterprise activities in an appendix to the federal budget, the agency accepts numbers generated by the enterprises themselves and does not independently verify their accuracy. This, of course, can lead to significant misperceptions. In the fiscal year (FY) 1986 budget, for example, Freddie Mac estimated that its FY 1986 activities would result in a net increase of outstanding mortgage-backed securities of $10.6 billion. In actuality, Freddie Mac's estimate was about $40 billion

[5]Alfred E. DelliBovi, Department of Housing and Urban Development, "Testimony on HUD Oversight of FNMA and FHLMC," in U.S. Senate Committee on Banking, Housing, and Urban Affairs, Subcommittee on Housing and Urban Affairs, *Roundtable Hearing on the Safety and Soundness of Fannie Mae and Freddie Mac* (Washington, D.C.: GPO, 7 February 1990), p. 19.

below the actual increase in its outstanding mortgage-backed securities that year, which amounted to $54.9 billion.[6]

Within the legislative branch, the Congressional Budget Office and the General Accounting Office (GAO) are increasingly allocating resources to analyzing government-sponsored enterprises and their activities. In addition, the 1989 Financial Institutions Reform, Recovery, and Enforcement Act (FIRREA) has improved on this state of affairs, at least for the short run. Provisions of the act require the Treasury Department and the GAO to publish annual reports, in 1990 and 1991, on the degree and kinds of risks involved in the activities of the enterprises as well as on their market-value net worth. The GAO is also required to determine appropriate capital standards that may be applied to each enterprise. The 1990 *Reports* of the Treasury and GAO provide an impressive amount of detail that is conspicuously absent from earlier government reports; nevertheless, they are based entirely on information provided by the enterprises. The study teams lacked the resources, available to regulators of banks and thrift institutions, to examine firsthand the records, transactions, and activities of the enterprises.

A Preliminary Assessment of the Financial Condition of the Enterprises

The private sector has generated some information about the financial condition of government-sponsored enterprises. Standard & Poor's Corporation, a national securities rating service for investors, presented preliminary information to the Senate Banking Committee in late 1989. That testimony is summarized in table 7–1.

Standard & Poor's (S&P) was careful to add caveats to its testimony. First, the ratings are based only on enterprise financial statements and other public information. S&P did not review

[6]Compare Office of Management and Budget, *Budget for Fiscal Year 1986* (Washington, D.C.: GPO, 1985), p. I-14, with Office of Management and Budget, *Budget for Fiscal Year 1988* (Washington, D.C.: GPO, 1987), p. IV-12.

TABLE 7-1

Standard & Poor's Preliminary Assessment of the Potential Risk to the Federal Government of the Implicit Guarantee, 31 October 1989

Enterprise	Assessment
Fannie Mae	At least investment grade ("BBB")
Freddie Mac	At least investment grade ("BBB")
Federal Home Loan Banks	At the high end of the investment-grade scale ("AAA" or close)
Farm Credit System	At the high end of the noninvestment-grade range ("BB" or close)
Sallie Mae	At the high end of the investment-grade range ("AAA" or close)

Source: Statement of Frank Rizzo, Standard & Poor's Corporation, in U.S. Senate Committee on Banking, Housing, and Urban Affairs, *The Safety and Soundness of Government Sponsored Enterprises, pp. 9–14.*
Note: The term *investment grade* means that an enterprise security, if federal backing were disregarded, would be rated "AAA," "AA," "A," or "BBB"; *noninvestment grade* is a junk-bond rating of "BB" or below.

important elements of financial quality control, such as underwriting and servicing standards or financial operating systems. Second, the FCS rating is based on the assumption that the full $4 billion bailout stands behind FCS obligations, and not just the amount of taxpayer money used by the FCS at the time of the 1989 testimony. Third, the ratings can change from time to time. In 1987, for example, S&P's preliminary assessment of Fannie Mae gave the enterprise a below-investment-grade rating:

> Relative to large savings and loan institutions, which its current business profile most resembles, the company's financial performance and risk profile, including asset quality, and profitability, asset and liability management and capitalization would put FNMA in the "BB" debt rating category.[7]

Between the 1987 S&P report and 1989, Fannie Mae retained a significant part of its earnings and continued to improve its asset quality.

Standard & Poor's preliminary assessment is intended to help

[7]Communication, Thomas G. Gillis, managing director, Standard & Poor's Corporation, to Susan E. Woodward, deputy assistant secretary for economic affairs, HUD, 23 Sept. 1987; cited in Department of Housing and Urban Development, Office of Policy Development and Research, *1987 Report to Congress on the Federal National Mortgage Association* (Washington, D.C.: Department of Housing and Urban Development, 27 Sept. 1989), p. 49.

the federal government begin to appraise taxpayers' contingent liability in the event another enterprise threatens to fail. The S&P testimony stressed that, for investors, there is no cause to worry even if an enterprise's financial position is unimpressive. Regardless of their balance sheets, "Standard & Poor's believes the debt of all these GSE's to be 'AAA' quality based on the implicit support of the federal government."[8] In other words, investors need not worry even if taxpayers should.

[8]Statement of Frank Rizzo, Standard & Poor's Corporation, in U.S. Senate Committee on Banking, Housing, and Urban Affairs, p. 14.

8

Supervising Enterprise Safety and Soundness

Everyone will agree that the first desideratum of a bank, or a system of banking, is that it should be safe.

—Ferdinand Pecora, *Wall Street under Oath*

Regulation of Enterprise Safety and Soundness to Compensate for the Lack of Market Discipline

As we have seen in earlier chapters, the federal government's guarantee of enterprise lending, which removes much of the usual market discipline, makes effective government regulation essential to containing the enterprises' risk taking and assuring their long-term financial viability.[1]

To illustrate this point further and thereby strengthen the conclusion, let's suppose that you are asked to cosign an automobile loan note for your neighbor. As cosigner, you require assurances that your neighbor remains financially responsible and that the automobile will not be used in an excessively risky way. Also as cosigner, you want to be sure that that loan payments are made promptly and that the automobile is not lent to more risky drivers. Now, we can extend our hypothetical example to say that the

[1]See appendix B for a list of some of the economic literature on this issue, as it applies to banks, thrifts, other institutions, and credit programs with federal backing.

government is the cosigner and the enterprise is the neighbor holding the loan and driving the automobile. Mere verbal assurances from enterprise managers (or the neighbor) do not substitute for oversight and prudent rules defining the government's (or the cosigner's) rights to limit its risks.

As with the cosigner's interest in the automobile note, no other party adequately protects the government's interest in the safety and soundness of government-sponsored enterprises. Various parties do have interests, but these at times coincide, diverge, or even conflict with those of the government. Like a cosigner, the government is reassured by these other parties that it does not need to become intrusive or burdensome; trust is said to be important to a good relationship. Only when something goes wrong (as it did with the Farm Credit System, Fannie Mae, and the thrift industry in the past decade) does the government discover that its confidence is misplaced and that its guarantee is on the line.

Regulation is not an assured solution for problems caused when the government's implicit guarantee distorts normal market incentives. As the regulatory history of the Farm Credit System or of thrift institutions governed by the Federal Home Loan Bank Board shows, regulators can be influenced by the institutions they regulate. Congress, in particular, may be sensitive to constituencies with an interest in increasing rather than reducing the federal government's risk exposure. For example, even as the Farm Credit System banks struggled to keep their portfolios above water, desperate farm borrowers persuaded members of Congress to pressure the banks to be more lenient in handling delinquent loans. Similarly, the Federal Home Loan Bank Board came under considerable pressure to refrain from promptly closing thrift institutions with negative net worth, even though this greatly compounded the federal government's risk exposure.

Another difficulty with regulation is that the regulators have been generally unsuccessful in detecting high-risk problems soon enough. This is tied to regulators' tendency to focus on past risk-related problems rather than on newly emerging ones. Also, management has an incentive to shift risk away from regulated and into unregulated areas. Even the best regulatory supervision cannot provide complete protection against the federal government's risk exposure. Nevertheless, effective regulation is needed to compensate for at least some of the diminished market discipline that results from the implicit federal guarantee of enterprise lending.

But what does effective enterprise regulation actually entail? To begin with, the regulator should be capable of overseeing enterprise safety and soundness and be properly motivated (that is, free of all conflicting motivations that might impede effective supervision). Further, the form of safety and soundness regulation follows logically from the federal government's role as implicit guarantor. Black, Miller, and Posner argue that efficient government regulation should resemble the measures adopted by either a private guarantor, which imposes controls on the firm whose obligations it guarantees, or by a private lender, which oversees the creditworthiness of a borrower.[2] The private lender is concerned about the capital and leverage of the borrower as well as the borrower's general management ability. The lender requires disclosure of material events and, under some conditions, may insist on direct supervision of the borrower's business. The private lender also specifies conditions of default, its rights upon default, and a process for asserting those rights. While the lender does not try to substitute for the borrower's judgment in general business decisions, it does take steps to prevent risky activities that would benefit the borrower at the lender's expense. This approach is applicable to regulation of the enterprises by the government to protect its financial stake in safety and soundness.

Why Capital Is Important

As the thrift debacle has taught, adequate capital is an important bulwark against financial failure. Capital standards must be set and enforced, because the federal guarantee diminishes market pressures that would otherwise require the maintenance of a significant capital cushion. For corporations without federal

[2]Fischer Black, Merton H. Miller, and Richard A. Posner, "An Approach to the Regulation of Bank Holding Companies," *Journal of Business* 51 (Mar. 1978): 382; see also Sherman J. Maisel, ed., *Risk and Capital Adequacy in Commercial Banks* (Chicago: University of Chicago Press, 1981), esp. chap. 6.

backing, the market itself imposes these capital requirements. Investors require assurance that they are placing their money with a firm that has enough capital to stay in business. Potential purchasers of company debt are wary of poorly capitalized, highly leveraged firms with high ratios of outstanding debt obligations to shareholder capital. This leverage can benefit shareholders but it disadvantages debt-holders.

While some shareholders may desire high leverage to enhance their returns, debt-holders look to companies that are well capitalized. The amount of a company's capital is important to debt-holders because it is shareholder capital that absorbs the first losses when an institution loses money. Debt-holders know that their risk of loss increases as the amount of shareholder capital decreases. Thus, as their risk goes up, debt-holders demand increased returns in the form of more generous yields on their debt securities; at some point, they may even refuse to purchase the firm's debt altogether.

By contrast, federally backed institutions such as banks, thrifts, and enterprises are largely protected from such debt-holder concerns. Debt-holders invest their money in federally insured deposits or enterprise obligations with little concern about an institution's creditworthiness. They look to the federal backing rather than to the capitalization or creditworthiness of the institution for their reassurance. As Black, Miller, and Posner point out, the federal government assumes the financial risk of the debt-holders that it is protecting. Moreover, the federal government must also assume the supervisory burdens not adequately performed by debt-holders; it must protect taxpayers by insisting on financial creditworthiness and an adequate amount of capital for banks, thrifts, and other federally supported institutions.[3]

While some federally backed financial institutions do maintain appropriate levels of capital without government supervision, many others have low levels of capital that do not adequately protect the federal government's stake as guarantor of federally insured deposits or enterprise obligations. This is largely caused by shareholders, who benefit from high leverage and thus object

---

[3]Black, Miller, and Posner, "An Approach to Regulation."

to any issuance of new stock, which dilutes shareholder returns and spreads the company's profits over a larger number of shares.

Like any other financial creditor, the government needs to protect against increases in its risk exposure. It can do so by limiting risk taking through such measures as setting limits on shareholder leverage. As shareholder leverage increases, taxpayers lose the protection of a cushion of capital, which buffers the government against downside losses. This is why capital standards are so important to protecting taxpayers against loss from the government-backed obligations of financial institutions.

The Current State of Enterprise Regulation

Safety and Soundness

Even after the regulatory failures of the Federal Home Loan Bank Board, the Department of Housing and Urban Development, and the Farm Credit Administration in the 1980s, the lessons of those failures are not always applied to the regulation of enterprise safety and soundness today.

One exception is the newly strengthened Farm Credit Administration (FCA), which regulates FCS institutions and Farmer Mac under statutory powers similar to those of federal bank regulators. The FCA has the authority to initiate cease-and-desist proceedings, to suspend or remove FCS institution officers and directors, to impose civil money penalties, to set and enforce capital adequacy standards, and to appoint conservators or receivers. The agency is also permitted to assess the regulated FCS institutions' supervisory costs, including the cost of examinations, and to pay FCA expenses from those assessments. However, the newly independent FCA appears to be unduly constrained by a combination of inadequate legal authority regarding Farmer Mac, and by the influence of key congressional committees responsive to the regulated Farm Credit institutions.

While the Department of Housing and Urban Development

(HUD) has some legal regulatory authority, it has shown little inclination or ability to supervise the safety and soundness of Fannie Mae and Freddie Mac. HUD has general regulatory authority to see that the purposes of the Fannie Mae and Freddie Mac charters are carried out; however, it lacks a clear mandate to regulate the enterprises' financial soundness.[4]

HUD also lacks the resources needed for effective regulation. Unlike other financial institution regulators, HUD is not authorized to assess Fannie Mae or Freddie Mac for the cost of maintaining a capable regulatory staff, one that is compensated at levels comparable to the salaries of federal bank regulators. HUD officials admitted to the GAO in 1985 that the department lacks the capacity and expertise to be a financial regulator responsible for supervising Fannie Mae's risk taking. Since then, Fannie Mae has doubled in size and HUD has become Freddie Mac's regulator as well. The department is likely to be overwhelmed if it attempts to become an active financial regulator of these two enterprises, which have a combined lending of well over half a trillion dollars. So far, HUD hasn't really tried. The responsibility for overseeing Fannie Mae has shifted among various HUD offices; none of them has been successful in developing an experienced supervisory staff able to monitor and regulate financial risk taking by the enterprise. Indeed, in 1989, the *Washington Post* reported that HUD lacks even a single full-time official responsible for overseeing Fannie Mae and Freddie Mac: "It's not as if we have to have someone watching them every day," a HUD spokesperson told the *Post.*[5] Furthermore, HUD has never used its authority to examine Fannie Mae, even though it has had that authority since 1968. Instead, HUD tends to concentrate on national housing and budget policies, such as the controversy over Fannie Mae's support of low-income housing in the late 1970s and over privatizing Fannie Mae in the 1980s. It tends not to focus on matters like Fannie Mae's financial safety and soundness.

[4]See, for example, U.S. Department of Housing and Urban Development, Office of Policy Development and Research, *1986 Report to Congress on the Federal National Mortgage Association* (Washington, D.C.: U.S. Department of Housing and Urban Development, 29 June 1987), Chapter 7.
[5]Jerry Knight, "Bailout of S&Ls Spurs Probes of Other Programs: Hill Examines Taxpayer Liability in Huge U.S.-Backed Enterprises," *Washington Post,* 15 Oct. 1989, pp. H-1, H-4.

The Financial Institutions Reform, Recovery, and Enforcement Act (FIRREA) of 1989 created a new federal agency—the Federal Housing Finance Board (FHFB)—to oversee safety and soundness and the activities of the Federal Home Loan Bank System. It appears that the FHFB will need some time, perhaps several years, to gain the staff and capability to supervise the $200 billion FHLBS. As of mid-1990, for example, the FHFB had only one examiner to inspect the financial condition of the twelve FHLBs. Finally, Sallie Mae has no financial regulator at all.

Capital Requirements

The federal government has not set consistent capital requirements for government-sponsored enterprises. Today, Fannie Mae is subject to a debt-to-capital ratio. However, the statute permits Fannie Mae to count subordinated obligations as a part of its capital, and (in contrast to the subordinated debt of commercial banks) an enterprise's subordinated obligations are implicitly backed by the federal government. This makes the capital requirement virtually meaningless.

The 1989 FIRREA legislation now imposes similar requirements on Freddie Mac. However, Freddie Mac stands to benefit from the statutory debt-to-capital requirement, which does not apply to off-balance sheet activities. This means that the debt-to-capital requirement applies to Freddie Mac's $35 billion of assets but not to its $272 billion of guaranteed mortgage-backed securities that are outstanding.

The absence of capital standards is reflected in the current low capitalization of Fannie Mae and Freddie Mac. Fannie Mae, at year-end 1989, had only $3 billion of shareholder capital to support $352 billion of assets and guaranteed securities; Freddie Mac had only $1.9 billion of shareholder equity to support $308 billion of assets and guarantees. These figures are substantially below the capital requirements established for commercial banks by the FDIC, the Comptroller of the Currency, and the Federal Reserve Board, as well as those imposed on thrifts since the enactment of FIRREA.

The Farm Credit Administration is responsible for setting capital standards for FCS institutions. The FCA has promulgated regulations requiring that most FCS institutions meet minimum risk-based capital requirements. These requirements involve a minimum ratio of permanent capital to risk-weighted assets of 7 percent, to be achieved by 1993. They also provide forbearance criteria for institutions that do not meet the capital-adequacy standards. In its 1990 *Report,* the Treasury questions whether the 7 percent requirement is adequate capitalization for the FCS. The Farm Credit Administration has not set any capital standards for Farmer Mac, the newest government-sponsored enterprise. There is some doubt whether the Farmer Mac legislation even permits the FCA to set such requirements.

The Federal Home Loan Bank System, required by its charter act to maintain a capital reserve, has maintained substantial capital, amounting to almost 8 percent of its assets at year-end 1989. In contrast, Sallie Mae has no capital requirements at all; however, it has maintained capital on its own. At year-end 1989, for example, Sallie Mae's capital amounted to about 2.9 percent of its assets.

Possible Effects of Improved Financial Regulation of the Enterprises

The effective regulation of enterprise safety and soundness would likely result in significant benefits for taxpayers, the federal government, enterprise competitors, borrowers, and shareholders, as well as the enterprises themselves. To understand the benefits that each of these groups would receive, we need first to clarify the various elements of effective financial regulation: (1) enhanced financial disclosures by the enterprises, (2) federal examination of enterprise safety and soundness, (3) federal supervision of the authority to forestall unsafe and unsound enterprise practices or conditions, (4) effective capital requirements comparable to those imposed on commercial banks, and (5) governmental authority to close or reorganize a failing enterprise.

Enhanced financial disclosures and federal examination would have few significant costs, except for enterprise managers fearful of publicizing added information about the financial condition of their institutions. Federal examination, supervision, and authority to intervene may inconvenience some enterprise managers and reduce the returns to some shareholders, but they would have offsetting benefits in promoting the long-term viability of the institutions. Effective capital requirements would be beneficial to taxpayers, the federal government, and competitors alike. However, capital requirements do involve some disadvantages for shareholders and, to a lesser extent, perhaps, borrowers. Some of these disadvantages can be reduced, though not eliminated, by technical refinements that minimize an enterprise's costs of raising more money from equity instead of from debt. Finally, prompt closure or reorganization of a failing enterprise would, on the one hand, reduce taxpayers' financial exposure. On the other hand, enterprise shareholders and borrowers would prefer to let an enterprise continue so that it has a chance to work itself back to solvency, as Fannie Mae did in the 1980s.

Enhanced Financial Disclosures

Enhanced financial disclosures can take a variety of forms, but two in particular provide the most useful information for the marketplace and the government. One is market-value reporting. The other is the Treasury Department proposal that each enterprise obtain and report an annual rating of its creditworthiness, without regard to the government guarantee.

As Freddie Mac has shown, for large specialized lenders such as enterprises, market-value accounting is a valuable management tool worth the cost to the company. Investors can use the improved information of market-value disclosures in making their investment decisions, and taxpayers and the federal government benefit from increased information about the financial viability of the enterprises. By analyzing market-value financial statements and interest-rate scenarios based on those statements, for example, congressional oversight committees might gain better insight into the actual public costs (in terms of financial risk) and benefits of each enterprise's line of business. For example, this could help answer questions about the value of large-scale mortgage portfolio lending: If market-value financial statements reveal significant interest-rate exposure, is this risk worth the benefits to home owners, compared to large-scale securitization of mortgages? Today it is difficult to obtain sufficient information to assist Congress and the executive branch with such a policy question.

Market-value accounting is not foolproof; many technical issues remain to be refined. Market-value disclosures are especially useful as supplements to the traditional financial reports based on cost accounting.

The Farm Credit System is likely to have the most difficulty with market-value accounting. Unlike the other enterprises, which purchase their loan assets and, therefore, can be expected to price them without great difficulty, FCS institutions purchase farm loans whose market value over the years may be difficult to estimate. Even so, market-value accounting will have clear benefits for the FCS. The most capable Farm Credit Banks already generate market-value reports and have found them useful instruments for enhancing managers' financial controls.

The Treasury Department has proposed another addition to enterprise financial disclosures. Today, enterprise obligations receive the top "AAA" credit rating, regardless of the financial condition of the institution, because of the strength of the federal government's implicit guarantee. Under the Treasury proposal, each enterprise would be required to obtain a financial rating of its debt obligations that disregards its government backing; that is, the rating would be based solely on the financial strength of the enterprise. This kind of disclosure would provide valuable market-based information about the financial state of the enterprises. Typically, rating agencies examine traditional kinds of risk—the credit risk of the loan portfolio and MBS business, interest-rate risk, management risk, and operations risk—based on extensive experience and models drawn from other financial institutions with comparable characteristics, such as banks, thrifts, and mortgage insurers, as the case may be.

From the Treasury's perspective, the ratings would also shed light on the extent of the government's actual financial exposure.

If the rating of an enterprise declines from one year to the next, this provides an important signal that the government's risk exposure is increasing. An appropriate response would be to increase federal supervision and oversight and to require the enterprise to reduce risk taking, to increase capital, or otherwise to return to a higher credit rating. By contrast, an enterprise whose rating increases may merit some reduction in regulatory constraints and capital requirements. Variations in the rating over time provide valuable information about the business policies and risk-taking ventures of an enterprise.

Enterprise competitors and borrowers are not likely to gain or lose much from the new market-value and credit-rating disclosures. One possible advantage of market-value reporting may be to increase enterprise responsiveness to market-driven events. This, in turn, would make the enterprises more effective competitors, especially against financial institutions that lack mastery of market-value accounting and that continue to respond to the distortions caused by cost-accounting principles.

Only one group stands to lose from the publication of enhanced financial disclosures: managers of institutions in declining financial circumstances. Suddenly the marketplace and the government may have improved information about the quality of management decisions. Market-value disclosures and annual credit ratings, while admittedly not providing completely accurate and timely information, can make it harder for enterprise managers to embed losses in their balance sheets for recognition by their successors several years too late. Given this clear set of benefits of enhanced disclosures compared to their costs, it will be interesting to see which enterprises prove most reluctant to implement market-value accounting and annual credit ratings on their own.

Federal Examination

Federal examination is the step beyond self-reporting of accurate market-based financial information. For large multibillion-dollar enterprises, federal examination would involve the presence of federal examiners to check credit quality of loans, measure interest-rate exposure, test management information and control systems, and generally oversee management's activities.

For taxpayers and the government, federal examination has proven essential in the effort to monitor the risk taking of commercial banks and now of thrift institutions as well. Examiners may fail to detect unsafe and unsound practices soon enough to forestall loss. Nevertheless, the federal government would be foolish to guarantee hundreds of billions of dollars of federal agency securities without checking for itself that its guarantee is properly used. Even if the risk is remote, the possible cost of even a single badly run enterprise getting into trouble is too high, given the billions of dollars at stake.

The costs of examination are not likely to be high for a $300 billion institution like Fannie Mae or for the $35 billion Sallie Mae. The enterprises generally find their staffing and administrative costs to be a small fraction of total expenses. Adding the costs of an effective examination staff (assuming that the regulator assesses the enterprises for its expenses) is unlikely to make much difference.

Given the competitive advantages of the enterprises in their markets, when adverse findings are disclosed on financial statements, their effects on competitors may be small. For one enterprise, though, federal examination may affect its customers. As examiners of the Farm Credit Administration begin to delve more deeply into issues such as loan documentation and credit quality, a preponderance of low-quality loans or forbearance in collecting on loans is likely to come to the regulator's attention more promptly than in earlier years.

For enterprise managers, federal examiners are a mixed bag. The most important question is likely to be whether the examiners are of high quality. To the extent that examiners fail to understand an institution's business, they are merely a burden, as some of the more capable FCS managers have complained. However, knowledgeable and efficient examiners can provide a useful source of information that often eludes top management's scrutiny. Especially as some of the enterprises swell to hundreds of billions of dollars in size, capable examiners may be able to point to early warning signs of mismanaged information and control systems or other operational activities.

If the federal government does decide to impose bank-type examination of enterprises, it will be in the interest of the government and the enterprises alike to assure that the examination staff is capable.

Federal Authority to Enforce Safety and Soundness and Capital Requirements

Safety and Soundness

If an institution is engaging in unsafe or unsound practices, it is in the taxpayer's interest to empower a financial regulator to intervene. Similarly, if the unsafe or unsound practice involves competitive advantages, such as the FCS policy of predatory pricing in the late 1970s, competitors benefit from forestalling the practice.

Federal bank regulators use a variety of tools to help protect against unsafe or unsound practices. Many of these are codified in a single part of the law (12 U.S.C. § 1818) that can be applied to the regulation of enterprises as well. The tools include cease-and-desist orders, civil money penalties, and removal of directors and senior managers for cause. To enforce capital requirements, another part of the banking law empowers bank regulators to issue capital directives and impose penalties for violations. As with other federal agency actions, the regulator's use of these powers is reviewable in court and can be set aside if the regulatory intervention is arbitrary, unfounded, or otherwise does not meet the applicable standards of administrative law.

For shareholders, federal regulation is a mixed blessing. To the extent that the regulator stops unsafe or unsound practices by incapable managers, shareholders benefit because their investment is additionally protected. To the extent that excessive risk taking provides shareholders with excessive rewards (say, because management is making a large bet on the future trend of interest rates), regulatory intervention reduces the rewards as well as the risks. The issue is really whether the government wants to permit the enterprises to adopt high-risk, high-return strategies or more modest approaches that attract shareholders interested in steady but not exorbitant and possibly volatile returns.

Enterprise borrowers may also find the results mixed. Effective federal oversight may mean denial of credit to less creditworthy borrowers, which will hurt those unable to obtain similar credit elsewhere. However, as FCS borrowers learned, it is not worth having a loan unless the borrower can afford to repay it; too many borrowers took on extra FCS debt, only to lose their farms as a result. If the federal government seeks to help less creditworthy borrowers or institutions, it should provide grant assistance or other carefully targeted subsidies, not lend money to borrowers who are not likely to repay.

Other customers may benefit from increased federal attention to safety and soundness. A well-run enterprise is likely to be viable over the long term. Except for the unusual structure of the Farm Credit System, the enterprises are structured so that returns from extra risk taking go largely to shareholders rather than to customers. This means that customers tend to benefit from a long-term stable and viable enterprise, rather than from an institution that takes risks merely to reward shareholders.

Enterprise managers may be ambivalent about federal regulation. On the one hand, managers want to be captains of their ship; they cannot be expected to relish intervention by federal bureaucrats. On the other hand, the annoyance may be modestly offset by the presence of the regulator as an excuse to avoid risky ventures. It remains to be seen, for example, whether Freddie Mac's senior managers will be able to maintain their policy of avoiding large-scale portfolio lending, given the demands of investor-shareholders for high returns.

Federal regulation has proven itself to be an ineffective substitute for the market discipline that is lost when the government lends its guarantee. Yet taxpayers will be the major beneficiaries from effective federal regulation. When the federal government cosigns the obligations of a private institution, effective supervision is the only tool it has to monitor and set limits on the risks that enterprises may take with that credit.

Capital Requirements

To a large extent, capital requirements appear to be a zero-sum game between shareholders and taxpayers. As an enterprise increases capital, shareholders lose leverage and per-share earnings while taxpayers are better protected. Competitors may also benefit from parity of capital requirements. Today, higher capital requirements on banks and thrifts create a disadvantage compared to the enterprises that compete against them to buy mortgages and student loans, for example.

However, to the extent that the cost of enterprise operations is increased by capital requirements, enterprise borrowers may be disadvantaged. Capital usually costs more than debt, especially because of a feature of the income tax laws: An enterprise may deduct the interest paid on its obligations but not the dividends paid to its shareholders.

For some enterprises, the question of effects on borrowers has already been settled. FCS institutions are now subject to bank-type risk-based capital requirements (but not minimum capital requirements). As the Treasury points out in its 1990 *Report,* the FCS capital requirements need to be tightened to assure that borrower stock is actually at risk. However, since the 1987 FCS bailout, the applicability of bank-type capital requirements has not been disputed.

Increased capital requirements for Sallie Mae, if they were ever needed, would not disadvantage students, because the guaranteed student loan program is not structured to pass Sallie Mae's cost advantages on to student borrowers. The FHLBS, at least for now, is well capitalized of its own accord.

That leaves Fannie Mae and Freddie Mac, and the home buyers who benefit from their low cost of funds. But home buyers are taxpayers, too. The important question is whether, on balance, increased financial protection for taxpayers through bank-type capital requirements is worth whatever increase in mortgage rates that might result for home buyers. In practical terms, the question is somewhat different: How can one reduce the costs to Fannie Mae and Freddie Mac of raising capital so that they can continue to provide benefits to the residential mortgage market but with a greater margin of safety? One answer is to look again at the use of subordinated debt. Subordinated debt is advantageous as a source of capital because federal tax treatment permits the issuing corporation to deduct interest payments. By contrast, a company may not deduct dividends paid to equity investors.

Some serious drawbacks of subordinated debt must be addressed. First, subordinated debt must be of a very long maturity if it is to substitute for shareholder equity as capital. Second, enterprises must issue subordinated debt without the SEC exemption, freedom from investment limitations, and other indicators of federal agency status. Otherwise, subordinated debt has implicit federal backing and the holders are not at risk in the same way as equity holders.

One additional refinement may make subordinated debt an acceptable substitute for shareholder equity, at least for part of an enterprise's capital requirements: The debt should be structured to convert automatically into common stock under specified circumstances. For example, consider an enterprise whose net worth drops to, say, 2 percent of its total size. At that point, outstanding subordinated debt in an amount of, say, 1 percent of total size would automatically convert into common stock according to a predetermined formula. As net worth drops further, more such conversions could be triggered until the enterprise restores its net worth or else the regulator intervenes to close or reorganize the institution. Convertible subordinated debt would thus help provide a source of capital for enterprises while reducing costs, compared to requiring capital in the form of shareholder equity alone. This innovation would also benefit shareholders; their shares would not be diluted until the capital cushion was clearly needed. At that point of extreme leverage, many shareholders might welcome the equity infusion.

As with other elements of effective federal supervision, trade-offs between safety and soundness and other policy goals can be addressed carefully so that the enterprises are able to deliver significant benefits without posing unnecessary risks to taxpayers. Even with bank-type capital of, say, 3 or 4 percent of total lending, the enterprises can continue to provide significant benefits to their borrowers.

The Treasury's proposal that the enterprises maintain sufficient capital to achieve an "AAA" rating, without regard to the implicit guarantee—even if the final standard were set below the proposed "AAA" credit rating—would influence the way some of the enterprises conduct their business. For example, Fannie Mae would find it much more difficult than Freddie Mac to obtain a high credit rating because of the interest rate-risk on its huge portfolio. The need to obtain a higher rating, in turn, would encourage Fannie Mae to increase its MBS business and reduce its portfolio, probably without serious adverse effects on the housing market.

The possible effects of the Treasury's proposal on the FCS require special consideration. Indeed, it would probably not be economically feasible for the FCS to attempt to achieve the top credit rating.[6] But the setting of some other FCS standard—say, perhaps, "A"—to be achieved within five years (the transition period proposed by the Treasury), would encourage the FCS to be more financially disciplined and to improve the at-risk nature of its capital, build reserves, clarify the joint-and-several liability of all institutions, and generally strengthen itself financially. Given the cyclical nature of the agricultural economy and the reasonable possibility that it may again face stress in future years, a strengthened FCS would be a welcomed result of the credit-rating proposal.

Federal Authority to Close or Reorganize a Failing Enterprise

The major lesson of the recent large-scale failure of banks and thrifts is the need to close an institution *before* its market value becomes negative. The ordinary company without federal backing fails when its liabilities exceed its assets and investors refuse to lend any more money. With the implicit guarantee, though, banks, thrifts, and government-sponsored enterprises can continue to do business long after they lose their capital and experience major financial losses. At that point, management can feel intense pressure to take high-stakes gambles, such as on interest rates or by purchasing high-risk, high-yielding assets. Unfortunately, most of these gambles are likely to fail, thereby compounding taxpayer losses when the government finally closes the institution.

The prompt closure or reorganization of a failing regulated company is often hindered by the widely recognized inability of regulators to detect unsafe and unsound conditions before con-

---

[6]Testimony of Thomas Gillis, managing director, Standard & Poor's Corporation, cited in Senate, Committee on Banking, Housing and Urban Affairs, *The Safety and Soundness of Government Sponsored Enterprises* (Hearing) (Washington, D.C.: Government Printing Office, 31 Oct. 1989), p. 95.

siderable financial damage has already occurred.[7] Although the experiences of the 1980s have caused the federal government to provide bank regulators and the FCA (with respect to most FCS institutions but possibly not the new Farmer Mac) with strengthened authority to appoint conservators and receivers to reorganize or close failed regulated institutions, most enterprise charter acts lack this provision.

Managers of a faltering enterprise are not likely to welcome giving the government the power to oust them from control; they would prefer to try to solve the financial problems themselves. Similarly, shareholders may not want the government to intervene, for they will also benefit from another chance to keep the company going, as opposed to the government impairing the value of their stock. Shareholders would probably argue, for example, that Fannie Mae's change of management successfully revived the failing enterprise in 1981, and was accomplished without regulatory intervention. However, according to HUD, Fannie Mae's nominal regulator, those management strategies were actually an attempt "to generate new income through growth and risk-taking."[8] Thus, as with the failing thrift institutions, the decision to close or reorganize a faltering enterprise is a zero-sum game between taxpayers and shareholders: While taxpayers stand to lose from high-risk gambles that may fail, shareholders stand to gain from those that may succeed.

Enterprise creditors are likely to welcome a well-defined set of rules and procedures governing their rights during conservatorship or receivership. Further, enterprise customers are not likely to suffer if the government is empowered to reorganize a failing enterprise. Even if the government appoints a receiver, as the FCA did for the Federal Land Bank of Jackson, Mississippi, in 1988, Congress is likely to try to assure a flow of enterprise credit to the borrowers previously served by the institution.

The regulatory authority to close or reorganize a faltering institution is justified on practical grounds. Without such author-

---

[7]Richard E. Randall, "Can the Market Evaluate Asset Quality Exposure in Banks?" *New England Economic Review* (July/Aug. 1989): 13.

[8]Department of Housing and Urban Development, *1987 Report to Congress on the Federal National Mortgage Association* (Washington, D.C.: Department of Housing and Urban Development, 27 Sept. 1989), p. 28.

ity, the regulator must maintain greater intrusive supervision of an institution to protect against excessive risk taking. As a result, too much weight is placed on the supervisory process as it becomes more involved in an institution's daily activities. From a practical standpoint, then, enterprises and taxpayers alike would benefit from limiting the supervision of safety and soundness to the level of regulatory oversight common to commercial banks, supplemented by the regulator's authority to appoint a conservator or receiver.

The Politics of Improving Federal Supervision of the Enterprises

The case for imposing effective financial regulation on the enterprises is strong. The hundreds of failed thrift institutions that loom before us represent perhaps the most striking example of what can happen when the government fails effectively to regulate the financial safety and soundness of such institutions. And the recent financial breakdown of the Farm Credit System and its ties to regulatory shortcomings only strengthens what is already obvious.

Unfortunately, regulatory lapses are not accidental. Indeed, they reflect a serious dynamic that needs to be overcome before the proposals discussed earlier can be implemented. That dynamic evolves as follows: When times are good and financial institutions are profitable, Congress and the executive branch tend not to see a need to apply stringent regulation of enterprise safety and soundness; "If it ain't broke, don't fix it" is a potent piece of conventional wisdom. Calls for strict regulation usually come only after something goes wrong. By this time, of course, the damage is already done. And when government-sponsored enterprises are involved, the damage may include billions of dollars of mistakes. Consider the evolution of the perceived state of the Farm Credit System from 1982 to 1987, for example. Prior to 1982, the FCS was viewed as a premiere government-sponsored enterprise. Then, in 1982, the FCS spent most of its time rebutting the efforts of the Reagan administration to remove its implicit federal guarantee and convert it into a self-supporting private institution. In 1983, the Farm Credit Administration reported some loan losses but claimed that they "represent[ed] a small percentage of the loans outstanding." The FCA again reported financial stress in 1984, but explained that it would be able to cover those losses and remain financially sound. In 1985, the FCS called on Congress for financial help after reporting a $2.7 billion loss for that year. Then, in 1986, the FCS reported an additional $1.9 billion in losses. Finally, in 1987, Congress enacted a $4 billion FCS bailout program.[9]

It was only after the FCA announced the pending FCS insolvency that Congress insisted on more strict regulation to curb FCS losses. By then, though, it was too late. As one ranking agricultural committee member asked the FCS regulator, "As the governor—and I guess the buck stops at your desk in this organization—why didn't you do something about unsafe and unsound banking practices?"[10]

It may be unappealing to impose effective regulation in good times, but when bad times hit, the damage may already be done. Much of the attention then shifts to the plight of those affected by the failed financial institution. Especially when borrower defaults or delinquencies are involved, the regulator faces considerable pressure not to force the institution to foreclose on its bad loans. Borrower relief became a major issue in the 1987 Farm Credit legislation, as desperate FCS farm borrowers contacted their members of Congress. It is also apparent in federal efforts to deal with thrift institution insolvencies. Indeed, with congressional support, the FHLBB significantly reduced its capital requirements in the early 1980s to accommodate thrifts in financial difficulty. While this stratagem permitted the regulator to avoid applying enforcement measures against many troubled thrifts, it did not alleviate the poor financial practices of literally hundreds of insolvent institutions. Especially because bad times can mean that considerable financial mismanagement or misjudgment has already occurred, imposing financial discipline after the fact often comes too late to forestall harm.

[9]Farm Credit Administration, *Annual Reports* (McLean, Va.: FCA, 1983–1987).
[10]House of Representatives, Committee on Agriculture, *Agricultural Credit Conditions* [Hearings before the Subcommittee on Conservation, Credit, and Rural Development] (Washington, D.C.: Government Printing Office, 30 Oct. 1985), p. 343.

Thus, there is a practical case for effective regulation of enterprise financial soundness. The government has the opportunity now to learn from past regulatory failures; to impose regulation of safety and soundness before another enterprise gets into trouble. In today's unusual economic environment, financial viability is an essential goal for any institution or federal credit program. Given the current signs of weakness in government credit programs and private institutions, including record numbers of failing banks and thrifts, safety and soundness cannot be presumed. While congressional committees should keep for themselves the power to allocate benefits from enterprise lending, they will better serve themselves and their constituencies by delegating effective financial regulation to a hard-nosed regulatory agency and by imposing meaningful capital requirements. This is far wiser than risking the need to stand over the ruins of a once-proud financial institution and ask a weak regulator, "Why didn't you regulate safety and soundness?"

9

Enterprise Accountability

In these times it is not good enough for any financial institution,
be it a GSE or otherwise, to say, trust me. It is not good enough
to say there's never been a problem in the past. The public will
insist that their elected officials accept responsibility for these
federally chartered and supervised institutions. In order to keep
faith with the public trust we must lift the veils of Fannie Mae,
and Sallie Mae and Connie Lee, and even Freddie and Farmer Mac
and see just exactly what's going on behind there. And so I ask
again what is to be done?

—Representative J. J. Pickle, 19 June 1990

Government-sponsored enterprises are growing at an accelerating rate. In aggregate size, they doubled between 1985 and 1989
and grew by over twentyfold since 1970. New enterprises are
being created and, except for the Federal Home Loan Bank System and the convalescing Farm Credit System, the existing enterprises continue to expand.

The huge financial presence of the enterprises means that they
can deliver benefits to many borrowers; it also means that a
failing enterprise could threaten the well-being of domestic and
international investors as well as the thousands of financial institutions that hold their securities based on the government's implicit guarantee. Ultimately, as is the case with the thrift industry,
taxpayers will bear the brunt of any major losses. Even if the
probability of such losses is small, the potential cost is large.

One factor that can affect enterprise success or failure is ac-

188

countability. It is time, then, to devise effective tools to promote the accountability of government-sponsored enterprises. Most important among these is the protection of taxpayers, by assuring the financial safety and soundness of the enterprises. Also needed are improved congressional oversight and direction of the benefits of enterprise lending to serve the highest priority public needs.

Separating the Supervision of Enterprise Safety and Soundness from Oversight of Benefits

Centralized Regulation of Safety and Soundness

The history of financial regulators—the Farm Credit Administration before 1985, the Department of Housing and Urban Development, and the Federal Home Loan Bank Board—reveals the problems that can beset a federal agency or department when it has conflicting responsibilities. These include supervision or promotion of the allocation of benefits provided by the regulated institution and also of the institution's financial safety and soundness.

One solution to the problem is to separate the supervision of enterprise benefits from the supervision of safety and soundness. Regulation of safety and soundness of all government-sponsored enterprises could be centralized within a single regulatory agency. Issues involving the allocation of the benefits of enterprise lending, such as the kinds of borrowers they should serve or the extent to which they should be permitted to engage in new kinds of activities, could be left to Congress or to the appropriate executive department or oversight agency (such as HUD). Like the Office of the Comptroller of the Currency or the recently created Office of Thrift Supervision, the centralized financial regulator could be located within the Treasury Department or Federal Reserve Board because of their expertise in financial matters. Or, similar to the Federal Deposit Insurance Corporation, the centralized regulator could be structured as an independent agency responsible for supervising the safety and soundness of the enterprises. Treasury Undersecretary Robert Glauber suggested in testimony before the House Ways and Means Committee on May 14, 1990, that such a regulator might be established in the Federal Reserve, the FDIC, or the Treasury itself. In this environment, the centralized regulator could develop long-term expertise in assessing and regulating the financial soundness of the enterprises. Especially important, the regulator could apply lessons learned from one government-sponsored enterprise in overseeing the others and in providing guidance to Congress about structuring proposed new enterprises. In effect, the enterprises would no longer be treated as unique financial institutions; nor would their mix of public and private characteristics continue to engender considerable confusion among federal policymakers.

There are arguments against centralized regulation of government-sponsored enterprises. Traditional constituencies of the enterprises are concerned about the consequences of such regulation, even if it is limited to considerations of financial soundness. For example, Henry Schechter, director of the AFL-CIO Office of Housing and Monetary Policy, argues that

> There would be a loss of sympathetic understanding for the various types of financing programs to meet housing and other special needs, and perhaps prejudice toward greater restrictiveness than is necessary to avoid excessive risks.[1]

Similarly, supporters of Farm Credit System institutions point out that regulation of their unique cooperative structure requires a special sensitivity to the significant differences between cooperative principles and operations and those of traditional profit-oriented corporations. Sallie Mae and its supporters are likely to oppose being subjected to any regulation at all, especially given the corporation's tradition of exceptional financial soundness. Finally, some argue that a centralized regulator would lack necessary knowledge of the specialized markets for home mortgages and farm credit now found in HUD and the FCA.

There are political reasons why centralizing the regulation of

[1]Henry Schechter, personal communication to the author, 12 May 1987.

enterprises may not succeed. When the Treasury proposed this new approach in its 1990 *Report,* the chairs of the three enterprise authorizing committees of the House—Banking, Agriculture, and Education and Labor—wrote to Speaker Thomas S. Foley, expressing fear about the possible loss of partial authority over enterprises now completely within their jurisdiction. As an alternative to centralized regulation of the financial soundness of all of the enterprises, Congress could attempt to fashion a common regulatory structure for each enterprise under capable individual regulators. This, however, would make the regulators even more prone to regulatory capture than would be the case for a centralized financial regulator. Except for the Agriculture Committee, which explored the issue of safety and soundness only *after* the FCS failed, none of the authorizing committees or subcommittees of the House or Senate was concerned with oversight of financial soundness until after the House Ways and Means Committee inquired into the subject in three separate hearings.

A broad-based committee like Ways and Means is better able to deal with safety and soundness issues in a timely manner, because it is not responsible for delivering enterprise credit benefits to powerful constituents in the housing, agricultural, and educational sectors of the economy. In any event, the federal government needs to protect taxpayers from today's state of affairs, in which some of the largest enterprises lack effective financial supervision and sufficient capitalization.

The Allocation of Enterprise Benefits Raises Politically Charged Issues

Enterprise benefits consist of the public purposes served by enterprise lending. Depending on their particular structures, the enterprises can use their borrowing advantages to reduce borrowing costs and improve loan terms for home buyers, farmers, thrift institutions, or other borrowers in their designated markets.

Many times enterprises are created to serve carefully targeted purposes. Over time, though, the initial targeted purpose of an enterprise can change. As we saw in earlier chapters, a number of enterprises have obtained statutory changes permitting them to service a much broader market with less apparent connection to priority credit needs. Controversy over enterprise benefits can become politically charged, involving the contending interests of various kinds of borrowers seeking federally supported credit, enterprise competitors, firms doing business with the enterprises, and the enterprises themselves. The scope of authorized enterprise activities reflects a balance of power among interested constituencies, many of whom are close to the congressional authorizing committees responsible for enterprise legislation.

Congressional Oversight of the Allocation of Enterprise Benefits Is Needed

The issue of enterprise benefits tends to be too difficult for a federal agency to handle without congressional direction. Two recent cases illustrate this point. In 1987, the Federal Home Loan Bank Board tried to limit Freddie Mac to a $75 billion annual level of loan purchases. Even though many in the thrift industry supported the measure, Congress decisively rejected the FHLBB action and enacted instead legislation precluding the regulator from imposing such ceilings. By the end of 1987, Freddie Mac exceeded the fairly generous FHLBB ceiling and continued its rapid growth. Today, Freddie Mac has over $300 billion in mortgage-backed securities outstanding, and is larger in its lending activities than any major money-center bank in the United States.

The other example, discussed in chapter 5, involves Fannie Mae and its regulator, the Department of Housing and Urban Development (HUD). In the late 1970s, HUD demanded that Fannie Mae increase its support of low-income home buyers in central cities. In 1978, the department proposed regulations requiring Fannie Mae to direct at least 30 percent of its mortgage purchases to housing for low- and moderate-income families, and another 30 percent of its commitments to mortgages on properties in central cities. In the face of intense industry opposition, HUD rescinded its proposed regulatory requirements, later noting that "during this period, in the mid-to-late 1970s when FNMA's financial security did not seem to be threatened, the Department tried but failed to channel FNMA's activities into specific areas of public policy concerns."[2]

While counterexamples can be found of regulators successfully redirecting enterprise benefits to some extent, the basic point remains: For any significant change in the allocation of enterprise benefits, it is rare that an administrative agency or federal department can succeed without congressional backing. This conclusion is bolstered by a practical consideration. Because many details of the scope of enterprise authority are spelled out in the enabling legislation, any significant redirection of enterprise benefits is likely to require changes in the law and thereby congressional involvement. An agency's role in this regard would be limited to assuring that an enterprise properly observes the legal limits imposed by Congress and does not engage in acts beyond its legal authority. While matters of safety and soundness should be delegated if they are to be implemented properly, congressional committees prefer to keep the allocation of benefits to themselves.

Improving Congressional Oversight of Enterprise Benefits

Even though the ultimate decision about the allocation of enterprise benefits rests with Congress, a responsible agency or department can contribute considerably to the quality of information available to congressional decision makers. The technical details of enterprise charter acts are arcane and susceptible to misunderstanding by all but the most experienced practitioners in the field. A knowledgeable regulator would be able to assist members of Congress in making more informed decisions.

Too often misinformation prevails. For example, the House of Representatives in 1986 passed a bill (H.R. 5300) to create a new enterprise, the Corporation for Small Business Investment

[2]Department of Housing and Urban Development, *Analysis of the Development of the Regulations Governing the Operations of the Federal National Mortgage Association,* cited in Department of Housing and Urban Development, *1986 Report to Congress on the Federal National Mortgage Association* (Washington, D.C.: Department of Housing and Urban Development, 29 June 1987), p. 166.

(COSBI). Buried in part of that bill (section 9010) was a provision permitting COSBI to act "without regard to any other law," except as Congress expressly applied such laws to the COSBI charter act. It is unlikely that members of Congress understood that they were voting to create a corporation that arguably would be exempt from civil and criminal laws that everyone else is required to obey. Proponents of the bill told congressional staff that the complicated provision was mere technical "boiler plate."[3] On this understanding, leading members of the House and Senate introduced the bill several times in several different years with that language included.

Congressional committees would especially benefit from technical analysis and recommendations concerning the structure of the federal legislation governing an enterprise. The legislative structure can profoundly affect the way an enterprise allocates its benefits and the extent it passes on its borrowing advantages by lending at favorable rates to its customers. Congress also needs to oversee the allocation of enterprise benefits as markets change over time. Benefits provided by an enterprise under its charter legislation need to be evaluated periodically in terms of (1) the degree to which the enterprise is passing on its borrowing advantages to ultimate borrowers, rather than merely keeping the benefits for shareholders; and (2) the degree to which those benefits are flowing to the borrowers with the highest priority credit needs.

Today's enterprises differ significantly in these two respects. Because of the structure of the federal Guaranteed Student Loan Program and because of its own pricing policies, Sallie Mae passes on virtually none of its borrowing advantages and tax benefits to students in the form of lowered interest rates on student loans. Instead, its federal agency credit benefits accrue almost exclusively to the corporate shareholders. At the other extreme, the Farm Credit System banks have engaged in overly generous loan pricing during certain periods in the past, and have actually passed to borrowers greater benefits than the FCS could afford to sustain.

The enterprises also differ significantly in the degree to which

[3]Personal communication, Senate Small Business Committee Staff, 1988.

they serve the highest priority credit needs. Congress generally begins by trying to target the benefits of enterprise activities to meet specific perceived public priorities. Over time, as markets and policies change, and as enterprises seek to expand their permitted activities, Congress tends to react by expanding the statutory purposes. When this is done through a small technical amendment contained in a large piece of legislation, the amount of congressional scrutiny may be less than adequate.

Questions of public purpose are among the most difficult to address for government-sponsored enterprises. The ongoing question for Congress is whether the benefits of an enterprise, in terms of the public purposes actually served, are targeted to the most deserving borrowers among the many who could make a claim for federally supported credit. Other questions of public purpose arise from the peculiar characteristics of government-sponsored enterprises: To what extent is an enterprise the best instrument to serve public purposes that Congress considers important? And, even if Congress is free legally, to what extent does it consider itself free morally or politically to confine or redirect the public purposes served by an enterprise if this would adversely affect the investment of enterprise shareholders?

Congressional oversight would be helped immensely if the responsible congressional committees required the relevant administrative agency or executive department to prepare an annual report on the allocation of the benefits from enterprise activities and recommendations for improvement. Given the proverbial tendency of regulators to be captured by the regulated institutions, such a report should be supplemented by reports from a central source with analytic capabilities, such as the Congressional Budget Office or the President's Council of Economic Advisers.

Finally, the congressional consideration of benefits and costs of enterprise operations might be enhanced by including a twenty-year sunset provision in each enterprise charter act. A twenty-year sunset, as was provided in the charters of the first and second Banks of the United States, would seem to be an appropriate period of time. Twenty years is long enough to permit an enterprise to lend billions of dollars to its directed beneficiaries, but short enough to permit in-depth congressional review of the inevitable political and economic changes over that period of time. Whatever such mechanical devices are adopted, federal control of enterprise benefits is best left to congressional oversight committees with analytic support from the appropriate executive agencies and departments.

The Future of Government-Sponsored Enterprises

In the 1990s, the federal government is likely to come to grips with its burgeoning credit programs, including government-sponsored enterprises. America's financial markets today are linked with international markets, and are consequently much more volatile than ever before. For example, 1990 brought a sudden drop in the previously extensive investment in U.S. government securities by Japanese and German financial institutions. Government-sponsored enterprises must be designed, capitalized, managed, and regulated to withstand periods of economic stress. The costs of prudent management and oversight are little compared to taking the chance, no matter how small, of a major loss. The thrift collapse is a $300 billion lesson from which the government is likely to learn at least something valuable.

The large size of some enterprises is another issue that Congress will have to address. Fannie Mae and Freddie Mac, already two of the largest financial institutions in the country, are growing by tens of billions of dollars a year. Together they already hold or guarantee one-fourth of all of the residential mortgages in the United States and little prevents them from buying up a much larger market share. With the failure of the thrift industry, their growth rate seems to be accelerating even more.

Such huge institutions represent an uncomfortable concentration of risk. If anything happens to management quality or prudence (for example, if Fannie Mae is again tempted to play the interest-rate yield curve or if a lower-quality management team took control of one of the enterprises), the financial consequences could rival those of the thrift industry. The federal government is clearly better protected if it diversifies this kind of risk.

One immediate solution would be to turn the Federal Home Loan Bank System into one or more competitors to Fannie Mae and Freddie Mac, operating under a similar charter. The public purpose of the FHLBS is increasingly coming into question, especially with indications that the public purpose of a separate thrift industry itself is under scrutiny. An elegant solution to two problems at once would be to give one or more Federal Home Loan Banks the authority to become national mortgage associations. This would provide a new public purpose for the FHLBS; it would also benefit home buyers. Increased competition among a larger number of secondary market lenders would help pass on federal agency credit benefits to home buyers and reduce the amount captured by shareholders. The major drawback of this idea is the prospect that increased secondary market competition would further depress the profitability of thrift institutions and commercial banks trying to hold mortgages in portfolio. The future of the thrift industry needs to be decided before any major decisions can be made about the future of the FHLBS.

An alternative solution, favored by some private competitors of Fannie Mae and Freddie Mac, would be to roll back the mortgage limits of the two enterprises, say, to the size of the mortgage of the median-income American family. This would help to direct the benefits of federal agency credit to the most needful middle- and lower-income families rather than also to higher-income families that can more easily fend for themselves in the credit markets. The enterprises already claim that the average mortgage they purchase each year is far below the statutory limit, and this restriction, especially if imposed prospectively, may not pose much of a financial hardship on Fannie Mae or Freddie Mac. Congress must weigh the choices carefully, but it must come to grips with the large size of these federally sponsored financial institutions.

The future of the Farm Credit System is an open-ended question. The three Banks for Cooperatives, now permitted to serve a national market, are likely to continue to thrive. The other FCS institutions are having some trouble sorting out their relationships among the various cooperative institutions. One especially troubling issue is whether many FCS associations will become distinct from FCS banks, thereby increasing the financial fragmentation of the system into smaller and possibly less well-managed units. Effective federal regulation is especially important for the Farm Credit System; the well-managed FCS banks, jointly and individually liable on obligations of the entire system, need protection against once again being dragged into financial difficulty by the weaker institutions.

One positive development has been the legislation establishing the Farm Credit System Insurance Corporation (FCSIC). FCS institutions are assessed a modest fee on performing loans and a somewhat higher fee on nonperforming loans; proceeds are paid into the FCSIC and are to be used to pay off investors in FCS consolidated obligations before borrower stock is tapped to avoid a default. The question remains, however, whether the FCSIC will become an effective and well-funded, risk-based insurance system or merely a substitute for inadequate capital in the Farm Credit System as a whole. As the bank and thrift insurance funds have shown, taxpayers are best protected by the combination of meaningful capitalization of each institution, effective regulatory oversight, and an insurance corporation that is sufficiently funded to protect against taxpayer losses over the long term.

As the FCS returns to financial health, it is reasonable to ask whether other rural credit needs—for water treatment and infrastructure projects, rural home loans, and rural small business loans—can be made prudently. Often the lending limits imposed on commercial banks create impediments to serving creditworthy rural borrowers. It is in overcoming such market imperfections that a government-sponsored enterprise fills its most important role. Again, however, careful analysis is called for rather than mere assertions of need.

Sallie Mae presents a somewhat different issue because of its healthy financial status and because it is not structured to pass on its federal benefits to student borrowers. Unlike the other enterprises, Sallie Mae does not need federal backing to earn a top credit rating from the investment community. In 1987, the enterprise tentatively explored but rejected the possibility of giving up its implicit federal guarantee. By dropping the federal guarantee, Sallie Mae would free itself from the likelihood that Congress will ultimately create a federal regulator of its safety and soundness. Also, the enterprise would become a federal corporation similar to Comsat, the National Cooperative Bank, and the Corporation for Public Broadcasting. While Sallie Mae's lending powers would probably not change, the institution would face significant external pressure to negotiate and redefine its authority. Educational and lending institutions concerned about higher-education finance, for example, would likely insist on participating in these decisions.

FICO and REFCORP are a bad idea, because their activities could be replaced by lower-cost financing through the Treasury's Federal Financing Bank. The federal government created each of these enterprises with a slightly different financial structure: FICO is backed by an implicit federal guarantee, whereas REFCORP has both the federal guarantee and an explicit guarantee of repayments of principal on its obligations. FICO and REFCORP, in turn, differ slightly from the FCS Financial Assistance Corporation (FAC), whose obligations are expressly guaranteed by the federal government. While FICO, REFCORP, and the FAC are intended to help fund a federal government bailout, it is distinctly cheaper to borrow at federal government rates. Moreover, in the early 1990s, as the known dimensions of the thrift bailout continued to grow, the executive branch considered yet other forms of off-budget federally backed borrowing. Such haphazard expansion and misuse of government-sponsored institutions is unfair to taxpayers.

If the federal government insists on using government-sponsored enterprises like FICO and REFCORP as a device to create the illusion that a financial bailout is being funded off-budget, then only one such enterprise should exist. That one enterprise could serve as the funding vehicle for all bailout programs. As the volume of this enterprise's outstanding debt obligations grew, its spreads would narrow and its borrowing costs would come increasingly close to the baseline level of Treasury borrowings. Only Wall Street investment firms and knowledgeable investors benefit from the inefficient proliferation of institutions like FICO, REFCORP, and the FAC.

The other government-sponsored enterprises can be valuable instruments of federal policy. When properly designed and operated, their public benefits can outweigh the costs. Unfortunately, inattention to the cost–benefit issue of enterprise lending has meant fewer benefits and greater risk exposure for taxpayers. The government needs to address the issue soon, before another enterprise faces major financial losses and before yet more constituencies develop a vested interest in receiving enterprise benefits that serve a low-priority public purpose. When they work well, government-sponsored enterprises are too valuable to let fail; if they do fail, though, the cost to society is potentially great. To ensure that the enterprises work well, they must be made accountable to public needs and the legitimate concerns of taxpayers. It is time to end today's state of risk.

Appendix A[*]

Laws, Cases, and Other Legal Sources on Government-Sponsored Enterprises

---

The Laws Establishing the Enterprises

Government-sponsored enterprises are established by federal law. In order of their creation, the enterprises are chartered under the following statutes:

- *Farm Credit System (FCS):* 12 U.S.C. §§ 2001–2279aa. The Federal Land Banks (FLBs) were established in 1916, the Federal Intermediate Credit Banks (FICBs) in 1923, and the Banks for Cooperatives (BCs) in 1933. The 1987 legislation combined the FLBs and FICBs into the Farm Credit Banks (FCBs). To-

---

[*]This appendix uses certain abbreviations to refer to federal laws, federal court cases, and federal regulations. For federal laws, "Pub. L. No." means "Public Law Number," "Stat." refers to "Statutes at Large," and "U.S.C." means "United States Code." The symbol "§" means the "Section" of a law or regulation. For federal regulations, the term "CFR" means the "Code of Federal Regulations," published annually. Finally, federal case law involves a variety of abbreviations. The most important are "U.S." and "S.Ct.," referring to two different publications of U.S. Supreme Court decisions; "F. 2d," referring to the *Federal Reporter,* Second Edition, which contains decisions of the Federal Courts of Appeal; and "F.Supp.," meaning the *Federal Supplement* reports of U.S. District Court decisions. Finally, "Del. Code Ann." means the "Delaware Code, Annotated."

202 A State of Risk

gether, the FCBs and BCs and Farm Credit associations constitute today's Farm Credit System.

- *Federal Home Loan Bank System (FHLBS):* 12 U.S.C. §§ 1421–1449. The Federal Home Loan Banks were established in 1932 by the Federal Home Loan Bank Act (Chap. 552, 47 Stat. 725).

- *Federal National Mortgage Association (Fannie Mae):* 12 U.S.C. §§ 1716–1723d. Fannie Mae originated with the National Housing Act of 1934 (Pub. L. No. 73–479, 48 Stat. 246), which authorized the establishment of National Mortgage Associations. In 1938, the Reconstruction Finance Corporation established the Federal National Mortgage Association as a subsidiary. Fannie Mae's charter was codified in the Housing Act of 1954 (Pub. L. No. 83–560, 68 Stat. 590). The Housing and Urban Development Act of 1968 (Pub. L. No. 90–448, 82 Stat. 536) partitioned Fannie Mae into a privately financed secondary market institution, today's Fannie Mae, and a government agency called the Government National Mortgage Association, today's Ginnie Mae.

- *Federal Home Loan Mortgage Corporation (Freddie Mac):* 12 U.S.C. §§ 1451–1459. Freddie Mac was established in 1970 by the Emergency Home Finance Act (Pub. L. No. 91–351, 84 Stat. 451).

- *Student Loan Marketing Association (Sallie Mae):* 20 U.S.C. § 1087-2. Sallie Mae was established by the Education Amendments of 1972 (Pub. L. No. 92–318, 86 Stat. 265).

- *Federal Agricultural Mortgage Corporation (Farmer Mac):* 12 U.S.C. §§ 2279aa et seq. Farmer Mac was established by the Agricultural Credit Act of 1987 (Pub. L. No. 100–233).

- *Financing Corporation (FICO):* 12 U.S.C. § 1441. FICO was established by the Federal Savings and Loan Insurance Corporation Recapitalization Act of 1987 (Pub. L. No. 100–86).

- *Resolution Funding Corporation (REFCORP):* 12 U.S.C. § 1441b. REFCORP was established by the Financial Institutions Reform, Recovery, and Enforcement Act of 1989 (Pub. L. No. 101–73).

The charter act of an enterprise serves a dual legal purpose: It substitutes for the business corporation law of a state and for the articles of incorporation of the particular company chartered under that state law. The enabling legislation for the FCS, FHLBS, and FICO provides that individual institutions shall be chartered by their regulator. Depending on the particular statutory language, some regulators are authorized to withdraw the charters they granted (see, for example, *Fahey v. O'Melveny & Myers*, 200 F.2d 420 [9th Cir. 1952]).

Legal Authority for Enterprise Activities

Government-sponsored enterprises may carry out only those activities expressly authorized by the language of their enabling legislation, as well as powers incidental to that express authority. See, for example, *Association of Data Processing Service Organizations v. Federal Home Loan Bank Board*, 568 F.2d 478 (6th Cir. 1977)[1]; and *Accord, Central Bank, N.A. v. Federal Home Loan Bank of San Francisco*, 430 F.Supp. 1080 (N.D. Calif., 1977), vacated and remanded, 620 F.2d 309 (9th Cir. 1980).

Enterprise charter acts are quite rigid. On a number of issues, legislative history may not be available to provide sufficient guidance about the scope of enterprise authority. As markets change and technologies develop, an enterprise may find the technical language of its charter act provisions to be extremely confining. In this regard, the enterprise charter act is quite different from the broad and flexible provisions of most state corporation laws (compare, for example, Del. Code. Ann. Title VIII, § 121a [1953]). To deal with newly developing issues not anticipated when an enterprise charter act was enacted, federal legislation or regulatory clarification is sometimes required.

The federal government amends enterprise charter acts quite frequently. Indeed, the government has considerable leeway in amending the terms of a charter act even if such amendments are detrimental to the interests of private shareholders. According to *Fahey v. O'Melveny & Myers*, for example, "shareholders in Federal Home Loan Banks have no vested interest under the statute in the continued existence of a particular Federal Home Loan Bank or

---

[1]As noted in chapter 5, the holding in the ADAPSO case—that the FHLBS is not authorized to provide data-processing services to its member thrift institutions—was superseded by the 1989 changes to the Federal Home Loan Bank Act (12 *U.S.C.* § 1431).

any legally protected private rights which would enable them to invoke the due process clause" (200 F.2d 446 [9th Cir. 1952]). See also *Union Pacific Railroad Co. v. U.S. (Sinking Fund Cases)*, 99 U.S. 700 (1878). Congress reserves authority, by way of amendment, to alter the rights, privileges, and immunities it has granted to an enterprise in its charter.

Legal Elements of the Implicit Federal Guarantee of Enterprise Obligations

The implicit federal guarantee arises from laws that give enterprise obligations and mortgage-backed securities (MBSs) many of the investment attributes of federal government securities. This is known as giving federal agency status to enterprise securities.

Many elements of the implicit federal guarantee—such as the line of credit from the enterprise to the Treasury, the exemption of enterprise obligations and MBSs from SEC registration requirements, the eligibility of enterprise obligations and MBSs as lawful investments for federal fiduciary trust and public funds—are found in the enterprise charter acts.

Other elements of the implicit federal guarantee are found in separate statutes. The National Bank Act (12 U.S.C. 24), the Home Owners' Loan Act of 1933 (12 U.S.C. § 1464 [c]), and the Federal Credit Union Act (12 U.S.C. § 1757) exempt national banks, thrift institutions, and credit unions, respectively, from usual investment limitations on their holdings of enterprise obligations or other securities. Also, the Secondary Mortgage Market Enhancement Act of 1984 (15 U.S.C. § 77[r][1][a]) authorizes business entities to hold Fannie Mae and Freddie Mac MBSs to the same extent they are authorized by state or federal law to hold obligations issued by the United States, and preempting conflicting state laws. The 1984 act also authorizes business entities to hold MBSs issued by other companies, but only if those MBSs have a high investment-grade rating.

Finally, the rules and regulations of government agencies like the Internal Revenue Service and the Federal Reserve Board may confer federal agency status on enterprise obligations and securities for specific purposes.

Government-Sponsored Enterprises as Federal Instrumentalities

Under the law, the enterprises are considered instrumentalities, not agencies, of the U.S. government. The distinction is important. As a general rule, government agencies are subject to federal appointment of their senior officers, civil service and federal procurement laws, the Freedom of Information Act, the federal budget, and other direct federal management controls. In contrast, federal instrumentalities are usually privately owned institutions supervised but not directly managed by the U. S. government. (This distinction is discussed at length in Ronald C. Moe and Thomas H. Stanton, "Government-Sponsored Enterprises as Federal Instrumentalities: Reconciling Private Management with Public Accountability," *Public Administration Review* [July/Aug. 1989]: 321–29). With respect to the budget treatment of government-sponsored enterprises, see President's Commission on Budget Concepts, *Report of the President's Commission on Budget Concepts* (Washington, D.C.: GPO, October 1967), pp. 29–30.

The law governing federal instrumentalities is largely based on two great cases involving the Second Bank of the United States: *McCulloch v. Maryland,* 17 U.S. (4 Wheat.) 316 (1819), and *Osborn v. Bank of the United States,* 22 U.S. (9 Wheat.) 738 (1824).

Among the cases defining government-sponsored enterprises as federal instrumentalities, see *Smith v. Kansas City Title and Trust Company, et al.,* 255 U.S. 180 (1920); *Federal Land Bank v. Bismarck Lumber Co.,* 314 U.S. 95 (1941); *Federal Land Bank v. Priddy,* 295 U.S. 229 (1935); *Fahey v. O'Melveny & Myers,* 200 F.2d 420 (9th Cir. 1952); *Association of Data Processing, Inc. v. Federal Home Loan Bank,* 568 F.2d 478 (6th Cir. 1977); *Northrip v. Federal National Mortgage Association,* 527 F.2d 23 (6th Cir. 1975); and *Rust v. Johnson,* 597 F.2d 174 (9th Cir. 1979).

Another set of legal cases, based on McCulloch and Osborn, similarly defines banks as federal instrumentalities: *First National Bank v. Missouri,* 263 U.S. 640 (1924); *First National Bank v. Fellows,* 244 U.S. 416 (1917); *Easton v. Iowa,* 188 U.S. 220 (1903); and *Davis v. Elmira Savings Bank,* 161 U.S. 275 (1896).

The U.S. government may use a variety of institutions, including entities formed under state law, as federal instrumentalities; see *Westfall v. United States,* 274 U.S. 256, 47 S.Ct. 629 (1927) (state bank, member of the Federal Reserve System, as a federal instrumentality); and *United States v. Brown,* 384 F. Supp. 1151 (E.D. Mich., 1974), reversed (affirmed on this issue), 557 F.2d 54, 559 (6th Cir. 1977) (entity formed under state law as a federal instrumentality).

The Benefits of Federal Instrumentality Status

Government-sponsored enterprises benefit from their status as instruments of federal policy for some purposes and from their status as private firms for others. In the first case, an enterprise's charter act and other applicable federal legislation can preempt it from potentially burdensome state laws (see *Federal National Mortgage Association v. Lefkowitz,* 390 F.Supp. 1364 [S.D.N.Y. 1975]; and *Rust v. Johnson,* 597 F.2d 174 [9th Cir. 1979] and taxes (see *Laurens Federal Savings and Loan Association v. South Carolina Tax Commission,* 365 U.S. 517, 81 S.Ct. 719 [1961]). In the second case, as a private institution, an enterprise is not subject to constitutional due-process requirements (see *Roberts v. Cameron-Brown Company,* 556 F.2d 356 [5th Cir. 1977]; and *Fidelity Financial Corporation v. Federal Home Loan Bank of San Francisco,* 589 F.Supp. 885 [N.D. Calif., 1983], affirmed, 792 F.2d 1432 [9th Cir. 1986]).

As federal instrumentalities, enterprises are probably not eligible to become a debtor under the Bankruptcy Code. The federal government has never permitted a federal corporation to become insolvent, and the applicable law is not clear in this regard. However, a set of interlocking definitions in the Bankruptcy Code suggests that a federal instrumentality, except when expressly authorized by federal law, cannot claim bankruptcy under the code. 11 U.S.C. § 101(30) defines a "person" to exclude a "governmental unit," and 11 U.S.C. §§ 109 and 101(12) preclude entities other than "persons" (or municipalities) from becoming debtors under Chapters 7 and 11 of the Bankruptcy Code. Finally, 11 U.S.C. § 101(21) defines a "governmental unit" to include an instrumentality of the United States.

Insolvent banks and thrifts are reorganized or closed by their federal regulators and are placed in conservatorship or receivership, respectively. Similarly, the Farm Credit Administration

(FCA) is authorized to appoint conservators or receivers to re-structure or close insolvent FCS institutions (12 U.S.C. § 2183). Again, because of the unusual statutory language of Farmer Mac's charter, the FCA may lack the authority to appoint a con-servator or receiver for Farmer Mac if that enterprise became insolvent. The Federal Housing Finance Board (FHFB), as regula-tor of the FHLBS, has broad but unspecified authority to reorga-nize insolvent Federal Home Loan Banks (see *Fahey v. O'Melveny v. Myers,* 200 F.2d 420 [9th Cir. 1952]). The FHFB's statutory authority includes the right to charter an FHLB, and this includes the right to dissolve it. The important distinction seems to be between (1) the enterprises chartered by Congress, and (2) the FCS and FHLBS, whose member institutions are chartered by a federal regulator. The current charters for the former enterprises lack express provisions defining creditors' rights or procedures in the event of insolvency.

The Responsibility of Enterprise Directors

Federal law prescribes that the boards of directors of most gov-ernment-sponsored enterprises shall include a minority of pub-licly appointed members and a majority of shareholder-elected members. One-third of Sallie Me's twenty-one directors, five of Fannie Mae's eighteen directors, and five of Freddie Mac's eigh-teen directors are appointed by the president of the United States. The boards of the Federal Home Loan Banks similarly contain a minority of directors appointed by the Federal Housing Finance Board. The Farm Credit institutions do not have publicly ap-pointed directors on their boards, except that one-third of Farmer Mac's directors are appointed by the president of the United States and confirmed by the Senate.

As a general rule, all enterprise directors owe a fiduciary re-sponsibility to their shareholders and the corporation. There ex-ists no basis for distinguishing publicly appointed directors from shareholder-elected ones in this regard. All enterprise directors, publicly appointed and shareholder-elected alike, are subject to personal liability for breaching their fiduciary responsibilities.

(This is discussed in "Personal Liability of Directors of Federal Government Corporations," *Case Western Law Review* 30 [Summer 1980]: 733–79; and Herman Schwartz, "Governmentally Appointed Directors in a Private Corporation—The Communications Satellite Act of 1962," *Harvard Law Review* 79 [December 1965]: 350–64.)

Legal Accountability

The enterprises are exempt from certain forms of accountability applicable to federal government agencies, such as the Freedom of Information Act and federal budget controls. They are also free from forms of accountability applicable to private companies, such as some of the investor rights available under state corporation laws and federal securities laws. (In this regard, see "FNMA and the Rights of Private Investors: Her Heart Still Belongs to Daddy," *Georgetown Law Journal* 59 [Nov. 1970]: 369–92.)

Increasingly stringent rules restricting private rights of action make it difficult for competitors or shareholders or even customers to bring successful court action against an enterprise. A federal district court has held, for example, that neither competitors nor shareholders may challenge Sallie Mae's action on grounds that the enterprise acted beyond the scope of its authority under law (*First American Federal Savings and Loan Association et al. v. Student Loan Marketing Association,* no. 84–1014–CIV–5 [E.D.N.C., 1985]). In contrast, because of provisions in the Federal Home Loan Bank Act, softened in 1989, prohibiting Federal Home Loan Banks from engaging in the business of banking, federal courts held that banks and other competitors could challenge actions of the FHLBS on grounds that they exceed lawful authority (*Association of Data Processing Service Organizations, Inc. v. Federal Home Loan Bank Board,* 568 F.2d 478 [6th Cir. 1977]; and *Central Bank, N.A. v. Federal Home Loan Bank of San Francisco,* 430 F.Supp. 1080 [N.D. Calif. 1977], vacated and remanded 620 F.2d 309 [9th Cir. 1980]).

However, more recent decisions have challenged the ADAPSO reasoning, arguing that only the regulator (now the FHFB) may challenge FHLBS acts beyond the scope of legal authority (*Fidelity Financial Corp. v. Federal Home Loan Bank of San Francisco,* 589 F. Supp.

885 [1983], affirmed, 792 F.2d 1432 [9th Cir. 1986]). The severe limitations on private rights to enforce in court the provisions of enterprise charter acts mean that regulators and Congress must be responsible for overseeing each enterprise's compliance with the legal limits on its authority.

Federal Regulation

By law, the Department of Housing and Urban Development (HUD) is responsible for regulating Fannie Mae and Freddie Mac (12 U.S.C. §§ 1716 *et sea.* and § 1451 *et sea.*). The Farm Credit Administration (FCA) regulates the FCS institutions and Farmer Mac (12 U.S.C. §§ 2241 *et sea.* and 2279aa-ll). The newly established Federal Housing Finance Board (FHFB) regulates the FHLBS (12 U.S.C. §§ 1421 *et sea.*). Sallie Mae has no financial regulator; the Higher Education Act expressly states that the authority of the departments of Education and Treasury to approve Sallie Mae obligations shall not be construed to permit the departments "to limit, control, or constrain" the activities of Sallie Mae (20 U.S.C. 1087-2[h][2]).

Some enterprise charter acts provide that the Secretary of the Treasury shall approve the issuance, maturities, and rates of interest of obligations as well as the issuance of MBSs. Compare 12 U.S.C. §§ 1719(b), (d), and (3) and 1455(j) and (k) (Fannie Mae and Freddie Mac obligations and MBSs approved by Treasury) with 31 U.S.C. § 1908 (FCS institutions need only consult with the Treasury before issuing obligations).

A review of the powers of enterprise regulators reveals that (except for the FCA since the 1985 enactment of the Farm Credit Amendments Act) they lack many of the enforcement powers and powers to set and enforce capital standards available to federal bank regulators (compare 12 U.S.C. §§ 1818 and 3907 with the regulatory authority of the federal government under the various enterprise charter acts). Only the FCA and FHFB are authorized to assess regulated enterprises, the FCS institutions (including Farmer Mac) and the FHLBS, respectively, for the costs of examination and supervision (see 12 *U.S.C.* §§ 2250 and 1438). Such authority is provided by law for all federal bank regulators. The other enterprise regulator, HUD, must pay expenses out of appropriated funds to engage in supervisory activities with respect to Fannie Mae or Freddie Mac.

The regulations of HUD with respect to Fannie Mae are codified at 24 C.F.R. part 81; of the FHFB at 12 C.F.R. parts 900 *et sea*.; and of the FCA at 12 C.F.R. parts 600 *et sea*.

Additional Legal Writings

The legal literature concerning government-sponsored enterprises is surprisingly sparse. Some of the more informative articles include the following: Dirk Adams and Rodney Peck, "The Federal Home Loan Banks and the Home Finance System," 43 *Business Lawyer* (May 1988): 833–864; Richard Bartke, "Fannie Mae and the Secondary Mortgage Market," 66 *Northwestern University Law Review* (March/April 1971): 1–78; and Richard Bartke, "Home Financing at the Crossroads—A Study of the Federal Home Loan Mortgage Corporation," 48 *Indiana Law Journal* (Fall 1972): 1–42. A brief but good overview of the Farm Credit System is Anne Dewey, "The Farm Credit System," *Federal Bar News and Journal* 36 (July/Aug. 1989): 287–289.

A variety of enterprise-related laws and cases are well analyzed in Raymond Natter, "Legal Status of the Federal National Mortgage Association" (Congressional Research Service, Library of Congress, monograph, 19 Jan. 1982); and Thomas H. Stanton, "Government Sponsored Enterprises: Their Benefits and Costs as Instruments of Federal Policy" (Washington, D.C.: Banking Research Fund of the Association of Reserve City Bankers, monograph, Apr. 1988).

Among the literature published by the U.S. government, the most useful regarding the enterprises and their regulators are Treasury Department, *Report of the Secretary of the Treasury on Government Sponsored Enterprises* (Washington, D.C.: GPO, May 1990); and General Accounting Office, *Government-Sponsored Enterprises: Government's Exposure to Risk* (Washington, D.C.: GPO, August 1990).

Appendix B

References

Overview of Government-Sponsored Enterprises and Related Institutions

Public Administration

Goldberg, Sidney, D., and Harold Seidman. *The Government Corporation: Elements of a Model Charter.* Washington, D.C.: Public Administrative Service, 1953.

Moe, Ronald C. "Administering Public Functions at the Margin of Government: The Case of Federal Corporations." Washington, D.C.: Congressional Research Service, Library of Congress, 1 Dec. 1983.

———., and Thomas H. Stanton. "Government-Sponsored Enterprises as Federal Instrumentalities: Reconciling Private Management with Public Accountability." *Public Administration Review* 49 (July/Aug. 1989) : 321–29.

Musolf, Lloyd D. "American Mixed Enterprise and Government Responsibility." *Western Political Quarterly* 24 (Dec. 1971): 789–806.

———. *Uncle Sam's Private Profit Seeking Corporations.* Lexington, Mass.: D.C. Heath and Co., 1983.

National Academy of Public Administration. *Report on Government Corporations.* Volume 1. A report based on a study by a panel of the National Academy of Public Administration for the Office of Management and Budget. Washington, D.C.: Government Printing Office, Aug. 1981.

Pecora, Ferdinand. *Wall Street Under Oath: The Story of Our Modern Money Changers.* New York: Simon & Schuster, 1939.

Seidman, Harold. "Government Sponsored Enterprise in the United States." In *The New Political Economy,* edited by Bruce L. R. Smith. London: Macmillan, 1975.

———. "Government Sponsored Enterprises: One View." *Public Budgeting & Finance* 9 (Autumn 1989): 76–80.

──────. "Public Enterprise Autonomy: Need for a New Theory." *International Review of Administrative Sciences* 49 (Jan. 1983): 65–72.

──────. "Public Enterprise in the United States." *Annals of Public and Cooperative Economy* 11 (March 1983): 3–18.

──────. "The Theory of the Autonomous Government Corporation: A Critical Appraisal." *Public Administration Review* 12 (Spring 1952): 89–96.

──────, and Robert Gilmour. *Politics, Position, and Power: From the Positive to the Regulatory State.* 4th ed. New York: Oxford University Press, 1986.

Stanton, Thomas H. "Government Sponsored Enterprises: Another View." *Public Budgeting & Finance* 9 (Autumn 1989): 81–86.

──────. "Increasing the Accountability of Government Sponsored Enterprises: First Steps." *Public Administration Review* (Sept./Oct. 1990): 590–93.

Economics and Finance

Bosworth, Barry P., Andrew S. Carron, and Elisabeth H. Rhyne. *The Economics of Federal Credit Programs.* Washington, D.C.: Brookings Institution, 1987.

Greider, William. *The Trouble with Money: A Prescription for America's Fever.* Knoxville: Whittle Direct Books, 1989.

Moran, Michael J. "The Federally Sponsored Credit Agencies: An Overview." *Federal Reserve Bulletin* 71 (June 1985) : 373–88.

Standard & Poor's Corporation. *S&P's Structured Finance Criteria.* New York: Standard & Poor's, 1988.

Stanton, Thomas H. "GSEs also Need Better Supervision." *Financier* 13 (Oct. 1989): 33–36.

Stigum, Marcia. *The Money Market.* rev. ed. Homewood, Ill.: Dow Jones-Irwin, 1983.

Federal Government Documents

Congressional Budget Office. *An Analysis of the Administration's Credit Budget for Fiscal Year 1991.* Washington, D.C.: Government Printing Office, Apr. 1990.

──────. *Credit Reform: Comparable Budget Costs for Cash and Credit.* Washington, D.C.: Government Printing Office, Dec. 1989.

Council of Economic Advisors. "The Federal Role in Credit Markets." In *Economic Report of the President.* Washington, D.C.: Government Printing Office, Feb. 1986, pp. 189–212.

Executive Office of the President. Office of Management and Budget. "Special Analysis F: Federal Credit Programs." In *Special Analyses: Budget of the United States Government, Fiscal Year 1990.* Washington, D.C.: Government Printing Office, 1989.

General Accounting Office. *Government-Sponsored Enterprises: Government's Exposure to Risks.* Washington, D.C.: Government Printing Office, 1990.

House of Representatives. Committee on Government Operations. *Amending the Government Corporation Control Act.* Hearing before a subcommittee. Washington, D.C.: Government Printing Office, Feb. 1958.

————. Committee on Ways and Means. *Federal Credit Reform and Borrowing by Off-Budget Agencies.* Hearing. Washington, D.C.: Government Printing Office, 18 Apr. 1989.

————. *Oversight Hearing on Government Sponsored Enterprises.* Hearing. Washington, D.C.: Government Printing Office, 26 Sept. 1989.

President's Commission on Budget Concepts. *Report of the President's Commission on Budget Concepts.* Washington, D.C.: Government Printing Office, Oct. 1967.

Senate. Committee on Banking, Housing and Urban Affairs. *The Safety and Soundness of Government Sponsored Enterprises.* Hearing. Washington, D.C.: Government Printing Office, 31 Oct. 1989.

Treasury Department. *Report of the Secretary of the Treasury on Government Sponsored Enterprises.* Washington, D.C.: Government Printing Office, May 1990.

Financial History

Bagehot, Walter. *Lombard Street: A Description of the Money Market.* 4th ed. London: Henry S. King and Co., 1873.

Baird, Frieda, and Claude L. Benner. *Ten Years of Federal Intermediate Credits.* Washington, D.C.: Brookings Institution, 1933.

Bolles, Albert S. *The Financial History of the United States, from 1789 to 1860.* New York: D. Appleton, 1883.

Conant, Charles A. *A History of Modern Banks of Issue.* New York: Putnam's, 1896.

Dewey, Davis R. *Financial History of the United States.* 8th ed. New York: Putnam's, 1922.

Dunbar, Charles F. *Chapters on the Theory and History of Banking.* 2nd ed. New York: 1909.

Eccles, Marriner S. *Beckoning Frontiers: Public and Personal Recollections* (esp. chap. 6). New York: Knopf, 1951.

Hammond, Bray. *Banks and Politics in America from the Revolution to the Civil War.* Princeton, N.J.: Princeton University Press, 1957.

Hoag, W. Gifford. *The Farm Credit System: A History of Financial Self-Help.* Danville, Ill.: The Interstate, 1976.

Olson, James S. *Saving Capitalism: The Reconstruction Finance Corporation and the New Deal.* Princeton, N.J.: Princeton University Press, 1988.

Rufener, Louis A. *Money and Banking in the United States.* Cambridge, Mass.: Houghton Mifflin, 1934.

Stokes, W. N., Jr. *Credit to Farmers: The Story of Federal Intermediate Banks and Production Credit Associations.* Washington, D.C.: Federal Intermediate Credit Banks, 1973.

The Individual Enterprises

Fannie Mae and Freddie Mac

Department of Housing and Urban Development. Office of Policy Development and Research. *1986 Report to Congress on the Federal National Mortgage Association.* Washington, D.C.: Government Printing Office, 29 June 1987.

——. *1987 Report to Congress on the Federal National Mortgage Association.* Washington, D.C.: Government Printing Office, 27 Sept. 1989.

Federal Home Loan Mortgage Corporation. *Task Force Report.* Washington, D.C.: Freddie Mac Advisory Committee, 17 Oct. 1986.

General Accounting Office. *The Federal National Mortgage Association in a Changing Economic Environment.* Washington, D.C.: Government Printing Office, GAO/RCED-85-102, 15 Apr. 1985.

——. *The Federal National Mortgage Association in a Changing Economic Environment* (supplement). Symposium. Washington, D.C.: Government Printing Office, RCED-85-102A, 17 July 1985.

Gray, Jonathan E., and Joan M. McGettigan. *The Federal National Mortgage Association (Fannie Mae): Strategic Analysis/Financial Forecast.* New York: Sanford C. Bernstein, 1989.

Hendershott, Patric. "The Future of the Thrifts as Home Mortgage Portfolio Lenders." *The Future of the Thrift Industry: Proceedings of the 14th Annual Conference.* San Francisco: Federal Home Loan Bank of San Francisco, 8–9 Dec. 1989.

House of Representatives. *National Housing Act.* Hearings on H.R. 9620. Washington, D.C.: Government Printing Office, 1934.

Kane, Edward J. *Valuing and Eliminating Subsidies Associated with Conjectural Treasury Guarantees of FNMA Liabilities.* Final report of research undertaken for Department of Housing and Urban Development. Washington, D.C.: Government Printing Office, 30 Aug. 1985.

Matlack, Carol. "Getting Their Way." *National Journal,* 27 October 1990, pp. 2584–2588.

Pittman, Edward L. "Economic and Regulatory Developments Affecting Mortgage Related Securities." *Notre Dame Law Review* 64 (Apr. 1989): 486–551.

Seiders, David F. "The Future of Secondary Mortgage Markets: Economic Forces and Federal Policies." In *Housing Finance Review.* Washington, D.C.: Federal Home Loan Mortgage Corporation, July 1984.

Senate. Committee on Banking and Urban Affairs. *Housing and Urban Development Act of 1968, Parts I and II.* Hearings. Washington, D.C.: Government Printing Office, 1968.

———. Committee on Banking, Housing, and Urban Affairs. *Federal National Mortgage Association Charter Act.* Hearing. Subcommittee on Housing and Urban Affairs. Washington, D.C.: Government Printing Office, 1977.

Thygerson, Kenneth J., and Carolyn Brown. "Mortgages and Mortgage-Backed Securities." In *Handbook of Financial Markets: Securities, Options and Futures.* 2nd ed., edited by Frank J. Fabozzi and Frank G. Zarb. Homewood, Ill.: Dow Jones-Irwin, 1986.

Weicher, John C. "The Future Structure of the Housing Finance System." AEI occasional papers. Washington, D.C.: American Enterprise Institute, Nov. 1987.

Woodward, Susan E., "Policy Issues in the Privatization of FNMA and FHLMC." In *Expanded Competitive Markets and the Thrift Industry: Proceedings of the Thirteenth Annual Conference.* San Francisco: Federal Home Loan Bank of San Francisco, Dec. 1987.

Federal Home Loan Bank System

Adams, Dirk, and Rodney Peck. "The Federal Home Loan Banks and the Home Finance System." *Business Lawyer* 43 (May 1988): 833–64.

Federal Home Loan Bank System. *A Guide to the Federal Home Loan Bank System.* 5th ed. Washington, D.C.: FHLB System Publication Corp., 1987.

General Accounting Office. *Housing Finance: Agency Issuance of Real Estate Mortgage Investment Conduits.* Washington, D.C.: Government Printing Office, GGD-88-111, Sept. 1988.

House of Representatives. Committee on Banking and Currency. *Creation of a System of Federal Home Loan Banks.* Hearings. Washington, D.C.: Government Printing Office, Mar. 1932.

Senate. Committee on Banking and Currency. *Creation of a System of Federal Home Loan Banks.* Washington, D.C.: Government Printing Office, Jan. 1932.

Farm Credit System and Farmer Mac

Farm Credit Administration. *Annual Report.* McLean, Va.: FCA, published annually.

General Accounting Office. *Farm Credit: Actions Needed on Major Management Issues.* Washington, D.C.: Government Printing Office, GGD-87-51, Apr. 1987.

———. *The Farm Credit System: An Analysis of Financial Condition.* Washington, D.C.: Government Printing Office, 1986.

———. *Federal Agricultural Mortgage Corporation: Secondary Market Development and Risk Implications.* Washington, D.C.: Government Printing Office, RCED-90-118, May 1990.

———. *Federal Agricultural Mortgage Corporation: Underwriting Standards Issues Facing the New Secondary Market.* Washington, D.C.: Government Printing Office, RCED-89-106 BR, May 1989.

Hiemstra, Stephen W., Steven R. Koenig, and David Freshwater. *Prospects for a Secondary Market for Farm Mortgages.* U.S. Department of Agriculture, Economic Research Service. Washington, D.C.: Government Printing Office, Dec. 1988.

House of Representatives. Committee on Agriculture. *Agricultural Credit Conditions.* Hearings. Subcommittee on Conservation, Credit, and Rural Development. Washington, D.C.: Government Printing Office, 1985.

———. *Farm Credit Act Amendments of 1955.* Report 99–425 (to accompany H.R. 3792). Washington, D.C.: Government Printing Office, 6 Dec. 1985.

Sunbury, Ben. *The Fall of the Farm Credit Empire.* Ames: Iowa State University Press, 1990.

Sallie Mae

Congressional Budget Office. *Government-Sponsored Enterprises and Their Implicit Federal Subsidy: The Case of Sallie Mae.* Washington, D.C.: Government Printing Office, Dec. 1985.

General Accounting Office. *Secondary Market Activities of the Student Loan Marketing Association.* Washington, D.C.: Government Printing Office, HRD-84-51, 18 May 1984.

FICO and REFCORP and Other Enterprises

Stanton, Thomas H. "Government Sponsored Enterprises: Another View." *Public Budgeting & Finance* 9 (Autumn 1989): 81–86.

———. "Pending Legislation Would End Impasse over SBA Program: Congress May Create a New Corporation to Aid Small Business, but Has Drafted the Law in a Way That May Ultimately Expose the Government to Significant Financial Losses," *Legal Times,* 6 Oct. 1986, pp. 24–26.

Issues Concerning Banks and Thrift Institutions

Bank Regulation

Aspinwall, Richard C., and Robert A. Eisenbeis. *Handbook for Banking Strategy.* New York: Wiley, 1985.

Benston, George J., Robert A. Eisenbeis, Paul M. Horvitz, Edward J. Kane, and George G. Kaufman. *Perspectives on Safe & Sound Banking.* Cambridge, Mass.: MIT Press (American Bankers Association), 1986.

Black, Fischer, Merton H. Miller, and Richard A. Posner. "An Approach to the Regulation of Bank Holding Companies." *Journal of Business* 51 (Mar. 1978): 379–412.

Clarke, Robert L. "Banking in Troubled Times: What Hurts? What Helps?" Washington, D.C.: Office of Comptroller of the Currency, 20 June 1988.

Federal Deposit Insurance Corporation. *Deposit Insurance for the 90's: Meeting the Challenge.* FDIC staff study. Washington, D.C.: Federal Deposit Insurance Corporation, 4 Jan. 1989.

Flannery, Mark J. "Deposit Insurance Creates a Need for Bank Regulation." *Business Review* (Jan./Feb. 1982): 17–27.

Furlong, Frederick T., and Michael C. Keeley. "Bank Capital Regulation and Asset Risk." *Economic Review* (Spring 1987): 20–40.

General Accounting Office. *Bank Failures: Independent Audits Needed to Strengthen Internal Control and Bank Management.* Washington, D.C.: Government Printing Office, AFMD-89-25, May 1989.

Golembe, Carter H., and David S. Holland. *Federal Regulation of Banking, 1986– 1987.* Washington, D.C.: Golembe Associates, 1986.

Guttentag, Jack M., and Richard J. Herring. "Restructuring Depository Institutions." Paper presented at the 13th Annual Conference of the Federal Home Loan Bank of San Francisco, 10 December 1987.

———. "Disaster Myopia in International Banking." *Essays in International Finance* 164 (September 1986).

Kane, Edward, J. *The Gathering Crisis in Federal Deposit Insurance.* Cambridge, Mass.: MIT Press, 1985.

Lash, Nicholas A. *Banking Laws and Regulations: An Economic Perspective.* Englewood Cliffs, N.J.: Prentice-Hall, 1987.

Litan, Robert E. *What Should Banks Do?* Washington, D.C.: Brookings Institution, 1987.

Maisel, Sherman J., ed. *Risk and Capital Adequacy in Commercial Banks* (esp. chap. 6). Chicago: University of Chicago Press, 1981.

Mitchell, Karlyn. "Capital Adequacy at Commercial Banks." *Economic Review* 69 (Sept./Oct. 1984): 17–30.

Office of the Comptroller of the Currency. *Bank Failure: An Evaluation of the Factors Contributing to the Failure of National Banks.* Washington, D.C.: Comptroller of the Currency, 1988.

Randall, Richard E. "Can the Market Evaluate Asset Quality Exposure in Banks?" *New England Economic Review* (July/Aug. 1989): 3–24.

Stigum, Marcia L., and Rene O. Branch, Jr. *Managing Bank Assets and Liabilities.* Homewood, Ill.: Dow Jones-Irwin, 1983.

Regulation of Thrift Institutions

Brumbaugh, R. Dan, Jr. *Thrifts Under Siege: Restoring Order to American Banking.* Cambridge, Mass.: Ballinger, 1988.

General Accounting Office. *Failed Financial Institutions: Reasons, Costs, Remedies and Unresolved Issues.* Testimony of Frederick D. Wolf. Washington, D.C.: Government Printing Office, T-AFMC-89-1, 13 Jan. 1989.

———. *Thrift Failures: Costly Failures Resulted from Regulatory Violations and Unsafe Practices.* Washington, D.C.: Government Printing Office, AFMD-89-62, June 1989.

Mayer, Martin. *The Greatest-Ever Bank Robbery: The Collapse of the Savings and Loan Industry.* New York: Scribner's, 1990.

Failed Financial Institutions

House of Representatives. Committee on Banking, Finance and Urban Affairs. *Continental Illinois National Bank: Report of an Inquiry into Its Federal Supervision and Assistance.* Staff study. Subcommittee on Financial Institutions Supervision, Regulation and Insurance. Washington, D.C.: Government Printing Office, 1984.

Sprague, Irvine H. *Bailout.* New York: Basic Books, 1986.

Index

accountability: financial, 162–164, 188–196; legal, 208–209
accounting standards: Financial Accounting Standards Board (FASB), 140; generally accepted accounting principles, 3–4, 7, 134, 148–149; market-value accounting, 128, 148–152, 175–176; off–balance sheet lending, 132–136, 137, 140, 150
advances: Fannie Mae and Freddie Mac, 50–52, 109–110; Federal Home Loan Bank System, 21, 50–52, 98–99, 119–120, 140–141; Sallie Mae, 50–52, 143, 145
agricultural lending: Farm Credit System, 50, 180, 198; Farmer Mac, 23–24, 49–50, 94, 124–125; rural commercial lenders, 117–118
American Savings and Loan, 6
Association of Data Processing Service Organizations (ADAPSO) v. Federal Home Loan Bank Board. See incidental powers

Bank of the United States, xxiv, 195
bankruptcy. *See* insolvency

banks. *See* commercial banks
banks for cooperatives. *See* Farm Credit System (FCS)
Basle Accords. *See* capital
Bowsher, Charles A., 12. *See also* U.S. General Accounting Office
Brendsel, Leland, 73, 150. *See also* Freddie Mac
Brumbaugh, R. Dan, 3–4, 89

capital: and risk taking, 4–6, 29, 162, 169–171; and competitive advantage, 78, 79, 89; minimum standards, 169–171, 173–174; protected capital of Farm Credit System, 141–143, 174, 181; risk-based standards, 78; shareholder equity, 19, 61, 132, 134–136, 138, 145–146, 158; subordinated debt, 173, 181–182
Carter administration, 118
Citicorp, 14, 88, 137–138
collateralized mortgage obligations (CMOs). *See* mortgage-backed securities (MBSs)
College Construction Loan Insurance Association (Connie Lee), 124

commercial banks: as customers of
government-sponsored
enterprises, 78; competition
with government-sponsored
enterprises, 27–28, 86–88, 91,
114, 117–118, 160, 180–181;
geographic restrictions, 79–80;
investments in federal agency
securities, 43, 45; lending limits,
compared to government-
sponsored enterprises, 17–18,
59, 69, 86–87, 121, 129, 153
competition: "crowding out," 27,
95–97; enterprise advantages,
27–28, 36–37, 76–81, 180–181;
enterprise disadvantages, 81–83;
Fannie Mae and Freddie Mac,
113–115; Farm Credit System,
117–118, 160; Federal Home
Loan Bank System, 90, 109,
110, 197; Sallie Mae, 86–88,
114
Congress. See U.S. Congress
Congressional Budget Office (CBO),
xxviii, 89, 162, 195
Continental Illinois Corporation,
26
contingent liability, 132–136,
138
cooperative: Farm Credit System, 20,
67, 95, 141–143; Federal Home
Loan Bank System, 20, 68
Corporation for Small Business
Investment (COSBI), xx, 25,
123, 193–194
Cranston, Senator Alan, xxiii, xxiv,
62, 120
credit ratings, 27, 29, 77, 78, 159,
160, 164–166, 175–177, 182–183,
198 See also Standard & Poor's
credit risk, 30, 77, 134, 140–141,
145, 155–156
customer services: Farm Credit
System, 52, 57, 117–118; Federal
Home Loan Bank System, 33,
57, 90, 121–122, 140

deposit insurance: compared to
implicit federal guarantee, 8–10,
26–29
derivative mortgage-backed
securities. See mortgage-backed
securities (MBSs)
directors: fiduciary responsibility of,
60, 66–67, 208; government-
appointed, 65–68, 207;
shareholder-elected, 65–67, 111,
112
diversification of risk, 30–31, 129,
196

economies of scale: issuing
mortgage-backed securities,
44–45, 77, 93; operations, 23,
70–71, 80–81, 83–84
Economist, The, 115–116
examination: as supervisory tool,
174–175, 177–178; of
commercial banks and thrift
institutions, 6–7, 164; of Farm
Credit System institutions, 178

Fahey v. O'Melveny & Myers, 203,
204
Fannie Mae: capitalization, 37,
135–136, 173, 181–183;
competitors, 88–91; and
Department of Housing and
Urban Development, 29–30,
59–60, 67, 119, 121, 162–163,
171–173, 184, 192–193, 209;
financial risks, 9, 129–136, 161,
165, 184, 196; history and
origins, 21–22, 33, 99–100, 122,
202; innovations by, 33, 86,
92–93; lending powers, 50–52,
197; low-income housing
program, 11, 59–60, 61–64,
118–119, 192–193; mortgage-
backed securities, 45–49,
132–136; political influence of,
xxiii, 10, 37, 71, 113–115,
118–119, 192–193; portfolio

lending, 129–132; profitability, 136; public purpose, 33, 58–64, 101–104, 110–111, 126, 1971 sources of income, 45, 48, 54–58

Farm Credit Administration: dominated by regulated institutions, 30, 168, 185–186; regulatory powers (after 1985), 73, 163, 171, 173–174, 178, 184, 209

Farm Credit System (FCS): average-cost pricing, 77–78, 159–161; capitalization, 141–143, 181, 183; congressional oversight, 185–186; cooperative structure, 32, 67, 73–74, 97, 141–143, 190; Financial Assistance Corporation, 124–125, 143, 199; financial failure of, 9, 67, 94–95, 124–125, 143, 159–161, 162–163, 185–186; financial risks, 9, 159–161, 165, 198; history and origins, 20, 97–98, 121, 201–202; innovations by, 86; lending activities, 50, 180, 198; political influence of, 168; profitability, 141–143; public purpose, 15, 32, 58–60, 126, 198; services to borrowers, 52, 57, 117–118; sources of income, 52

Farm Credit System Financial Assistance Corporation, 124–125, 143, 199

Farm Credit System Insurance Corporation, 154, 198

Farmer Mac: capitalization, 174; Farmers Home Administration Loans, 24, 50; financial role, 49–50, 94; history and origins, 23–24, 124–125, 202; mortgage-backed securities, 49–50, 94; regulation and supervision, 171, 174, 184; sources of income, stockholders, 24, 67–68

federal agency, 205

federal agency credit market, 39–41, 44, 146. *See also* implicit federal guarantee

Federal Deposit Insurance Corporation (FDIC), 8, 190

Federal Financing Bank. *See* Treasury Department

Federal Home Loan Bank Act of 1932, 20–21, 202

Federal Home Loan Bank Board (FHLBB): and thrift institutions, 4–7, 55, 168, 186; as Freddie Mac's board of directors, 22, 110, 192. *See also* Office of Thrift Supervision; Federal Housing Finance Board

Federal Home Loan Bank of San Francisco, 119–120

Federal Home Loan Bank System (FHLBS): advances to thrift institutions, 21, 50–52, 98–99, 119–120, 140–141; capitalization, 19, 141, 174, 181; cooperative structure, 20, 68; financial activity, 40–41, 108; financial risks, 140–141, 165; history and origins, 20–21, 33, 98–99, 121–122, 202; low-income housing program, 62, 64; political influence, 119–120; profitability, 141; public purpose, 33, 59, 62, 64, 98–99, 101–102; 108–110, 119–120, 126, 197, 203, 208–209; services to thrift institutions, 33, 57, 90, 121–122, 140; sources of income, 57–58; taxes, 82

Federal Home Loan Mortgage Corporation. *See* Freddie Mac

Federal Housing Finance Board (FHFB), 66, 163, 173, 207, 209–210. *See also* Federal Home Loan Bank Board (FHLBB)

federal instrumentality:

government-sponsored
enterprise as, 80–81, 205–207
Federal Intermediate Credit Banks.
See Farm Credit System (FCS)
Federal Land Banks. See Farm Credit
System (FCS)
Federal National Mortgage
Association. See Fannie Mae
Federal Reserve System, 3, 11, 43,
121, 205
Federal Savings and Loan Insurance
Corporation (FSLIC), 26–27, 140
Financial Accounting Standards
Board (FASB), 140
Financing Corporation (FICO), 18,
26; history and origins, 24, 108,
124–125, 146–148, 202; public
purpose, 148, 199
Financial disclosures: federal agency
securities, 128; financial
statements, 128–152;
market-value disclosures,
148–152, 164, 175–176
Financial Institutions, Reform,
Recovery, and Enforcement Act
of 1989 (FIRREA), xxii, 50, 89,
110–111, 164, 173
Fox, Edward A., 39, 60, 72. See also
Sallie Mae
Freddie Mac: capitalization, 158,
173, 181–183; competitors,
88–91; Federal Home Loan Bank
Board and, 22, 110, 192; history
and origins, 22–23, 122–123,
202; innovations by, 86, 128;
lending authority, 50–52, 197;
low-income housing programs,
11, 61–64; mortgage-backed
securities, 45–49, 137–138;
political influence of, xxiii, 10,
110, 192; portfolio lending,
136–137; profitability, 138;
public purpose, 58–60, 101–104,
126, 197; regulation and
supervision, 163–164; risks, 62,
138; sources of income, 45, 48,
54–57, 58–64

Garn–St. Germain Depository
Institutions Act of 1982, 5
Generally accepted accounting
principles (GAAP), 3–4, 7, 134
Glass-Steagall Act of 1933, 83
Glauber, Undersecretary Robert R.,
190. See also Treasury
Department
Government National Mortgage
Association (Ginnie Mae) and
Fannie Mae, 21; mortgage-
backed securities, 46, 49, 86,
93–94
government-sponsored enterprises
(GSEs): as specialized lenders,
30–31, 59; compared to banks,
17–18, 59, 69, 86–87, 121, 129,
153; compared to thrift
institutions, 8, 17–18, 59, 79–81,
153, 162, 185–187; competitive
advantages, 27–28, 36–37,
76–81, 180–181; defined, 17;
history and development; 16,
20–25, 86, 97–101, 121–125;
implicit federal guarantee of,
9–10, 25–27, 41–44, 77–78,
146–147, 157–162, 184, 203–204;
innovations by, 33, 85–86,
92–93; lending activities, 54–56;
management quality, 69–74;
ownership and control, 60–61,
64–69; political influence of,
10–12, 37, 190–191; public
purpose, 31–33, 38, 76, 191–196;
statutory restrictions, 15, 58–60,
107–108, 203–204; volume, size
and growth of, 18–19, 34–36,
138, 143, 156–157, 188, 196
Gradison, Representative Bill, xxii,
120
Greenspan, Chairman Alan, 11. See
also Federal Reserve System
Greider, William, 127
Guaranteed Student Loan Program
(GSLP): and lenders, 87–88; and
Sallie Mae, 84, 87–88, 100, 104,
194

Harris, Secretary Patricia R., 59, 119.
See also Housing and Urban
Development, Department of
Hemel, Eric I., 8, 107
home-equity loans, 52
Housing and Urban Development,
Department of: and Fannie Mae
and Freddie Mac, 29–30, 59–60,
67, 119, 121, 162, 171–173,
184, 192–193, 209; Ginnie Mae,
21

implicit federal guarantee: benefits
of, 77–78; consequences of,
9–10, 28; nature of, 25–27, 28,
41–44, 146–147, 204–205; and
risk taking, 157–162, 184
incidental powers: Federal Home
Loan Bank System, 58, 109–110,
203, 208–209; legal issues
concerning, 203–204, 208–209;
Sallie Mae, 58, 108–109, 112,
208
insolvency: bankruptcy, 2, 206–207;
conservatorship or receivership,
183–185, 207; gambling, 2, 4–6,
183–185
interest rate(s): Regulation Q, 3, 9;
yield curve, 55, 129–130, 196
interest-rate risk, 3, 30, 55, 129–132,
134, 140, 148, 156, 161
investment bankers, xxiv, 11, 89–91,
114–115, 136

Jackson, President Andrew, xxiv. *See
also* Bank of the United States
Johnson, James A., 71. *See also* Fannie
Mae

lending powers: congressional
oversight, 107–112, 116–121,
125–127, 193–196; pressures to
expand, 81–83; primary versus
secondary market, 40, 59, 91–94;
public purpose, 31–33, 38,
58–64, 76, 191–196. *See also*
incidental powers

liquidity: debt securities, 44–45;
mortgage-backed securities,
44–45, 77, 93
low-income housing: Fannie Mae
and Freddie Mac, 11, 59–64,
118–119, 192–193; Fannie Mae
controversy with HUD, 59, 119;
Federal Home Loan Bank
System program, 62, 64

management, 69–74, 85, 154–155, 196
management and operations risks, 9,
30, 69, 134, 154–155, 156–157,
184, 198
market discipline, 157–162, 167–168
market efficiency, 96–103
market risk, 30, 129, 155
Maxwell, David, O., 14, 62, 72, 83,
114. *See also* Fannie Mae
moral hazard, 28, 157–162
mortgage bankers, 93–94, 122–123
mortgage instruments, 86, 92–94
mortgage-backed securities (MBSs),
45–47: derivative securities, 156;
Fannie Mae and Freddie Mac,
22, 89–91, 132–138; Farmer
Mac, 24; Federal Home Loan
Bank System, 83; financial
attributes, 159; Ginnie Mae, 22;
guarantee fees, 56; innovations
in, 93; pass-through securities,
47; prepayment risk, 47, 150;
REMICs, 47–49, 91, 110–111,
113–115; swap transactions,
52–54, 77, 114
Murray, James E., 59. *See also* Fannie
Mae

National Housing Act of 1934, 21,
202
National Infrastructure Bank, xxii
national mortgage associations, 21,
197, 202
Nixon administration, 100

Office of Comptroller of the
Currency (OCC), 8

Office of Management and Budget
(OMB), xxviii, 7, 163–164
Office of Thrift Supervision (OTS),
7–8
Omnibus Budget Reconciliation Act
of 1981, 109

pass-through securities. See
mortgage-backed securities
pension and trust funds, 43, 204
Pickle, Representative J. J.,
xxii–xxiii, 120, 188
portfolio lending, 129–132, 136–137,
175–176, 197
prepayment risk, 47, 150
Production Credit Associations. See
Farm Credit System (FCS)
Proxmire, Senator William, 118–119
public purpose: of government-
sponsored enterprises, 31–33,
38, 58–64, 76, 191–196; of thrift
institutions, 10

Reagan administration, 111–112,
120
real estate mortgage investment
conduit securities (REMICs). See
mortgage-backed securities
(MBSs)
Reconstruction Finance Corporation
(RFC), 21, 122
regulation. See Department of
Housing and Urban
Development; Farm Credit
Administration; Federal Home
Loan Bank Board; Federal
Housing Finance Board;
supervision, financial
residential mortgage market:
conforming mortgages, 38, 77,
116–117; Fannie Mae and
Freddie Mac, 84, 88, 91–94;
mortgage bankers, 93–94,
122–123; secondary mortgage
market, 91–94; private mortgage
insurance, 92; servicing, 93;
thrift institutions, 88–89, 114

Resolution Funding Corporation
(REFCORP), 18, 26; history and
origins, 24, 108, 125, 202; public
purpose, 199
risk, financial: credit risk, 30, 77,
134, 140–141, 145, 155–156;
interest-rate risk, 3, 30, 55,
129–132, 134, 140, 148, 156,
161; management risk, 69,
154–155, 184; market risk, 30,
129, 155; operations risk, 30,
134, 156–157; prepayment risk,
147, 150; specialized lenders,
30–31, 145; taxpayer exposure
to, 153–154, 164–166
risk taking: Fannie Mae, 161; Farm
Credit System, 159–161; Freddie
Mac, 62–63; thrift institutions,
2–10, 55, 149, 162; and federal
supervision, 163–164, 168–169,
177–178, 198
Roosevelt administration, 21, 122

safety and soundness: economic
principles, 167–171; federal
supervision, 171–174, 179–180,
198. See also capital; moral
hazard; risk, financial; risk
taking
Sallie Mae: accountability, 208, 209;
capitalization, 143, 145, 181;
competitors, 86–88, 114;
congressional oversight, 12, 112,
123; Connie Lee, 124; financial
risks, 108, 145, 157, 162, 165;
history and origins, 23, 100–101,
123, 202; home equity loans, 52;
innovations by, 85–86; lending
activity, 50–52, 143–145;
ownership and control, 68–69;
profitability, 61, 145–146; public
purpose, 60, 102, 107–108, 126,
198; sources of income, 54–56,
58. See also Guaranteed Student
Loan Program (GSLP)
savings and loan associations. See
thrift institutions

Schechter, Henry, 190
secondary mortgage market. *See*
    Fannie Mae; Freddie Mac;
    Ginnie Mae; residential
    mortgage market
Securities and Exchange Commission
    (SEC), 44, 128, 204
Seidman, Harold, xxvii
servicing: mortgage loans, 93;
    student loans, 157
shareholders, 170–171: cooperative
    shareholders, 67–69;
    investor-shareholders, 22, 179,
    180; shareholder rights, 60,
    208
small business investment companies
    (SBICs). *See* Corporation for
    Small Business Investment
    (COSBI)
Stafford Student Loan Program. *See*
    Guaranteed Student Loan
    Program (GSLP)
Standard & Poor's, xxv, 9, 159,
    164–166
Student Loan Marketing
    Association. *See* Sallie Mae
subsidy benefits, 31–34, 96–97,
    179–180, 182; for farmers and
    ranchers, 31, 97, 104–105, 126;
    for homeowners, 103–105,
    181–183; for students, 39, 60,
    104–105
supervision, financial: capital-
    adequacy standards, 180–183;
    regulatory capture, 185–187,
    191, 192–193; regulatory tools,
    169–171, 179–180, 183–185;
    safety and soundness, 29, 37,
    171–174, 179–180, 185–187. *See*
    also examination

Tax Reform Act of 1986, 48–49, 79,
    91

taxation of government-sponsored
    enterprises, 25, 36, 44, 78–79, 82
thrift institution(s): and Federal
    Home Loan Bank System, 33,
    108, 121–122, 140; and Fannie
    Mae and Freddie Mac, 23,
    52–53, 88–89, 113–115, 117,
    122–123; financial failure of,
    2–10, 12–13, 55–56, 149, 162;
    investment in federal agency
    securities, 43; legal restrictions,
    3, 99; political influence of, 2,
    5–7, 10, 121–123, 168; qualified
    thrift lender test, 52; Sallie Mae
    acquisition of, 108–109, 112;
    similarities and differences
    compared to government-
    sponsored enterprises, 2–10,
    17–18, 59, 79–81, 153, 162,
    185–187
Thygerson, Kenneth, 75, 103
Treasury Department: line of credit
    (backstop), 44; regulatory
    authority, 43, 123, 209; safety
    and soundness proposals, 10–12,
    29, 63, 175–176, 182–183,
    189–191; study of government-
    sponsored enterprises, xxii–xxiii,
    69, 85, 145, 157, 164, 174–177,
    210

user fees, 120
U.S. Congress: and powers of
    government-sponsored
    enterprises, 60, 63, 108–112,
    116, 192–196; oversight,
    xxiii–xxv, 121–124, 185–187,
    192–196
U.S. General Accounting Office, 113;
    study of government-sponsored
    enterprises, xxii–xxiv, 164, 210
U.S. League of Savings Institutions,
    112